D0853442

GIANTS
OF THE
LOST
WORLD

GIANTS L**O**ST WORLD

OF THE

DINOSAURS AND OTHER EXTINCT MONSTERS OF SOUTH AMERICA

Donald R. Prothero

SMITHSONIAN BOOKS

WASHINGTON, DC

This book may be purchased for educational, business, or sales promotional use. For information, please write: Special Markets Department, Smithsonian Books, P. O. Box 37012, MRC 513, Washington, DC 20013

Published by Smithsonian Books
Director: Carolyn Gleason
Managing Editor: Christina Wiginton
Production Editor: Laura Harger
Editorial Assistant: Jaime Schwender
Edited by Gregory McNamee
Designed by Gary Tooth

Library of Congress Cataloging-in-Publication Data

Prothero, Donald R.
Giants of the lost world : dinosaurs and other extinct monsters of South America / by Donald R. Prothero.
Other titles: Lost world | Dinosaurs and other extinct monsters of South America
Description: Washington, D.C. : Smithsonian Books, [2016] | Includes index.
Identifiers: LCCN 2015047514 | ISBN 9781588345738
Subjects: LCSH: Dinosaurs—South America. | Extinct animals—South America. | Doyle, Arthur Conan, 1859–1930. Lost world.
Classification: LCC QE861.9.S68 P76 2016 | DDC 567.9098—dc23
LC record available at http://lccn.loc.gov/2015047514

Manufactured in the United States of America
20   19   18   17   16   5   4   3   2   1

Dedicated to the pioneers of South American paleozoology

Georges Cuvier

Charles Darwin

Alfred Russel Wallace

Peter Wilhelm Lund

Florentino and Carlos Ameghino

John Bell Hatcher

William Berryman Scott

George Gaylord Simpson

José Bonaparte

Carlos de Paula Couto

Rosendo Pascual

without whom this story would never be known

CONTENTS

INTRODUCTION: The Lost World ix

1. The Island Continent 1

2. Tyrant Lizard Kings 17

3. Giants among Giants 31

4. Demise of the Dinosaurs 45

5. Living Dinosaurs 61

6. Land of the Reptilian Monsters 73

7. The Old Timers I: Killer Opossums 83

8. The Old Timers II: Pseudo-Elephants, 95
   Pseudo-Hippos, and Pseudo-Horses

9. The Old Timers III: The Slow Folk 111

10. The Castaways 123

11. Invasion! 135

12. Where Have All the Mammals Gone? 157

EPILOGUE: The Sixth Extinction 165

ACKNOWLEDGMENTS 168

INDEX 169

Figure 0.1. Sir Arthur Conan Doyle, author of the Sherlock Holmes detective stories and *The Lost World*.

INTRODUCTION

The Lost World

The Lost World was a work of fiction by Sir Arthur Conan Doyle, the author of the Sherlock Holmes stories, but it was based on the newly made discovery of actual isolated plateaus in the Amazonian jungles of South America inhabited by unique creatures unknown to science. Not even Doyle could have imagined the extinct gigantic creatures that really did exist in the prehistoric past of South America.

Sherlock Holmes just wouldn't die.

His creator, Sir Arthur Conan Doyle (figure 0.1), had written the first short story about the legendary detective back in 1886. By 1893, he had written twenty-four short stories and two novels. He was tired of the task of churning out several Holmes stories a year for *Strand Magazine*. Like many a writer with one very successful book series, Conan Doyle was afraid of being typecast as the author of Sherlock Holmes and nothing else. He wanted to work on historical fiction instead. In November 1891, he had written to his mother, "I think of slaying Holmes . . . and winding him up for good and all. He takes my mind from better things." His mother wrote back, "You won't! You can't! You mustn't!" But in 1893, he published "The Final Problem," in which Holmes and his nemesis, Dr. Moriarty, fight to the death at Reichenbach Falls and Holmes falls to his doom—or so it appears.

When readers cried out for more Sherlock Holmes stories, Conan Doyle realized that he had underestimated the popularity of his most famous character. In addition, his other writings did not sell very well. After an eight-year hiatus, he relented and wrote "The Hound of the Baskervilles," the most famous Holmes story ever. In 1903, Conan Doyle brought the short stories back again with "The Adventure of the Empty House." In this story, Holmes reveals that he escaped the fall that killed Moriarty but had to remain in hiding for a year to flush out his henchman, Colonel Sebastian Moran, whom Holmes caught trying to assassinate him. Conan Doyle then dutifully wrote thirty-two more Sherlock Holmes stories and one more novel until 1927, three years before his death at age seventy-one, never again daring to alienate his loyal readers.

In 1911, though, Conan Doyle got an inspiration for a story and a character that might compete for popularity with Sherlock Holmes. He heard a lecture on February 11 at the Royal Geographical Society about the Huanchaca Plateau in Bolivia given by a good friend of his, the noted explorer Percy Harrison Fawcett. Fawcett was famous for his perilous expeditions in South America, where he nearly starved to death more than once. Many of the fearless explorers featured in the comic books and adventure movies of the 1950s were based on Fawcett. These, in turn, may have been the inspiration for popular modern movie characters such as Allan Quatermain and Indiana Jones.

As Fawcett wrote in his posthumous memoirs,

> Monsters from the dawn of man's existence might still roam these heights unchallenged, imprisoned and protected by unscalable cliffs. So thought Conan Doyle when later in London I spoke of these hills and showed photographs of them. He mentioned an idea for a novel on Central South America and asked for information, which I told him I should be glad to supply. The fruit of it was his *Lost World* in 1912, appearing as a serial in the *Strand Magazine*, and subsequently in the form of a book that achieved widespread popularity.

Conan Doyle was influenced not only by Fawcett's discoveries but also by the first blooming of "dinomania." Although fragmentary dinosaur fossils had been found in England as early as 1824, they were too incomplete to build a complete skeleton. Except for some large lizardlike models sculpted by Waterhouse Hawkins for the Great Exhibition of 1851, there were few reconstructions or images of dinosaurs available for public consumption, since the fossils were too piecemeal. Most of them were just a few bones, not enough to even to grasp their enormousness. So far, dinosaurs had still not made much of a dent in the public consciousness.

At the beginning of the twentieth century, however, museums in the United States began to mount large skeletons of dinosaurs, such as *Brontosaurus* (now *Apatosaurus*), *Stegosaurus*, *Allosaurus*, *Triceratops*, and

Tyrannosaurus rex, that had been recently found in Colorado, Wyoming, and Montana. They also commissioned paintings and sculptures of these beasts, giving people an image of "dinosaur" for the very first time. Soon dinosaurs were a huge fad and their images were everywhere, and the phrases "as dead as a dinosaur" and "like a dinosaur" entered the public language as well.

The lucky accident of hearing Fawcett's accounts, combined with the popularity of dinosaurs in the public imagination, gave Conan Doyle an idea for a story. In 1912, he published a novel entitled *The Lost World*, in which dinosaurs still survive on an isolated plateau in South America, forgotten by time. The featured dinosaurs are those known to science at the time: *Iguanodon* and *Megalosaurus* (found in England in the 1820s and 1830s) and *Stegosaurus* (figure 0.2) and *Allosaurus* (found in Colorado and Wyoming in the 1880s), but not the *Brontosaurus* or *T. rex* or *Triceratops* seen in many later film versions of the novel. There are also the flying reptiles known from Germany, *Pterodactylus*, and the English *Dimorphodon*, as well as an anachronistic mixture of extinct mammals and giant birds originally found by Darwin during his voyage aboard HMS *Beagle* to South America from 1831 to 1836 (see chapters 5–9). Naturally, there also must be primitive humans in this fictional prehistoric menagerie, represented by

Figure 0.2. Original plate from the 1912 edition of *The Lost World*, showing *Stegosaurus* as artists then reconstructed it.

Pithecanthropus or "Java man," based on one of the earliest human fossils, which had been discovered in Java just twenty years earlier.

More important for Conan Doyle, the novel gave him a chance to create a new, dynamic character that soon became his most popular creation other than Sherlock Holmes. The story begins with a journalist, Edward Malone, who hears about the amazing discoveries of these living dinosaurs from a blustering, bearded, bombastic scientist-explorer, Professor George Edward Challenger. Conan Doyle, speaking through Malone, describes Challenger this way:

> His appearance made me gasp. I was prepared for something strange, but not for so overpowering a personality as this. It was his size, which took one's breath away—his size and his imposing presence. His head was enormous, the largest I have ever seen upon a human being. I am sure that his top hat, had I ventured to don it, would have slipped over me entirely and rested on my shoulders. He had the face and beard, which I associate with an Assyrian bull; the former florid, the latter so black as almost to have a suspicion of blue, spade-shaped and rippling down over his chest. The hair was peculiar, plastered down in front in a long, curving wisp over his massive forehead. The eyes were blue-grey under great black tufts, very clear, very critical, and very masterful. A huge spread of shoulders and a chest like a barrel were the other parts of him which appeared above the table, save for two enormous hands covered with long black hair. This and a bellowing, roaring, rumbling voice made up my first impression of the notorious Professor Challenger.

Conan Doyle painted a portrait of a brilliant scientist and explorer with the ingenuity and smarts to get out of any dangerous situation. Many people have pointed out that these features of Challenger were closely modeled on Percy Fawcett. Nevertheless, Challenger is rude, crude, loud, boisterous, and without social inhibitions, and he is always violating people's sensibilities and ignoring the cautiousness of his scientific colleagues. Like Sherlock Holmes, whom Conan Doyle based on Joseph Bell, a beloved professor at his medical school at the University of Edinburgh, Challenger was based on real people: Percy Fawcett and William Rutherford, a professor of physiology who had also taught Conan Doyle in medical school.

In the original story, other scientists dispute Challenger's claims. Frustrated with their skepticism, he dares them to go to South America to see for themselves. The expedition includes not only Malone, who is the narrator of the story, and Challenger, but also his chief critic, Professor

Summerlee, as well as big-game hunter Lord John Roxton (figure 0.3). After reaching their destination, they are abandoned by the superstitious natives who had been hired to help them and then have many adventures on the plateau. They are nearly killed by the dinosaurs, captured and held prisoner by the "ape-men," help the native people on the plateau win a battle with the ape-men, and barely escape with their lives. The explorers finally return to England triumphant, only to have other scientists ridicule their claims once again. But Challenger brings home a special package that provides a surprise twist to the ending. The story is available free online, so I will not spoil it for you. It is definitely worth reading, even more than a century after it was published.

The Lost World was a smashing success, and it spawned several other Professor Challenger stories, even though Conan Doyle never could abandon writing about Sherlock Holmes. The original novel led to a famous 1925 silent movie based on the novel, with groundbreaking stop-motion animation of the dinosaurs by Willis O'Brien, who later worked on Merian Cooper's film *King Kong*. The animated dinosaurs may look crude and jerky by today's standards, but they were frighteningly real to audiences of that

Figure 0.3. Frontispiece of the original 1912 edition of *The Lost World*, with actors made up to look like Conan Doyle's conception of the four main characters (*left to right*): Edward Malone, Professor Summerlee, Professor George Edward Challenger, and Lord John Roxton.

time. *The Lost World* was remade five times, each movie increasingly different from the original Conan Doyle story, as well as inspiring many radio plays and several TV shows, the most recent produced in 2011.

Conan Doyle's premise that dinosaurs survive today in some isolated place was not really new. In 1864, just twenty years after the existence of dinosaurs was first announced by science, Jules Verne had them living underground in *Journey to the Center of the Earth*. This seemed to be forgotten, though, until Conan Doyle's 1912 novel spawned an entire genre of science fiction stories following its basic plot lines. The earliest was the 1915 novel *Plutonia*, by the Russian Vladimir Obruchev, about dinosaurs living underground in Siberia. In 1916, Tarzan creator Edgar Rice Burroughs wrote *The Land That Time Forgot*, another lost world discovered, in this case, by a German U-boat captain. There have been dozens of later stories influenced by *The Lost World*, the most famous being Michael Crichton's *Jurassic Park*. Crichton went as far as entitle his 1995 sequel *The Lost World*. Even children's cartoons have this plot line, and *Ice Age: Dawn of the Dinosaurs* (1999) has the characters breaking through a cavern floor and finding a lost world of dinosaurs beneath. Conan Doyle's novel spawned a standard science fiction trope that never seems to go out of style.

It turns out that there are many such isolated plateaus in the border zone from Bolivia and Brazil to Venezuela and Guyana (figure 0.4). They are known as tablelands or *tepuis*, "houses of the gods" in the Pemon language spoken in the upper Amazon Basin. These plateaus are erosional remnants of a thick layer of billion-year-old sandstone in the core of the oldest rocks in South America. This layer sits above a granite basement that is even older, and together they once covered most of the headwaters of the northern Amazon Basin. Today more than 115 *tepuis* have been described, all that is left of this sandstone layer. They are found at the headwaters of the major rivers of tropical South America: the Amazon, the Orinoco, and the Rio Negro.

The *tepuis* are about 1,000–3,000 meters (3,300–10,000 ft) higher than the surrounding tropical rainforest basins. Their sides are sheer cliffs hundreds of meters high. Angel Falls in Venezuela, the largest waterfall in the world, drops 979 meters (3,212 ft) off the side of one of the *tepuis*. The tops of the tablelands are deeply eroded into soft sandstone, forming caverns and many weird rock formations. There are sinkholes 300 meters (1,000 ft) across. The largest quartzite cave in the world, Abismo Guy Collet, is 671 meters (2,200 ft) deep and is found on a *tepui*.

Figure 0.4. Kukenan *tepui*, one of largest *tepuis* in South America and the model for the Maple White Land plateau described in Conan Doyle's *The Lost World* (photograph by Paolo Costa Baldi, license GFDL/CC-BY-SA 3.0).

Towering above the landscape at high altitude, *tepuis* have a much cooler climate than the dense tropical jungles around them, making them true "ecological islands." Some are cloaked in fog and clouds the year round. They all receive the torrential tropical rains that fall in the region. With their distinctive climate and vegetation, *tepuis* harbor completely different animals than do the jungles below the cliffs. Instead of the Amazonian forests dominated by jaguars, tapirs, capybaras, and many smaller animals, *tepuis* have their own unique assemblage of animals and plants. These creatures are not lost dinosaurs trapped by time, as envisioned by Conan Doyle. Instead, they are unique species of smaller mammals, birds, reptiles, and amphibians. Among the species not found anywhere else are two species of opossums, weasels, bats, several rodents related to guinea pigs and chinchillas, and three species of climbing rats. There are forty-one species of birds found nowhere else, including species of tinamous, parakeets, parrotlets, nightjars, and swifts.

The reptiles are mostly snakes that occur both in the lowlands and on the *tepuis*, including deadly venomous bushmasters and fer-de-lance pit vipers, plus coral snakes. There are also many species of iguanas and tegu lizards. The amphibians include a wide variety of frogs (especially tree frogs) and salamanders.

Biologists long thought that all of these animals had been completely isolated since erosion had separated the sandstone caprock into each individual *tepui*. However, recent research has shown that the tree frogs are descended from ancestors in the Amazonian basin, which had evolved independently as each one crawled to a summit. Nonetheless, most of the species are currently separated from their relatives in the rainforest below them, and many have had enough time and isolation to evolve into new species. For that reason, most of the *tepuis* are now in protected areas, including many national parks as well as other kinds of designated protected ecoregions, so that poachers and animal collectors do not raid the vulnerable forests or hikers or climbers trample the delicate vegetation and start fires.

Sadly, the research on life on the *tepuis* goes very slowly because it is difficult for anyone to reach them and there is very little funding for such basic biological fieldwork. Most big-money biology today is cellular and molecular biology, and field biologists and ecologists have to struggle to get research funds. Despite this, the most recent research shows that these lost worlds are now doomed because of climate change. As the planet warms, the cool, protected habitats of these "islands in the sky" are now vanishing. Some of the recently discovered species have already gone extinct in the short time since they were found. Such creatures have nowhere to go if the climate changes their habitat, since there are no other places on the earth like the *tepuis*. Conan Doyle thought the tablelands were inhabited by prehistoric species not yet extinct, but in reality the real inhabitants of these lost worlds are actually vanishing.

But Conan Doyle's idea that South America was a sort of lost world of terrifying prehistoric monsters was not a fantasy. In fact, South America was an isolated island-continent throughout most of its history, from at least 150 million years ago until just a few million years ago. The fantastic dinosaurs that he imagined *did* live in South America. They were just extinct, and they had to be dug up out of the rocks, not captured on an isolated plateau. In fact, South America has an incredible history as a land where many very strange creatures evolved and died out. From the time it broke away from the supercontinent of Gondwana, it harbored the biggest creatures ever to roam the planet. South America was truly a land of giants, including the largest animals ever to live on land. In fact, record-breaking reptiles are the norm for South America. They include the largest snake ever found, as well as a gigantic turtle and many other impressive specimens.

The idea for this book came from an interesting twist of fate, courtesy of my friend and colleague Ken Campbell Jr., who worked with me to establish the paleomagnetic dating of the fossils he was collecting from the Peruvian Amazon. I tell the story of the jawbone he brought me in chapter 11, the fossil of a long-extinct group of deerlike mammals known as palaeomerycids—whose presence there forced us to rethink how animals populated the South American continent. I presented this research at a number of different scientific conferences, and I published scientific work on it. Then I was asked to give a talk at the South Pasadena Senior Center, where I often give guest lectures, and I put our discovery in the framework of the "Island Continent" narrative that described most of South America for the past 60 million years, when it was a continent as isolated as any island from the rest of the world. I talked about some of the huge dinosaurs, snakes, turtles, alligators, birds, and other beasts that had roamed the Lost World. When I read Arthur Conan Doyle's book of that title to my boys at bedtime, I realized it was the perfect hook to connect all the pieces of the story.

The book you are now reading is the result. In it, emulating Professor Challenger, we will travel alongside numerous explorers, from Charles Darwin to the modern generation of paleontologists, as they discover and document this lost world of giants.

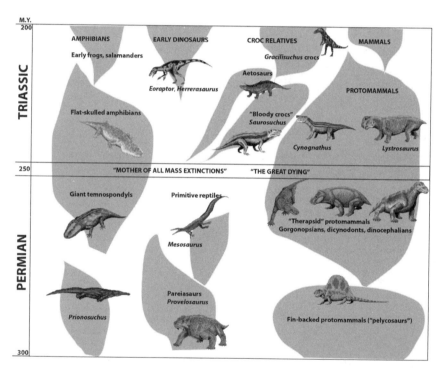

M.Y.

TRIASSIC

PERMIAN

200

250

300

AMPHIBIANS

Early frogs, salamanders

Flat-skulled amphibians

EARLY DINOSAURS

Eoraptor, Herrerasaurus

CROC RELATIVES

Gracilisuchus crocs

Aetosaurs

"Bloody crocs"
Saurosuchus

Cynognathus

MAMMALS

PROTOMAMMALS

Lystrosaurus

"MOTHER OF ALL MASS EXTINCTIONS"   "THE GREAT DYING"

Giant temnospondyls

Primitive reptiles

Mesosaurus

Prionosuchus

Pareiasaurs
Provelosaurus

"Therapsid" protomammals
Gorgonopsians, dicynodonts, dinocephalians

Fin-backed protomammals ("pelycosaurs")

Figure 1.1. Simplified diagram of the pattern of diversification of land animals during the Permian and Triassic across Pangea (including South America). During the Early-Middle Permian, the dominant creatures were the fin-backed protomammals known as pelycosaurs, plus huge crocodilelike amphibians (*Prionosuchus* and temnospondyls) and a variety of primitive reptiles such as the hippolike pareiasaurs and the little lake predator *Mesosaurus*. By the Late Permian, more advanced "therapsid" protomammals, such as the predatory gorgonopsians, the thick-skulled dinocephalians, and the dicynodonts, with tusks and toothless beaks, ruled the landscape. These creatures were decimated during the great Permian extinction event. (Illustration by E.T. Prothero.)

1

The Island Continent

The island continent of South America formed as part of a gigantic supercontinent about 250 million years ago. This supercontinent, Pangea, hosted a variety of strange and huge creatures, including the largest amphibian that ever lived. By the time South America began to break away from the rest of the supercontinent, it also began to have its own unique collection of dinosaurs and other prehistoric creatures.

The Christmas Gift That Changed the World

A well-chosen holiday gift can be a source of delight and wonder for its lucky recipient. It can also alter the course of that person's life—and indeed of history. For Winston Churchill, a set of lead soldiers marked the beginning of a distinguished military career, while for Steve Jobs, a build-it-yourself radio kit was the initiation into the world of electronics. For Alfred Wegener, a world atlas was inspiration enough to revolutionize our understanding of the world itself—even if that atlas was not meant for him.

Born in Berlin in 1880, Wegener (figure 1.2) was an unlikely revolutionary, the pious son of a clergyman. He initially studied classics before switching to astronomy, meteorology, and climatology, but he never had much formal training in geology. By 1905, he was working at a meteorological observatory. In 1906, the twenty-six-year-old organized and led the first of four expeditions to Greenland to understand climate in polar regions.

Wegener then became an instructor in meteorology at the University of Marburg, where he worked with the legendary climatologist Wladimir Köppen, who developed a climate classification scheme that is still used

Figure 1.2. Alfred Wegener in the polar shelter hut on his final, and fatal, expedition to Greenland in 1930.

today, one that I teach it to my meteorology class every year. Renowned as a teacher who could explain things clearly and precisely, Wegener published a textbook in meteorology, *Thermodynamics of the Atmosphere* (1910), which would become a standard in the field.

During the Christmas holidays in 1910, Wegener happened to glance at a world atlas that was a gift for one of his friends. As he recalled later, he was struck by how well the Atlantic coasts of South America and Africa seemed to fit together. Many people had noticed this almost as soon as the first good maps of the Atlantic were drafted back in the 1500s, but Wegener did not stop there. He began to collect evidence from the distribution of fossils, from the rocks that indicated ancient climates and ancient latitudes of continents, and from other data that suggested that all the continents had once been united into one supercontinent he called Pangea, whose name means "all lands" in Greek. By 1912, he had given a few lectures on his ideas and published three short papers in a German geographical journal on the subject. In 1913, Wegener married Köppen's daughter and then ran his second Greenland expedition, spending the winter on the ice—where he very nearly starved to death before he and his companion were rescued.

When World War I broke out in 1914, Wegener was drafted into the Kaiser's army, as was nearly every able-bodied young man in Germany at the time. After he was twice wounded, the German High Command decided that Wegener was no longer fit to be trench fodder. They sent him to work in the army weather service, where he traveled among weather stations all over German-held Europe. Despite all this traveling and army duties, he managed to finish writing a book, *On the Origin of Continents and Oceans*, which was published late in 1915. The book had little immediate impact because of the wartime restrictions, but Wegener remained remarkably productive for a busy active-duty officer, publishing another twenty papers in meteorology and climatology before the war ended.

When peace came, Wegener obtained a position at the German Naval Observatory in Hamburg, then transferred to the University of Hamburg, and finally accepted a secure post at the University of Graz. During this time, he wrote an influential book with his father-in-law on the climates of the geological past. But his ideas about drifting continents (figure 1.3) were not widely read or accepted, especially not in the geological community in Europe and the United States. He presented them at the 1926 meeting

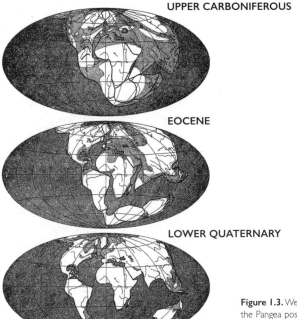

UPPER CARBONIFEROUS

EOCENE

LOWER QUATERNARY

Figure 1.3. Wegener's original reconstruction of the Pangea positions of the continents 250 million years ago (Ma). (From Wegener, *Die Entstehung der Kontinente und Ozeane*, 1915.)

of the American Association of Petroleum Geologists in New York City, where his audience roundly rejected his theories. His theories continued to be scorned by geologists, but Wegener kept working hard, gathering data in Greenland in 1929. In 1930, he led his fourth and last big expedition to Greenland, the largest he had ever mounted, with propeller-driven ice sleds and much innovative equipment. In November 1930, he and a partner were returning from a supply run to their remote camp in the center of the Greenland ice sheet when they ran out of food and hit a patch of bad weather. Wegener, fifty years old, froze to death. His partner buried Wegener on the Greenland ice sheet, where he still rests today under many feet of ice. Wegener never lived to see any support for his ideas, which would gain wide acceptance four decades later.

On the Origin of Continents and Oceans was a masterful compilation of all the evidence of ancient geography available at the time. Many people had wondered whether Africa and South America fit together, but Wegener showed that the fit also included India, Madagascar, Australia, and Antarctica. As a climatologist, he was particularly impressed by the way certain deposits are strongly controlled by climate and latitude: ice caps on the poles, rainforests in the tropics, and desert deposits in the mid-latitude high-pressure belt between 10° and 40° north and south of the equator. But when he took the map back to the Permian Period (250–300 Ma, or million years ago), the location of those ancient deposits made no sense on a modern globe. The south polar ice sheets extended from South America to Africa and apparently stretched across the equator to India, which is a climatological absurdity. Only if you put the continents back into their Permian configuration as part of a single supercontinent, Pangea, did they make sense.

If the continents had not moved, then why did the bedrock scratches carved by the rocks pushed along by ancient Permian glaciers run from Africa to South America? That would require the glacier to jump into the Atlantic, flow in a straight line across the Atlantic Ocean from Africa to Brazil, and then jump back out of the ocean—another absurdity. Likewise, all the ancient Permian desert deposits and coal swamps of tropical Permian rainforests made sense only if they were put back in their Pangean locations, not their modern latitudes. Then even the ancient Precambrian bedrock in South America and Africa matched precisely, like pieces of a jigsaw puzzle.

Clinching all this was the evidence from the Permian fossils. South America was loaded with distinctive fossils that united it with other continents, especially Africa. There were distinctive extinct seed ferns known as *Glossopteris* found on all the continents of the southern landmass called

Gondwana. There were small swimming reptiles such as *Mesosaurus*, found in lakebeds in Brazil and South Africa, and protomammals such as the bulldog-sized beaked herbivore *Lystrosaurus* and the bearlike predator *Cynognathus* that could never have swum across the modern Atlantic Ocean (figure 1.4). To Wegener, and to any modern geologist, this evidence should have been clear and conclusive: The continents drift apart like the ice floes Wegener knew so well.

If the evidence was so solid, why were Wegener's ideas ridiculed and rejected? Why did geologists treat his ideas as crazy and call him a crackpot for another half-century after his book was published? Not all of it was due to the strength or weakness of his scientific evidence. There were also the effects of the sociology of science. First, Wegener was not a formally trained geologist, and there is natural reluctance to accept ideas from outside your scientific field that appear to violate your basic assumptions, such as the fixity of continents. Even more important, Wegener's evidence came mostly from the Southern Hemisphere, yet almost all the world's geologists back then lived in Europe or North America. Very few had ever traveled to South Africa or Brazil, which were long, expensive trips by ocean liner

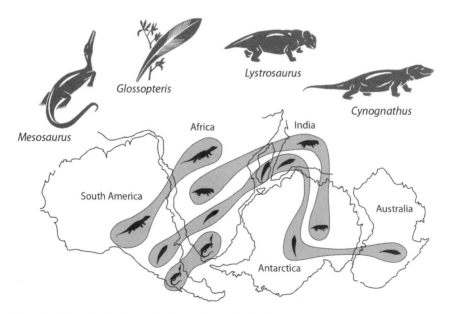

Figure 1.4. The distinctive plants and animals of the Permian link the various Gondwana continents together. The little aquatic reptile *Mesosaurus* and bearlike protomammal *Cynognathus* are both found in Brazil and South Africa. The dog-sized beaked protomammal *Lystrosaurus* is found in Africa, Madagascar, India, and Antarctica. The seed fern *Glossopteris* is found on all the Gondwana continents. (Redrawn from several sources.)

in those days. Naturally, the evidence is much more persuasive if you can see it in person, rather than read it in type and see it in the small, grainy black-and-white photos that were normal for journals back then. Indeed, Wegener's biggest boosters, such as South African geologist Alexander du Toit, were mostly in the Southern Hemisphere and could see the evidence firsthand. They pointed out that the Permian rocks of South Africa and Brazil were virtually identical; the only difference was that in one country they had Afrikaner names and in the other names in Portuguese.

Another supporter was British geologist Arthur Holmes, known as the "Father of the Geological Timescale" for his pioneering work in radiometric dating in 1913–15. He embraced Wegener's ideas—but then, he had worked as a geologist in Africa before returning to England. Holmes boldly published diagrams showing drifting continents and mantle currents pushing those continents around for the first time in his widely used geology textbooks in the 1920s, forty years before the geological community came to accept the notion.

But the controversy was not all due to the sociology of science. Wegener proposed no plausible mechanism to explain how continents drifted, and the ideas he floated, such as centrifugal force, were not very realistic. Geologists argued that if the continents had plowed across the ocean basins, there should be huge areas of oceanic crust crumpled up on their leading edges like the snow on a snowplow blade—and such deposits had never been found. Meanwhile, they dismissed the matches in rocks across the continents as inconclusive and concocted fantastic land bridges to explain how animals could have made their way across the Atlantic Ocean. They continued to denigrate Wegener and ridicule his ideas for decades. In the 1940s, leading American paleontologist George Gaylord Simpson even published numerous papers arguing that the fossils did not require continental drift. His home institution, the American Museum of Natural History, held a major symposium in 1949 dismissing all the evidence of moving continents.

Ironically, as the heap of scorn reached its peak, evidence was coming from an unexpected direction: the bottom of the ocean. Both Wegener and his critics were completely ignorant of what the oceanic crust was really like. In fact, the answers did not come until after World War II, when modern marine geology was born. By the late 1940s and 1950s, several oceanographic institutes had ships routinely crisscrossing the world's sea lanes, getting detailed surveys of seafloor depth and routinely collecting seismic, gravity, and magnetic data as well as sediment cores everywhere they went. By the late 1950s, scientists had the first real glimpse of what 70 percent of the earth's surface actually looked like, thanks to the first detailed maps of the seafloor by Marie Tharp and her partner Bruce Heezen.

Meanwhile, ancient magnetic data gathered from rocks on land showed that the continents had moved with respect to the magnetic poles of the earth. Other scientists had established that the earth's magnetic field flips back and forth from its modern direction to a direction 180° opposite what we measure today. This history of magnetic field reversal provided the final, crucial piece of data: the proof of seafloor spreading, demonstrated by Fred Vine and Drummond Matthews in 1963. It turned out that Wegener's critics were wrong. The continents *do* drift around the globe, but they do not crumple up the oceanic crust ahead of them because most of the oceanic crust slides beneath other plates and plunges back into the mantle.

I am fortunate in having lived to witness this scientific revolution. It began about the time I was born. When I was an undergraduate, from 1972 to 1976, geology instruction around the country was just beginning to make the transition from old ideas to plate tectonics. In graduate school at Lamont-Doherty Geological Observatory and Columbia University, I was taught by many of the pioneers of plate tectonics: Neil Opdyke, who first studied paleomagnetism in ocean cores; Lynn Sykes, who confirmed plate tectonics through seismology; Bill Ryan, pioneer of marine geology, who helped discover that the Mediterranean was a desert six million years ago; Walter Pitman, who figured out the complex pattern of magnetic stripes on the Pacific seafloor; Wally Broecker, who coined the term *global warming* and was a giant in both oceanography and climate change; Jim Hays, who helped discover the causes of the Ice Ages; and Bruce Heezen and Marie Tharp, who singlehandedly mapped the entire ocean floor. They were the generation that pushed the scientific revolution to its conclusion. But it all began a century ago with Wegener.

Monsters of Gondwana

Meanwhile, scholars were also working to connect the chronology of past life to the geological record, and in doing so they were building a fantastic fossil record for the supercontinent of Gondwana, especially the portion that later split off to become South America. That region, and now modern continent, has an excellent fossil record going back over 500 million years, with 3-meter-long (10-ft) sea scorpions, the gigantic relatives of the nautilus that we know as ammonites, and many other spectacular creatures.

During the Permian Period, as part of Gondwana, it shared many amazing creatures that spread across South America to Africa, India, Australia, and other parts of the ancient world.

In the Permian beds of South America, the little aquatic reptile *Mesosaurus* gave way to more impressive aquatic predators such as *Prionosuchus* (figure 1.5*a*–*b*). This immense amphibian, by far the largest fossil amphibian ever found, stretched up to 10 meters (33 ft) long and weighed at least 360 kilograms (more than 800 lbs); the skulls of some specimens are more than 1.6 meters (5.2 ft) long. It had a long, narrow snout like that of the modern fish-eating crocodilian known as the gavial (or gharial), with hundreds of sharp teeth. These were suitable for snagging aquatic creatures that lived in the lagoon deposits and riverbeds of northern Brazil, where it was found in the Pedra do Fogo Formation. Many smaller creatures were lunch for *Prionosuchus*, including sharks, primitive bony fish, lungfish, and even other large amphibians. The Pedra do Fogo Formation also yields numerous fossils of petrified trees, suggesting that these creatures lived in a humid, tropical swampy region during this time. But crocodiles had not yet evolved and would not do so until about 200 Ma, a full 70 million years after the amphibian *Prionosuchus* began filling its ecological niche in Brazil.

Even more impressive was the spectrum of bizarre land animals roaming the continents of Gondwana, particularly Brazil and South Africa. They included some truly spectacular creatures from every branch of the amphibians and reptiles, as well as the earliest ancestors of mammals. Although *Prionosuchus* was the biggest amphibian ever, the lakes and rivers of the Permian were teeming with a large number of flat-bodied,

Figure 1.5. The immense, crocodile-sized amphibian *Prionosuchus* from the Permian of Brazil. (*a*) Reconstruction of the animal in life (courtesy Nobumichi Tamura). (*b*) Size comparison with a human (courtesy @User: Smokeybjb/Wikimedia Commons/CC-BY-SA 3.0).

crocodile-shaped amphibians known as temnospondyls (see figure 1.1). In the early Permian, the largest amphibian was *Eryops*, a big temnospondyl over 2 meters (6.5 ft) long, with a robust tail and limbs and a broad, flat skull well over 60 centimeters (2 ft) long in big individuals. This was one of the largest terrestrial animals of the Early Permian, capable of hunting prey both in the water and on the land. The slightly more primitive *Edops*, from the Early Permian redbeds of Texas, had an even longer skull, and it would have been even larger than *Eryops* if its complete skeleton were known.

By the Late Permian, the huge temnospondyl amphibians had retreated to a completely aquatic lifestyle, possibly due to competition from all the large predators on land at the time. Temnospondyls straggled on into the Triassic (200–250 Ma), where they were 3-meter-long (10-ft) monsters that were still common in the swamps and lake deposits of places such as the Petrified Forest in Arizona. However, these last of the temnospondyls were completely aquatic, with weak legs that would never have carried them very far on land, flattened heads that looked upward only, and huge, flat bodies adapted to living in shallow water and feeding on aquatic prey.

In addition to huge amphibians in the water, the land abounded with some of the earliest reptiles. Most were small creatures about the size of a dog or a modern lizard. Some were truly huge, though, and to most modern eyes ugly. The weirdest of them all were the pareiasaurs, which resembled warty lizards trying to be hippos (figure 1.6). They were fat and stumpy-legged, with a short tail and a barrel-shaped trunk that housed a digestive tract large enough to feed on the relatively indigestible plant life of that time. Pareiasaurs had broad, rounded skulls made of thick, bony plates. Little bumps and knobs of bone armored their heads and their hides over their entire body. The biggest pareiasaurs, from Russia and South Africa, were the size of temnospondyls and weighed as much as 600 kilograms (1,300 lbs). Yet pareiasaurs had only small, leaf-shaped teeth, and apparently they were gentle herbivores, munching on the ferns and conifers that covered the Permian landscape. The Upper Permian Rio do Rasto Formation in Brazil yields a pareiasaur known as *Provelosaurus*, which was about 2.5 meters (8 ft) long.

Although amphibians that resembled crocodiles and pareiasaur reptiles that looked like hippos were important in the Permian, the dominant group of animals on Permian landscapes was the protomammals ("synapsids," to a paleontologist). The protomammals were a separate lineage that originated at the same time as true reptiles (about 320 Ma) and evolved in a different direction from those reptiles. At no time during their history

Figure 1.6. The warty, hippo-sized reptiles known as pareiasaurs were found all over Pangea in the Permian, from Brazil to South Africa to Siberia. Skeleton of the huge pareiasaur *Bradysaurus* (courtesy @User: Masur/Wikimedia Commons/CC-BY-SA 3.0).

were protomammals ever reptiles, which is why no modern paleontologist uses the obsolete and misleading term "mammal-like reptiles." Instead, the protomammals evolved to become the ancestors of all mammals today.

Protomammals came in every shape and size and ruled the landscape through the entire Permian, from 300 Ma to about 250 Ma. In the Early Permian, there were the familiar fin-backed protomammals (figure 1.7), such as the huge predator *Dimetrodon* and the herbivore *Edaphosaurus*. Although these creatures are often called dinosaurs, they are not—they are our distant relatives. *Dimetrodon* was over 4.6 meters (15 ft) long, with a sail that reached about 1.7 meters (5 ft) above the ground, and it weighed up to 250 kilograms (550 lbs). It had a narrow, compressed skull with strong, curved jaws sporting a wicked set of pointed, conical stabbing teeth. Scientists have argued about the function of their huge sail, with no real consensus as to what it was used for. It provided a big surface area for the skin of *Dimetrodon* and *Edaphosaurus*, which would have helped absorb the sun's rays and warm and cool their bodies faster in sun or shade. Other scientists point out that no other Permian animal had this feature, so it may not have been essential for warming and cooling their bodies. Instead, some scholars argue that the fin served as a device for signaling the size and strength of the animal as it competed with others for dominance and mating rights, just as the horns of antelopes, cattle, and sheep and the antlers of deer do today.

Figure 1.7. The largest animals of the Early Permian landscape were the finback protomammals *Edaphosaurus* (left) and *Dimetrodon* (right) (drawing by Mary P. Williams).

By the Late Permian, the finbacks were gone, replaced by a giant explosion of different kinds of protomammals. Some of these protomammals were among the first plant eaters ever to evolve. These included the squat creatures with a toothless beak and big canine tusks known as dicynodonts ("double dog teeth" in Greek), which reached 3.5 meters (11 ft) long and weighed up to 1,000 kilograms (1 ton). Some of them, such as *Kannemeyeria* from Africa, and others from India, China, and Argentina, had the same dimensions as the larger dicynodonts, about the size of an ox. Others, such as the little dicynodont *Lystrosaurus*, which we saw earlier, were about the size of a dog. In the Late Permian, the sheep-sized *Endothiodon* was found not only in Brazil but also in South Africa, Zambia, Zimbabwe, Tanzania, Mozambique, and even India, giving it a wide distribution across Gondwana.

The second group of herbivorous protomammals was known as the dinocephalians ("terrible heads"). They sported an array of warts and bumps and thick, bony battering rams on their heavily armored skulls. Some dinocephalians reached up to 4.5 meters (15 ft) in length and weighed up to 2 metric tonnes (4,400 lbs). One of these was *Pampaphoneus* (figure 1.8), a huge creature over 1.8 meters (6 ft) long from the Middle Permian of Brazil (about 265 Ma). It was one of the few dinocephalians to develop long, stabbing canines and sharp teeth for meat eating.

Preying upon these herbivores were ferocious carnivorous synapsids in impressively wide array. The most impressive were the saber-toothed gorgonopsians (figure 1.1), whose Greek name suggests the terror induced by the snake-headed monster Medusa. They had huge skulls with impressive stabbing canine teeth, strong jaw muscles for chewing, and powerfully built bodies. The largest were the size of a rhinoceros, with a skull 45 centimeters long, saber teeth over 12 centimeters long, and a long, sprawling

Figure 1.8. Reconstruction of *Pampaphoneus*, a large, predatory protomammal known as a dinocephalian (courtesy Nobumichi Tamura).

crocodilelike body up to 3.5 meters (11 ft) in length. Big Gorgons are found in the same beds in Brazil and South Africa with little *Endothiodon*, which must have been easy prey for the ferocious giants. Indeed, all of the Late Permian land animals, from the huge amphibians to the pareiasaur reptiles to the herbivorous dicynodonts and dinocephalians, were vulnerable to the Gorgons.

Catastrophe

Just as these creatures reached the peak of their evolutionary success at the end of the Permian, they were decimated by the greatest mass extinction in all of earth history. In fact, the Permian extinction wiped out 95 percent of the species in the ocean and at least 70 to 80 percent of all creatures on land as well. Paleontologists call it "the mother of all mass extinctions," since it was far more severe than any other extinction event, even the one that wiped out the dinosaurs. At one time, scientists attributed this event to the assembly of the Pangea supercontinent, which destroyed the shallow marine habitat for sea creatures when the oceans were crushed between the colliding continental blocks, but that event had occurred more than 50 million years earlier. Others have blamed it on the growth of the great Gondwana ice sheet, but that had occurred 100 million years earlier. A few scientists claimed the earth was hit by a giant meteor or comet (as happened at the end of the age of dinosaurs), but no claim of this impact has ever withstood the scrutiny of other scientists. None of the typical signs of impact, such as droplets of melted crustal rock splattered around the earth or rare elements such as iridium, which come from space rocks, has even been proven to exist.

Instead, the cause of the mother of all mass extinctions seems even more frightening: the biggest volcanic eruptions in all of earth history, its ancient lava flows still visible in northern Siberia, which triggered a massive super-greenhouse climate. The oceans then became supersaturated with carbon dioxide, making them too hot and acidic and killing nearly everything that lived there. The atmosphere was also low on oxygen and full of excess carbon dioxide, so land animals above a certain size nearly all vanished, and only a few smaller lineages of protomammals, reptiles, amphibians, and other land creatures made it through the hellish planet of the latest Permian and survived to the aftermath world of the earliest Triassic.

When the earth slowly began to recover after the Permian catastrophe, the oceans and land were first inhabited by just a handful of species that could survive in difficult conditions. These are often called "opportunistic" or "weedy" species. Scientists compare them to weeds that can quickly jump in and flourish where disturbances have killed most other life. In the oceans, most of the rich assemblage of Permian sea creatures, such as the trilobites and the two main groups of Paleozoic corals, had vanished forever. Some Paleozoic sea creatures, such as the sea lilies (crinoids) and lamp shells (brachiopods), barely made it through the catastrophe. Just a few surviving lineages managed to recover in the Triassic and became the ancestors of all later members of their group. All the Paleozoic corals vanished completely, and a new group of corals evolved from soft-bodied sea anemones. They were the ancestors of all corals living today.

On land, just a few groups of reptiles and protomammals survived, and soon they evolved to restore their rule over the landscape. The huge, warty pareiasaur reptiles did not make it, and neither did the thick-skulled dinocephalians. But the beaked, herbivorous dicynodonts, with their distinctive tusks, pulled through, as shown by the ubiquitous Gondwana resident *Lystrosaurus* (figures 1.1, 1.4). Soon these dicynodonts became huge, reaching the size of an ox. In the Middle Triassic of Brazil roamed the long-tusked dicynodont *Dinodontosaurus* ("terrible toothed lizard" in Greek), which reached 2.5 meters (8 ft) in length and weighed several hundred kilograms.

The surviving protomammals in the Triassic were a new evolutionary diversification and radiation of creatures that were much more like mammals than any of their Paleozoic ancestors. These included the bear-sized *Cynognathus* as well as a suite of smaller protomammals that looked much like weasels or raccoons. By the Middle Triassic, the badlands exposures of units such as the Chañares Formation and the Upper Triassic Ichigualasto Formation, both in Argentina, had become veritable graveyards of a riotous diversity of these advanced protomammals.

But the protomammals did not rule the Middle or Late Triassic unchallenged. They competed with a whole new group of animals, the archosaurs, or "ruling reptiles." Archosaurs are the group that became the ancestors of crocodiles, dinosaurs, and birds. Some of these archosaurs were pig-sized herbivores with beaks, known as rhynchosaurs. Others, known as aetosaurs, were gentle plant eaters about the size of crocodiles but had armor on their back fringed with a row of bony spikes.

The earliest ancestors of the crocodilians are represented by *Gracilisuchus* and *Luperosuchus* from the Chañares Formation and *Trialestes* from the Ichigualasto Formation, but they were nothing like modern crocodiles or alligators. They were only about the size of a chicken, about 30 centimeters (1 ft) long, with long, delicate bodies and limbs. Indeed, their hind limbs suggest that they hopped like kangaroos.

The most impressive of all these primitive archosaurs were the monster predators of the Triassic, the rauisuchids (also known as the erythrosuchids, or "bloody crocodiles"). They are not closely related to crocodiles but were even bigger than any alligator, with huge bodies and tails, a fully upright posture for rapid bursts of running in ambush, and big, deep skulls and jaws with recurved teeth for ripping the flesh from any other creature that they encountered. The most complete of these fossils was *Saurosuchus* from the Ichigualasto Formation, which was about 7 meters (23 ft) long, with a monstrous set of jaws over a meter (3.3 ft) long. Another "bloody croc" was *Fasolasuchus* from the same formation. It may have been up to 10 meters (33 ft) long, although the fossils are too incomplete to be sure about those size estimates. These were the dominant predators of Middle and Late Triassic times, killing and eating all other creatures on the landscape and pushing out the remaining lineages of protomammals, which were small dog-sized or weasel-sized creatures.

Dawn of the Dinosaurs

In 1988, a young paleontologist named Paul Sereno was just out of graduate school at Columbia University and newly hired at the University of Chicago. He was beginning his independent research career and looking for a place to make important discoveries. Paul and I had been classmates when we were both graduate students at Columbia and the American Museum of Natural History in the early 1980s. One of his first projects was collaborating with me on a project studying dwarf rhinoceroses, eventually yielding a joint scientific paper on the project. Paul then moved on to study dinosaurs. By the time he finished his doctorate, he had traveled around the world looking at dinosaurs in museums in China, Mongolia, and Russia, and he soon became one of the world's leading dinosaur experts.

For his first major scientific expedition, Paul raised the funds to go to the foothills of the Andes and collect in the Ichigualasto Formation. It was already famous for its abundant Late Triassic fossils, ranging from gigantic bloody crocs to a variety of archosaurs, protomammals, and even the very last of the giant, flat-bodied temnospondyl amphibians. Paul was happy to collect those fossils, but he was more interested in a fossil called *Herrerasaurus*, which was known only from isolated hind limb bones found by an Argentinian goatherd and given to paleontologist Osvaldo Reig in 1963 (see figure 1.1). What was known of it suggested that it was very close to being the most primitive dinosaur, but scholars had little to go on. A few other specimens had been collected, but what *Herrerasaurus* really was remained controversial. Three weeks into his 1988 field season in the Ichigualasto Formation, Paul found a nearly complete skeleton eroding out of a sandstone ledge. The specimen showed that *Herrerasaurus* (figure 1.9*a*)

Figure 1.9. The primitive dinosaur relatives from the Late Triassic of Argentina. (*a*) The large predator *Herrerasaurus* (courtesy Nobumichi Tamura). (*b*) The turkey-sized *Eoraptor* (courtesy Kentaro Ohno/CC-BY-SA 2.0).

was a lightly built bipedal dinosaur about 3.7 meters (12 ft) long, although exactly where it fits in the dinosaur family tree is still controversial.

In 1991, Paul and another team returned to Argentina to find more specimens from the Ichigualasto Formation. This time one of his Argentinian team members, Riccardo Martinez, found a complete skeleton of the oldest and most primitive dinosaur. Named *Eoraptor* ("dawn raptor") by Paul, it was a turkey-sized creature only about a meter (3.3 ft) long, but it had features that established it as the most primitive dinosaur known (figure 1.9*b*). Thus, South America produced not only the world's largest but also the earliest dinosaurs. In the next few chapters, we will look at some of these spectacular monsters of the Lost World.

CHAPTER **2** **Tyrant Lizard Kings**

It is well known that *Tyrannosaurus rex* was a giant meat-eater that ruled the late Age of Dinosaurs. But South America had its own impressive carnivorous dinosaurs, including one that had horns like a bull's, and also the biggest land predator of all time.

T. rex

Tyrannosaurus rex. The very name is the stuff of fascination and nightmares. Thanks to a century of publicity and promotion, *T. rex* is thought of as the ultimate giant predator, the killer with no mercy. It had been the star of movies for many years, usually portrayed as dragging its tail on the ground like a lizard. Then Michael Crichton and Steven Spielberg revolutionized its image as the most terrifying dinosaur of all in the movie *Jurassic Park* and its sequels, and since then the scientifically accurate image of running tyrannosaurs with their tails held out straight behind them has entered the public consciousness. Even so, the most recent of the series, *Jurassic World*, did not show the feathers that we now know covered most predatory dinosaurs, thanks to the discovery of several feathered tyrannosaurs found in China in recent years.

   Tyrannosaurus rex was by no means the largest land predator, or even the largest predatory dinosaur. That distinction belongs to other dinosaurs discussed later in this chapter. Nor was *T. rex* the most bizarre or remarkable of all the predatory dinosaurs. The fin-backed African predator *Spinosaurus* is a good candidate for the strangest-looking, though equally odd is the horned monster from the latest Cretaceous of Argentina, known as *Carnotaurus* (plate 1*a–b*; figure 2.2).

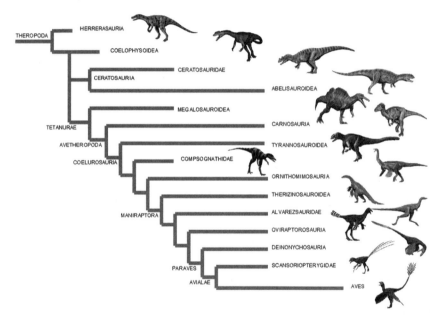

Figure 2.1. Family tree of the predatory dinosaurs, or theropods. The dominant South American groups included the Abelisauroidea (such as *Abelisaurus*, *Ekrixinatosaurus*, *Aucasaurus*, *Skorpiovenator*, and the horned *Carnotaurus*) and the Carnosauria such as *Giganotosaurus* and *Tyrannotitan* (related to *Carcharodontosaurus* of Africa) plus the spinosaurid *Irritator* and *Megaraptor* (related to the *Spinosaurus* of Africa). Also found in South America were the ostrichlike Alvarezsauroidea with stumpy front limbs, such as *Patagonykus*, *Alvarezsaurus*, *Achillesaurus*, and others. Deinonychosaurs (such as the familiar *Velociraptor*) are represented in South America by *Unquillosaurus*. (Illustration by Nobumichi Tamura.)

Figure 2.2. The bizarre bull-horned, snub-nosed predatory dinosaur *Carnotaurus* from the latest Cretaceous of Argentina. (*a*) Close-up of the tiny, useless forelimbs (photograph by D. R. Prothero). (*b*) Diagrams showing the extraordinary skull, with the huge horns and the short snout.

The Flesh Bull

Carnotaurus was the main villain of Disney's 2000 film *Dinosaur*, the first major studio film about dinosaurs made entirely with computer-graphic animation. Disney's artists originally planned to use *T. rex*, since it was more familiar, but they switched to *Carnotaurus* because the horns made it appear more devilish. Of course, the movie mixes together dinosaurs that lived on completely different continents millions of years apart, so the Late Cretaceous South American predator is shown chasing horned dinosaurs and duck-billed dinosaurs from much older beds in Canada and Montana. Since Disney's *Dinosaur*, *Carnotaurus* has appeared in other films, the kids' TV show *Dinosaur Train*, and cartoons.

Its horns are the most distinctive characteristic feature of *Carnotaurus*, whose name means "flesh bull" in Latin, referring to its large horns and flesh-eating ways. But the entire creature is distinct from other predatory dinosaurs in lots of ways besides the horns. It is the most specialized and distinctive member of a group of South American dinosaurs called abelisaurs, which occupied the top predator role during the latest Cretaceous in the Gondwana continents, especially South America, Madagascar, and India. By contrast, tyrannosaurs were the top predators in North America and Mongolia at the same time. Thus, tyrannosaurs and abelisaurs never came into contact. They were ecological equivalents living on different continents at the same time.·

Like most abelisaurs, *Carnotaurus* had a shorter snout than did tyrannosaurs, making it look snub-nosed when compared to *T. rex*. Like tyrannosaurs, it had a powerfully built, bull-like neck, so it could snap its head from side to side to rip flesh from its prey or wrestle with powerful creatures as they struggled. Its skull was lightly built and full of bony struts, so it was highly flexible. *Carnotaurus* could probably stretch its mouth around large prey items, a bit like snakes do. Its lower jaw was thin and shallow, not nearly as thick and robust as the jaw of tyrannosaurs. Its teeth were smaller and more slender than those of tyrannosaurs, so it was not as likely to bite as hard; instead, it used them more for nipping. Although the bite force of *Carnotaurus* was stronger than that of any living alligator, it was not as strong as that of tyrannosaurs. Thus, many paleontologists think *Carnotaurus* may have been adapted to quick, rapid biting of smaller prey or possibly to making quick, slashing wounds on larger prey rather than the bone-crushing power bites the tyrannosaurs used. *Carnotaurus* was the largest predator of its time, living alongside some remarkable large dinosaurs such as the spike-backed sauropod *Amargasaurus* (plate 4), so it seems likely that it preyed on dinosaurs close to its own size (or at least on their young).

Another feature of both tyrannosaurs and *Carnotaurus* was their small arms. The arms of *T. rex* were tiny, but those of *Carnotaurus* were even smaller proportionally (figure 2.2a). Most paleontologists think they were vestigial arms that were in the process of being lost and that were completely useless. The lower arm bone of *Carnotaurus* was much shorter than the upper arm bone, and its wrist bones never developed. It still had four fingers against the two of *T. rex*, but *Carnotaurus* had only two functional digits, the index and middle fingers, which were short and stubby. Its little finger was gone entirely, and only the middle finger still had a claw. The tip of the ring finger was missing, and in its place on the hand bone was a long, bony spur that stuck out of the hand. These tiny limbs clearly had no function, and they remind paleontologists of other dinosaurs that were in the process of losing their forelimbs and relying entirely on their mouth and hindlimbs.

Carnotaurus was smaller and more lightly built than *T. rex* or the other dinosaurs we will meet in this chapter. The complete skeleton of *Carnotaurus* is about 9 meters (30 ft) long, and so its body weight is estimated at about 1.35 metric tonnes (1.5 tons). Other abelisaurs, such as *Ekrixinatosaurus* and *Abelisaurus*, were also found in the Upper Cretaceous beds in Argentina. They were probably larger, but their fossils are too incomplete to be sure.

The long, slender hindlimbs of *Carnotaurus* suggest that it was among the fastest runners of all the large predatory dinosaurs. This is supported by the structure of the thighbone, which could withstand lots of bending and twisting, and the vertebrae of the hips and tail, which serve as the attachment points for its powerful leg muscles. Estimating its speed is difficult to do reliably, although it could certainly run faster than a human—something *T. rex* could not do, the movies notwithstanding. *Carnotaurus* was probably not as fast as an ostrich, which can top 69 kilometers (43 mi) per hour.

Unlike most dinosaurs, *Carnotaurus* is known from a complete skeleton (plate 1) with all its bones still connected, or what paleontologists call "articulated." It was found in a death pose, lying on its right side with its neck and head pulled back due to the tightening of the neck ligaments after death. Most dinosaurs are known from a few broken bones, with most of the parts missing. Even fewer are known with their bones articulated together as they were in life. Amazingly, *Carnotaurus* was preserved with skin impressions on several parts of its body. These impressions show a mosaic of polygon-shaped scales that did not overlap, scored with pairs of parallel grooves in several places. The scales of the head are less regular than those of the body. Unlike in tyrannosaurs, there is no evidence of feathers in *Carnotaurus*, so if it had any, they were in areas of the body for which no skin impressions are known.

Legendary South American paleontologist José Bonaparte and his crew discovered this amazing specimen in 1984 in the Upper Cretaceous La Colonia Formation, dating to about 70–72 Ma, making it one of the last predatory dinosaurs known in South America. *Carnotaurus* apparently lived in a coastal tidal flat and estuary setting, where the most common fossils are aquatic forms such as lungfish, turtles, snakes, crocodiles, and even plesiosaurs that swam ashore from deeper waters. The only other dinosaur from this formation is a possible duck-billed dinosaur, but other Late Cretaceous rocks nearby yield armored sauropods such as *Saltasaurus* and the spiky *Amargasaurus*, plus other duck-billed dinosaurs and even the armored ankylosaurs. Both the duckbills and ankylosaurs are related to fossils found in North America and are never seen in older rocks in Argentina, so they must have been immigrants from the north that crossed a land bridge in Central America during the Late Cretaceous.

Master of the Mesozoic

Before the 1940s, almost nothing was known of the dinosaurs and other Mesozoic fossils of South America. Many fossils of Cenozoic mammals had been collected and studied by people such as Charles Darwin in 1832 and by the Ameghino brothers in the 1870s and 1880s, but almost no one had collected many South American dinosaurs. This all changed almost entirely due to the effort of Bonaparte (figure 2.3), who found *Carnotaurus* and most of the dinosaurs discussed in this book. Although he is no relation to Napoleon Bonaparte, people have compared him to the emperor in terms of his drive and determination. Paleontologist Bob Bakker called him "Master of the Mesozoic." Bonaparte is widely considered to be the founder of dinosaurian paleontology in South America.

Bonaparte is responsible for finding and naming more than two dozen genera of fossils from the Mesozoic, 90 percent of which are still considered to be valid, unlike many names that turn out to be something else named before. These include the predatory dinosaurs such as *Carnotaurus* and its close relative *Abelisaurus*, plus other predatory dinosaurs such as *Ligabueino*, *Noasaurus*, *Piatnitzkysaurus*, and *Velocisaurus*. Bonaparte discovered or described numerous South American sauropods, including *Argentinosaurus* (perhaps the biggest of all land animals), *Antarctosaurus* (as large or possibly even bigger), *Andesaurus* (another giant close to *Argentinosaurus* in size), *Amargasaurus* (the spiky one), *Agustinia* (a brachiosaur), *Coloradisaurus*,

Figure 2.3. José Bonaparte after he received the 2008 Romer-Simpson Medal for lifetime achievement, the highest award of the Society of Vertebrate Paleontology. Left to right: Louis Jacobs of Southern Methodist University; Chuck Schaff of Harvard University; José Bonaparte; and Louis Taylor of the Denver Museum. (Photograph by M. Taylor; courtesy L. H. Taylor.)

Dinheirosaurus (from Portugal), *Lapparentosaurus* (from Madagascar), *Mussaurus* (a Triassic prosauropod ancestral to later giants), *Rayososaurus*, *Riojasaurus*, *Saltasaurus* (an armored titanosaur), *Volkheimeria*, and *Ligabuesaurus*. Bonaparte described and named *Herrerasaurus* from the Triassic beds of Argentina. No individual has ever found and named so many dinosaurs that are still considered real species, with the possible exception of two American pioneers of paleontology in the late 1800s, Edward Drinker Cope and Othniel C. Marsh. Bonaparte also found and named the South American duckbill *Kritosaurus australis*, which links Argentinian dinosaurs with *Kritosaurus* from the Late Cretaceous of Canada.

In addition to dinosaurs, Bonaparte found and described the primitive flightless bird *Patagopteryx* and the peculiar pterosaur known as *Pterodaustro*, which had a flamingolike filtering device on its lower jaw. Despite his reputation for finding dinosaurs, Bonaparte prefers to study mammals. He found some of the few Cretaceous mammals from South America belonging to strange groups known as gondwanatheres (unique to South America and Madagascar), plus docodonts and dryolestoids. Some of these mammals previously had been known only in the Jurassic of the Northern Hemisphere until Bonaparte found them in Argentina.

Born on June 14, 1928, Bonaparte celebrated his eighty-seventh birthday on the very day I wrote this chapter. I have been fortunate to meet him several times during my career. He was interested in my research on the dryolestoids, Jurassic mammals that are one of his favorite research topics. He is a modest man who seems self-effacing and humble when you talk to him. In an article in *Omni* from 1993, Don Lessem describes him this way: "Distinguished, sixtyish, he is a man of modest proportions. His large glasses and thinning pate, polished manners, neat attire, and scholarly parlance lend him the air of an academic, which he is, by practice if not training, ten months a year."

The son of an Italian sailor, Bonaparte was born in the provincial town of Rosario, Argentina, and grew up in Mercedes, about 100 kilometers (62 mi) west of Buenos Aires. Like most South American pioneers in paleontology, he never had any formal training, since there were no paleontologists in the country at that time to train people. The same was true of the Ameghino brothers, pioneers in discovering South America's Cenozoic mammals, as we will see in chapter 8. Bonaparte started collecting fossils at a young age, when a local retired fossil collector showed him some of his own finds. He made collecting fossils his obsession and passion. His house was soon full of fossils that he found in nearby riverbanks, and when it filled up, he created a museum in his town to house them. (They are now in the collection of the University of Tucumán.) In the late 1970s, he took a post at the National Museum of Natural Science in Buenos Aires, where he has been working and studying fossils ever since.

Like other Argentine pioneers in paleontology, Bonaparte has worked hard with very limited resources and focused on finding fossils no matter what the suffering and inconvenience for him and his crew. Many of his students complain that he is a hard taskmaster and can be extremely difficult. Bonaparte admits this, saying, "Yes, I can be tough, I suppose, but I work hard." Indeed, he is known as a workaholic, laboring sixteen hours a day, six days a week, and driving his crews just as relentlessly. He is also known to be stubborn and old-fashioned. For a long time, he rejected the new ways of classifying and analyzing the relationships of animals that swept through paleontology in the 1980s. A lot of his former students have mixed feelings about their time with him, yet he helped launch the careers of most of Argentina's current generation of dinosaur paleontologists. Don Lessem describes an expedition that Bonaparte undertook with University of Chicago paleontologist Paul Sereno into the Triassic beds that yielded *Herrerasaurus*:

> It's a desolate place like the Valley of the Moon in northwestern Argentina where Bonaparte and his dinosaurs are likely to be found, anytime from September to April. The conditions are harsh, the equipment primitive. Bonaparte and Sereno drove a rickety Renault with a broken fuel pump during their dig in the Valley of the Moon in 1988. An assistant had to perch on the roof much of the ride, dangling the fuel line. Bonaparte is accustomed to sleeping outdoors or in the sheep-shearing room of remote *estanzias* [*sic*], the vast Argentine ranches. He explored Argentina's Patagonian mountains on horseback, at least until he was turned back by fierce summer snow squalls.

Dinosaur paleontologist Peter Dodson says of Bonaparte, "Almost single-handedly he's responsible for Argentina becoming the sixth country in the world in kinds of dinosaurs. The United States is still first, but Bonaparte's shown that Argentina is so rich in dinosaurs from so many time periods that it may yet top us one day." Bob Bakker says, "We wouldn't know anything about South America's dinosaurs without him." Dinosaur encyclopedia author George Olshevsky writes, "His discoveries are fantastic. On a scale of one to ten of how strange a dinosaur could be, with a ten being the first dinosaur with wings, some of Bonaparte's finds are a nine."

Professional paleontologists appreciate him. Not only has Bonaparte received numerous awards and honors in his native Argentina, but in 2008 he was awarded the Romer-Simpson Medal of the Society of Vertebrate Paleontology, the highest award any vertebrate paleontologist can receive (figure 2.3). It is named after Alfred S. Romer and George Gaylord Simpson, two of the greatest paleontologists of the twentieth century, both of whom collected many fossils in Argentina during their careers and knew Bonaparte well in the 1930s, 1940s, and 1950s.

The Biggest Predator Ever?

So, if the biggest predatory dinosaur was not *Tyrannosaurus* and certainly not *Carnotaurus*, what was? Fans of the third *Jurassic Park* movie remember an immense creature with a long, crocodilelike snout and a sail on its back named *Spinosaurus* (figure 2.4). In the movie, it was much larger than *T. rex* and killed it easily. *Spinosaurus* was long thought to be much bigger than any other predator, but in 2014, new specimens were described and published. They showed that its appearance was very different than anyone had expected. Recovered by Paul Sereno and his crew from the Early Cretaceous of Egypt, Morocco, and Tunisia, *Spinosaurus* was no tyrannosaur with small arms, standing erect on its two long legs. Instead, its front and hind legs were about the same length, suggesting it walked and swam on all fours like a long-legged crocodile, rather than running on its hind legs like most predatory dinosaurs. Its skull has a long, narrow snout suitable for catching fish, rather than for attacking large animals such as *T. rex*. There were channels for nerves and blood vessels in the beak that would help it sense changes in the water around it, making it even more like a crocodile.

Chemical analysis of its bones showed that its diet was mainly fish and other aquatic creatures. It had dense limb bones that helped provide ballast in water, just as hippos do. With its short limbs, it probably did not hunt on land much but spent most of its time swimming; its long, delicate fingers and toes suggest that it had webbed feet as well. The function of the huge "sail" on its back is still controversial among paleontologists. It was not a true sail that would propel it across the water. To the contrary, the sail would have made it difficult for *Spinosaurus* to sink down and hide, as crocodiles do. Some have argued that it was a radiator surface to pick up or dump body heat, while other paleontologists think it was a feature for display, showing its size and stature to intimidate others of its species or to attract mates.

When German paleontologist Friedrich von Huene first reconstructed *Spinosaurus*, he estimated its size at 15 meters (~50 ft) and 6 metric tonnes

Figure 2.4. The newer, more crocodilelike version of *Spinosaurus*. Reconstruction of the animal in life (courtesy Nobumichi Tamura).

(6.6 tons) in weight. A 1988 study suggested a length of 15 meters (50 ft) but a weight of only 4 metric tonnes (4.4 tons). A 2007 study revised the size estimates to 12.6–14.3 meters (41–47 ft) in length and 12–21 metric tonnes (13.2–23 tons), shorter but heavier than previous estimates. The new specimens described by Sereno and Nizar Ibrahim are thought to be about 15.2 meters (50 ft) long, but the skeleton is a composite of several individuals (some juveniles) with a lot of the key bones missing, so the size is still not clearly established. Unlike the depiction in *Jurassic Park III*, *Spinosaurus* was clearly not a two-legged monster that towered over *T. rex* but a low-slung, crocodilelike aquatic dinosaur only slightly larger than *T. rex*.

South America had its own spinosaurs. The best known of these is *Irritator*, described by Dave Martill and others in 1996, from the Lower Cretaceous (110 Ma) Santana Formation of Brazil. The original specimen was collected by a poacher and then sold illegally. So much plaster and other material had been used to enhance the appearance and market value of the skull when scientists finally got to study it that Martill and colleagues got very irritated, hence its name. Its species name is *challengeri*, in honor of Conan Doyle's character who discovered the "Lost World."

Irritator is based mainly on a crocodilelike skull, which is 84 centimeters (33 in) long and strongly resembles the skull of *Spinosaurus* (figure 2.4). The rest of the body is not known (except for a few vertebrae that might belong to *Irritator*), so the true size of *Irritator* is hard to estimate. Some paleontologists suggest that it was as much as 8 meters (26 ft) in length, much smaller than the 12- to 15-meter length of *Spinosaurus*. *Irritator* was found in ancient Brazilian lakebeds of the Santana Formation, which are already famous for their extraordinarily well-preserved fossil fish, plus turtles, crocodiles, pterodactyls, and other Cretaceous creatures that lived in or near the water. It is very similar to *Spinosaurus*, an aquatic swimming predator much like a crocodile.

Besides the abelisaurs and spinosaurs, South America was home to many other groups of predatory dinosaurs as well (figure 2.1). Among these were the bizarre ostrichlike dinosaurs known as the Alvarezsauridae, such as *Patagonykus*, *Alvarezsaurus*, and *Achillesaurus*. This group had stumpy front limbs that were simply spikes with no fingers, previously documented in the Mongolian dinosaur *Mononykus*. Yet another theropod lineage was the *Velociraptor*-like deinonychosaurs, so famous from the *Jurassic Park* series. Although most of these creatures were found in Asia and North America, South America has its own representative of the "raptors," known as *Unquillosaurus*.

Despite these similarities to North American and Asian theropods, what is striking about South America is the lack of other predatory dinosaur groups. Tyrannosaurs never reached the Lost World; neither did the ostrichlike ornithomimids (such as *Gallimimus* from *Jurassic Park*). Even more surprising is the absence of the weird pot-bellied, giant-clawed herbivorous theropods known as therizinosaurs, which were common in Asia and North America but never got across the Panama land bridge.

If we want dinosaurs bigger than *T. rex* and *Spinosaurus*, we need to look at yet another group of predators, the carcharodontosaurs. Most of them were bigger than not only the tyrannosaurs but also the abelisaurs and spinosaurs. From the same beds in North Africa that yielded *Spinosaurus* came an even bigger dinosaur skull. It was named *Carcharodontosaurus* (figure 2.5) because its teeth were about the size and shape of those of the great white shark, *Carcharodon*. *Carcharodontosaurus* had a relatively long, tall skull that is much more lightly built than the skulls of tyrannosaurs, abelisaurs, or spinosaurs. The skull roof is composed of high, bony arches, with big openings on both sides of the skull that make it lighter and increase the area for attaching powerful jaw muscles. Only the skull of *Carcharodontosaurus* is

Figure 2.5. The immense skull of *Carcharo-dontosaurus* from the Lower Cretaceous of North Africa (courtesy P. Sereno).

known, plus a few other bones. Based on this limited evidence, the body of *Carcharodontosaurus* was about 12–13 meters (39–43 ft) long and weighed about 6–15 metric tonnes (6.6–16.5 tons), making it about the same size as *Spinosaurus* and large *T. rex*.

Who's the Biggest of Them All?

The skeletons of *Carcharodontosaurus* and *Spinosaurus* are too incomplete to reliably estimate their size, making it difficult to name definitively the biggest land predator of all time. Currently, the title goes to a different South American dinosaur. Originally discovered by amateur fossil hunter Ruben Dario Carolini in 1993, it was found in Lower Cretaceous beds in southern Argentina. In 1995, it was named *Giganotosaurus carolinii* by Rodolfo Coria and Leonardo Salgado (plate 2; figure 2.6). In Greek, its name translates as *Giga* ("big"), *-noto* ("southern"), and *-saurus* ("lizard"), pronounced GIG-a-NO-to-saur-us. (Unfortunately, many people misread the name and mispronounce it "GIGANTO-saurus.") *Giganotosaurus* lived in the Early Cretaceous, much earlier than abelisaurs or other predators; it lived beside sauropods such as the titanosaur *Andesaurus*, the diplodocids *Nopcsaspondylus* and *Limaysaurus*, and an array of other iguanodonts and small predatory dinosaurs related to *Velociraptor*.

About 70 percent of the skeleton of *Giganotosaurus* has been found, making it much more complete than the other contenders for "biggest land predator ever." Like its close relative *Carcharodontosaurus*, the skull of *Giganotosaurus* is built of high arches of bony struts, with lots of openings on the sides. Such a light skull is a big contrast to the massive, bulldoglike

Spinosaurus aegyptiacus - 17 m

Giganotosaurus carolinii - 13 m

Carcharodontosaurus saharicus - 12 m

Tyrannosaurus rex - 12 m

Mapusaurus roseae - 11 m

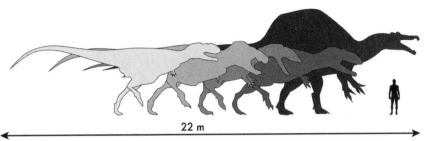

22 m

Figure 2.6. Comparison of the size of *Giganotosaurus* to other large predatory dinosaurs. The profile of *Spinosaurus* is based on the old, outdated reconstructions, so it is not really as large as shown here. (Adapted by Mary P. Williams from several sources, including Matt Martyniuk, http://creativecommons.org/licenses/by-sa/3.0/legalcode.)

skull of *T. rex*, so the bite force of *Giganotosaurus* was probably only a third as strong. Its broad teeth, resembling those of sharks, were better suited for producing slashing wounds than for biting down and crushing, as tyrannosaurs did. It probably gashed and disabled its prey from ambush, then disemboweled them and gorged itself while those unfortunate creatures slowly bled to death.

The nearly complete skeletons of *Giganotosaurus* are as much as 14.2 meters (47 ft) long, and this suggests that they weighed as much as 13.8 metric tonnes (15.2 tons). This is a bit longer than the largest *T. rex*, which was about 13 meters (43 ft) long and weighed only 8 metric tonnes (8.8 tons). Thus, until some other dinosaur is found that is both larger and more complete, *Giganotosaurus* holds the title of the largest land predator to have ever lived.

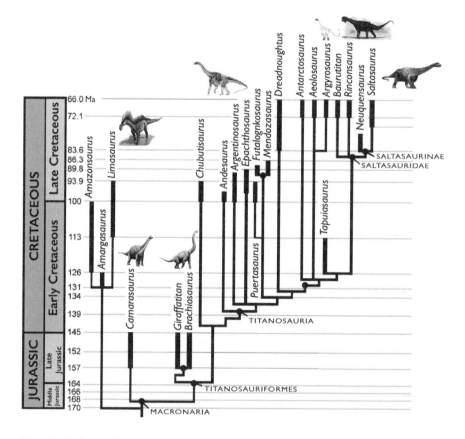

Figure 3.1. Family tree of sauropod evolution, focusing mostly on the dinosaurs of South America. The Lost World had a few diplodocines ("brontosaurs") such as *Limasaurus*, *Amazonsaurus*, and the spiky *Amargasaurus*, but there were no camarasaurs or brachiosaurs. Most South American sauropods were titanosaurs, ranging from the small *Saltasaurus* to the immense *Argentinosaurus*. (Drawing by E.T. Prothero, based on several sources.)

CHAPTER 3

Giants among Giants

Not only were the largest land predators of all time found in South America, but the largest dinosaurs ever found also come from the Lost World. These huge creatures had long necks and tails. Some even had spikes down their necks.

¡Mas Huevos!

In 1997 and 1998, Luis Chiappe and Lowell Dingus explored the barren washes of the 80-million-year-old Anacleto Formation on the flanks of the extinct Auca Mahuida volcano in northern Argentina. They had come to find the fossils of early birds that lived alongside the big dinosaurs, but instead they found the surface of the ground littered with hundreds of dinosaur eggs (figure 3.2). Most were about the size of softballs, but some were as big as small bowling balls. As they described it:

> Eggs were everywhere. As we strode across the mud-cracked flats exposed beneath the banded ridges of crimson rock that radiated under the searing Patagonian sun, crew members began kneeling down to examine small, dark gray fragments of rounded rocks with a curious texture. Picking up these chunks for closer inspection, we could see that the surface was sculpted into hundreds of small bumps and depressions. We knew immediately from the distinctive texture that we had found something startling—dinosaur eggs. A quiet but elated sense of amazement enveloped the crew. Our morning routine of casual prospecting had instantly turned into a moment of stunning discovery. With a bit of careful reconnaissance and a healthy dose of good luck, we had stumbled across a fantastic new site, the kind of site we had been hoping to discover our entire lives—remote, untouched, and crammed full of fossils

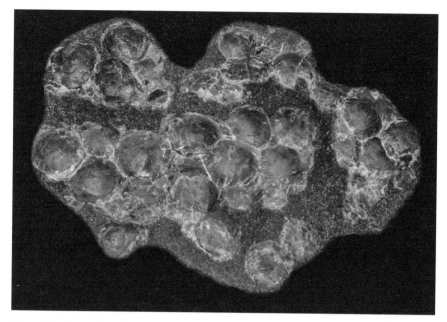

Figure 3.2. The original discovery site at Auca Mahuevo, Argentina, was covered with nests of sauropod eggs and fragments littering the ground. This photo shows typically dense masses of cantaloupe-sized eggs after cleaning (courtesy Luis M. Chiappe, Natural History Museum of Los Angeles County).

that no one had ever seen before. We slowly came to our senses and began to take stock. Scanning the scene around us, we were once again stunned by the sight of thousands of dinosaur egg fragments littered across the desolate Patagonian landscape. In many places the fragments of eggs were so abundant that we couldn't walk without stepping on pieces of fossil eggshell. These were not the small bones of ancient birds we had originally hoped to find, but serendipity, a common companion on paleontological expeditions, had not let us down.

Dingus, Chiappe, and their crew had stumbled across the largest concentration of dinosaur eggs ever found. Hundreds of them covered the area, which stretched for many meters. The eggs were so densely clustered that the rocks can be considered as "egg beds," more egg than rock. In just 25 square meters (269 sq ft) of one surface were more than two hundred complete dinosaur eggs, organized into clumps suggesting that each was an egg clutch in a discrete nesting site. Most of the clutches had between fifteen and thirty-four eggs. Each level in the rocks was another egg layer, too, showing that this nesting ground had been used for a long time. Not only that, but the close packing of nests showed that this was a communal nest site where herds of large sauropods would congregate during breeding season. There were remarkably few crushed eggs or eggshell fragments, suggesting that the site had been protected by the mothers guarding the perimeter but not walking among the eggs once they had been laid. The remarkable preservation of the eggs was due to the fact that large flash floods had buried the eggs—and had done so many times, because there were multiple egg layers in the rocks, covering a total thickness of 25 meters (75 ft). Although the region was officially called Auca Mahuida, the crew nicknamed this site "Auca Mahuevo" (a contraction of *mas huevos*, "more eggs" in Spanish).

When the scientists collected the best-preserved eggs and brought them back to the lab, they found that almost half had embryos in them. Some of the specimens even had casts of the skins of the embryos, as well as the outer egg membrane, the same membrane you must peel off when you eat a hard-boiled egg. The scientists were able to dissect out the tiny bones of baby sauropods, the group of long-necked, long-tailed giant dinosaurs that we once called "brontosaurs." The baby sauropods were too immature for scientists to estimate which adult dinosaur was their parent, because there are actually several different sauropods known from this time period in Argentina. But this was by far the best sauropod nesting site ever found.

Dinosaur eggs were a novelty when the American Museum of Natural History in New York first mounted expeditions to Mongolia in the 1920s. They were under the leadership of the daring explorer Roy Chapman Andrews, who many believe was the model for the movie character Indiana Jones. A few dinosaur eggs had been reported in 1859 in the Provence region of southern France, but mostly they were not recognized as dinosaur eggs. The American Museum expeditions originally went to Mongolia to find evidence of early humans evolving in Asia—which they did not, since early humans evolved in Africa. In place of early human fossils, the expeditions came back with a treasure trove of dinosaur fossils, along with spectacular giant mammals and many other impressive finds. The most famous of these discoveries were the large clutches of elongate dinosaur eggs found in the Flaming Cliffs, many still arranged in a circle as their mother had laid them.

The eggs and nests were a sensation when they were brought back to New York in 1923, and they helped raise enthusiasm and funds for further Mongolian expeditions throughout the rest of the decade. At the time, the American Museum scientists presumed that the eggs belonged to the most common dinosaur found in the Djadochta Formation of the

Flaming Cliffs, the ancestor of *Triceratops* known as *Protoceratops*. In 1995, however, a new expedition to Mongolia by the current staff of the American Museum found these same nests covered by the long-legged, predatory, ostrichlike dinosaur *Oviraptor* in a brooding posture, proving that it was the parent. Embryos inside some of the eggs were from *Oviraptor* as well, not *Protoceratops*. Ironically, scientists had named it *Oviraptor*, or "egg thief," in 1923 because they thought it was stealing the eggs in the nesting grounds, not that it was the mother of those eggs.

Since 1923, the discovery and study of dinosaur eggs has made huge strides. In 1978, paleontologist Jack Horner of the Museum of the Rockies in Bozeman, Montana, found huge clusters of eggs and nests of the duck-billed dinosaur *Maiasaura* ("good mother lizard"), which fed and protected its hatchlings until they were old enough to leave the nest. They also found nests of the small predator *Troodon*, which did not take care of its babies after they hatched but abandoned them to fend for themselves, as most reptiles do. During the 1980s and 1990s, more and more dinosaur eggs and nesting grounds have been identified, so it has become a major growth area for research in paleontology.

But Chiappe and Dingus's discovery was one of the most amazing of all dinosaur egg sites. These eggs have given us great insights into how dinosaurs grew from tiny babies the size of a Chihuahua when they hatched to monsters that could make the ground thunder beneath their feet as adults. The detailed study of their bone tissues shows that dinosaurs grew at extraordinary rates once they hatched, a rate of growth unmatched in any living animal. They had to grow rapidly to find food and to become large enough that the many huge predatory dinosaurs did not snack on them. Of course, those eggs that did hatch released hatchlings into a world where predators were all around them, from small carnivorous dinosaurs to the largest predators the world had ever seen (see chapter 2). One of these predators was *Aucasaurus*, found in the same beds with the eggs, a large carnivorous dinosaur with horns over its eyes like *Carnotaurus*. The scarcity of the skeletons of the huge adults suggested that like most animals, the vast majority of these hatchling and baby sauropods never survived to lay more eggs themselves.

King of the Giants

The largest land creatures that ever lived were the huge sauropods found in the Cretaceous rocks of South America. The biggest of all sauropods currently known from a reasonably complete skeleton was *Argentinosaurus*, from the Upper Cretaceous Huincul Formation of Patagonia, 95 million years in age (plate 3). A rancher found the first limb bones in 1987, mistaking them for petrified logs. Then they were brought to the attention of José Bonaparte, whom we met in the previous chapter. Bonaparte collected them and named them *Argentinosaurus huinculensis*. *Argentinosaurus* is not based on a complete skeleton, but it does have most of the backbone, hip region, some ribs, and a right shinbone.

Nevertheless, the individual bones are immense. Each vertebra in the backbone is over 1.59 meters (5.2 ft) tall, and the shinbone is 1.55 meters (more than 5 ft) long. Based on these specimens, *Argentinosaurus* was about 30–35 meters (98–115 ft) long and weighed 80–100 metric tonnes (88–110 tons). There is a reconstructed skeleton in the Museo Municipal Carmen Funes that is 40 meters (130 ft) long and 7.3 meters (24 ft) high. If these size estimates are correct, *Argentinosaurus* was the longest and heaviest land animal to have ever lived.

What about some of the other huge sauropod bones from the Cretaceous in Argentina, including *Antarctosaurus* and *Argyrosaurus*? Most of these species are based on a few leg bones, so it is impossible to tell whether they were much bigger than *Argentinosaurus*. The thighbones from *Antarctosaurus* are incredible, measuring 2.31 meters (7.6 ft) long (figure 3.3). *Argyrosaurus* was almost this size, with thighbones almost 2 meters (6.6 ft) long and upper arm bones 1.3 meters (4.3 ft) long. In 2007, *Futalognkosaurus* was found and described from the Late Cretaceous (87 Ma) of Argentina. The skeleton is about 70 percent complete. *Futalognkosaurus* may have reached 28 meters (92 ft) long, just slightly smaller than *Argentinosaurus*. In 2014, the science news was full of pictures of even larger limb bones from Argentina, but these fossils have not yet been formally described or published. In 2016, the American Museum of Natural History in New York displayed a huge titanosaur that may be even bigger than *Argentinosaurus*, although it still did not have a name at the time this was written. Its weight is estimated at about 70 metric tonnes (77 tons), or about five elephants. To sustain such a huge body, it would have an enormously long digestive tract to process its diet of coarse pine needles and cycad fronds and ferns. Its huge size suggests that it had an enormous four-chambered heart that weighed about 230 kilograms (500 lbs) and was about 2 meters (6.5 ft) in circumference. Such a heart would have pumped about 90 liters (24 gallons) of blood each time it beat, which would have been about every five seconds in such a large animal.

The Argentinian Cretaceous hosted not only the biggest but also the most bizarre sauropods. The strangest was *Amargasaurus* (plate 4), also

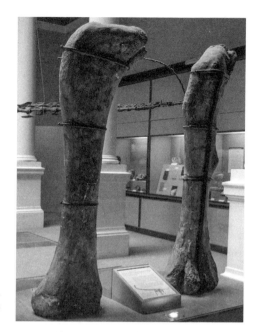

Figure 3.3. Thighbone of *Antarctosaurus*, a titanosaur from Argentina, with the largest leg bones of any animal ever found (courtesy R. Coria).

found and named by José Bonaparte. It was not huge by the standards of South America's giants, reaching only about 9 meters (30 ft) long. It had a weird skull with the nostrils on the top of its head, rather than at the tip of the snout. Its most bizarre feature is the elongated pair of spines at the top of each vertebra in its backbone, giving it a porcupinelike appearance.

No one knows what the spikes along its backbone were used for. Some have suggested that they were for defense, making it hard for a predator to chomp down on its neck or back. Others suggest that they were for display, to show other males and female of their species who was boss, the function of the antlers in deer and the horns in antelopes. Some paleontologists argue that instead of a row of paired spikes, these spines were covered by skin, giving the dinosaur a humped back resembling that of a buffalo. Others have argued that they supported a thin membrane of skin, somewhat like a sail. Whatever these spikes along the backbone were used for, they are not unique to *Amargasaurus*. They are found on predatory dinosaurs such as *Spinosaurus* from the Cretaceous of Egypt, as well as the herbivorous iguanodont *Ouranosaurus* from the same beds in Egypt.

Thunder Lizards

Over the past century, our understanding of the sauropods has come a long way. There are now hundreds of fossil species of sauropods, although it is difficult to decide which named sauropod species are real because of the scarcity of complete skeletons. Their limb bones are huge and durable, even if much of the skeleton has been scattered and washed away. Consequently, there are dozens of species of sauropods that are based on only a few fossils, usually a few vertebrae and occasionally the limbs. Even the relatively complete sauropods based on partial skeletons had the annoying habit of losing their heads before they were fossilized. There are just a few species known from nearly complete skeletons, *Apatosaurus, Diplodocus, Brachiosaurus, Camarasaurus, Argentinosaurus, Futalognkosaurus, Amargasaurus, Barosaurus,* and *Mamenchisaurus* among them.

The ancestors of these huge monsters were Triassic dinosaurs called prosauropods. These provide classic "missing links" between the big Jurassic monsters and their early dinosaur ancestors. The Late Triassic prosauropod *Plateosaurus* was 10 meters (33 ft) long, and weighed about 4,000 kilograms (8,800 lbs), yet it is tiny compared to its descendants. Prosauropods began to evolve a relatively long neck and tail. They could walk either on four feet or on two feet. Prosauropods still had long fingers for grasping, which changed in their giant descendants as their immense weight crushed their fingers down to stubby disks of bone.

A century ago, paleontologists thought of sauropods as sluggish, tail-dragging lizards of the swamps, supporting their immense weight by the buoyancy of water. But since the 1980s, new fossils have completely changed our understanding of sauropods and how they lived. The first major surprise comes from their trackways, which demonstrate that sauropods held their tails out straight, because there are no tail drag marks. Studies of the ecology and geology of sauropod-bearing rocks show that they lived not in swamps but in both coastal regions and even drier habitats. With their long strides, sauropods could walk a long way to feed on trees, using their long necks. In addition, their bodies were so full of weight-reducing air sacs that sauropods would float high in the water and could not dive, if they spent much time in water at all.

Sauropods have some puzzling features, including heads and mouths that were quite small for such immense animals. Their simple peglike or bladelike teeth were not very efficient at grinding up plants, particularly in contrast to duckbills and horned dinosaurs, which had dense clusters of hundreds of grinding teeth to chew lots of plant matter. These inefficient mouth and teeth suggest that sauropods fed on anything they could reach, especially needles on the tops of conifers and ferns in the undergrowth. Remember, in the Jurassic there were no grasses or other flowering plants yet. Based on sauropods' nearest living relatives, chickens and crocodiles, paleontologists have long thought that they had large gizzards to process large amounts of vegetation. There are a number of sauropod skeletons that seem to have polished grinding stones where the gizzard should be, although more recently this has been disputed.

Sauropod necks could not bend in tight curves, like the body of a snake does, but they were still more flexible and not as rigid as a fishing rod, as some paleontologists have argued. The vertebrae in the neck, back, and tail are marvels of lightweight construction. They are built entirely of bony struts and held together by many long tendons to make them light but very strong, with air sacs throughout to reduce weight.

Because of their immense size, sauropods needed massive limbs. Even though they walked on the tips of their toes, their incredible weight meant that their toe bones were crushed into short disks and rods of bone, just as they are in elephants. Because of their enormous size, sauropods could not walk very fast. Apparently, they walked in a slow but steady pace of a few miles per hour, but they could not trot. They were able to travel huge distances all the same simply because of their long stride.

Paleontologists have found many different groups of sauropods. Most familiar are the long-necked, whip-tailed diplodocines such as *Diplodocus* and *Apatosaurus* and the tall brachiosaurs with their long front legs, short hind legs, and giraffelike necks. However, both of these groups were rare in South America. Instead, the Lost World of South America was dominated by the small-headed, stocky titanosaurs, which also lived in Europe, Africa, and the other Gondwana continents, including Antarctica. In the Northern Hemisphere, sauropods were most diverse and dominant during the Late Jurassic. However, in the Gondwana continents in the Late Cretaceous, titanosaurs were still flourishing, even as they were vanishing from the Northern Hemisphere. The huge sauropods of the Cretaceous of Argentina were mostly titanosaurs, including the largest creatures ever to walk on land.

Who's on First?

What was the largest dinosaur—and largest land animal—ever? The problem with comparing sauropods is that most species are based on just a few limb bones or vertebrae, so it is hard to get reliable size estimates or make meaningful comparisons. Currently, the most completely known sauropod is based on a composite of five different specimens of *Giraffatitan* (formerly *Brachiosaurus*) found in the Upper Jurassic of East Africa and now on display at the Museum für Naturkunde in Berlin. It stands 13.5 meters

(44 ft) above the floor of the museum and is about 22.5 meters (74 ft) long. It would have weighed about 78 metric tonnes (86 tons). This is not the maximum, because there is one leg bone that is 13 percent larger than the bones of this famous mounted skeleton.

There are suggestions of even bigger dinosaurs, but they are based on just a few bones. For example, the huge brachiosaur from the Early Cretaceous of Oklahoma named *Sauroposeidon* had bones so huge that they were mistaken for tree trunks when they were first found. For this monster, we have only a few neck and leg bones, which suggest a creature that reached 17 meters (56 ft) in the air, taller than *Giraffatitan*. If you scale its bones up based on the Berlin specimen, *Sauroposeidon* was about 34 meters (112 ft) long and weighed around 50–60 metric tonnes (55–66 tons).

The latest alleged "largest dinosaur ever" was announced in 2014. It was named *Dreadnoughtus* because the paleontologists compared it to the huge "dreadnought" battleships of World War I that feared no other ship because of their huge size. *Dreadnoughtus* was claimed to be 70 percent complete, but only the back end of the animal and its forelimbs are known. Without the head, shoulders, or neck, its size is pure guesswork. More recently, a new reconstruction of *Dreadnoughtus* reduced its size considerably from the 59 metric tonnes originally estimated.

Then there is *Bruhathkayosaurus* from the Late Cretaceous of India. It is based on just a few specimens that were lost when floods swept through its storage area, so all we have now are simple line drawings and measurements of the original publication. If the measurements were accurate, *Bruhathkayosaurus* weighed about 175–220 metric tonnes (190–240 tons), although some scholars think it weighed no more than 139 metric tonnes.

Or what about *Amphicoelias fragillimus*? This was the name given by pioneering paleontologist Edward Drinker Cope in 1877 to a single backbone vertebra. All we know of this creature is one illustration, but if the measurements are accurate, it was the biggest creature ever to walk on land. The vertebra was apparently 2.7 meters (8.8 ft) tall, which would suggest that *Amphicoelias* was 40–60 meters (130–200 ft) long and up to 122 metric tonnes (135 tons), making it larger than any other dinosaur except *Bruhathkayosaurus*. Sadly, this single fossil of *Amphicoelias* disappeared from Cope's collections some time before he died in 1897, as no one could find it among the immense pile of bones in his cluttered house after his death. Back in those days, fossils were not impregnated with hardeners and protected by plaster jackets as they are now, so it probably just fell apart while it was in storage. Most paleontologists today think that this specimen was not nearly as big as Cope's diagram suggested, but that the scale on the drawing probably has a typographic error. *Amphicoelias* and *Bruhathkayosaurus* might have been the largest land animals ever, but their specimens are lost and their descriptions are inadequate. For now, the largest land animal ever is still *Argentinosaurus*.

How Many Kinds of Sauropods Were There?

Argentinosaurus, Antarctosaurus, Argyrosaurus, Futalognkosaurus, Dreadnoughtus, and many other names have been applied to immense titanosaurs from about the same time in one small region of Argentina (see figure 3.1). That is a great many huge animals of the same shape and nearly the same size to be living together. Some paleontologists look at this number of species and argue that it is not biologically realistic, given what we know of the ecology of large animals. This argument has come up many times, most recently in a highly publicized study in 2015 that argued that the diplodocine *Brontosaurus* was again a real species. For more than a century, paleontologists had agreed with Elmer Riggs's work in 1903, which showed that *Brontosaurus* and *Apatosaurus* were the same thing, and by the rules of zoology, *Apatosaurus* was named first and thus is the only correct name.

If the conclusions of the 2015 study by Emanuel Tschopp and co-authors are correct, the diplodocines were incredibly diverse during the Late Jurassic. In fact, in the Morrison Formation (Upper Jurassic, mainly Colorado-Utah-Wyoming) alone, they record fourteen different species in nine genera: *Suuwassea, Amphicoelias, Apatosaurus, Brontosaurus, Supersaurus, Diplodocus, Kaatedocus, Barosaurus,* and *Galeamopus*. These diplodocines were from a single formation that covers a limited geographic area and about 7–11 million years of time, plus several more specimens that have not been named yet. And that does not count the nondiplodocid sauropods, including the monstrously huge *Brachiosaurus*, as well as *Camarasaurus* and *Haplocanthosaurus*, two distantly related diplodocoids, and possibly several more creatures. In Carnegie Quarry at Dinosaur National Monument, probably representing a single biological fauna and a short interval of time, Tschopp and colleagues claim that the following species are real: the diplodocines *Apatosaurus louisae, Brontosaurus parvus, Diplodocus carnegii* and *D. hallorum, Barosaurus,* and *Camarasaurus* and *Haplocanthosaurus*. That makes at least seven distinct species of huge sauropods from a single interval of time, all crowding together and sharing common resources.

For many people, this is the best sauropod research, and indeed the thoroughness and rigor of the analysis are impressive. But as a paleontologist who has published taxonomy on large terrestrial vertebrates for more than thirty-five years, I found some issues troubling. This is an incredibly high diversity of animals for any limited time and place. If we were talking about species of small-bodied creatures, such as insects or rodents, there would be no problem. But huge land animals need lots of room to roam and feed. Ecological theory and studies of modern animals show that larger species require bigger home ranges. The principle of competitive exclusion suggests that no two species can compete for the same resources, and that problem is magnified for larger animals, which rarely share territory with their own competing populations, let alone closely related species. We know of no examples of large land vertebrates today that exist in high diversity and compete for the same resources. Even before poaching reduced their numbers, only one really big mammal—the elephant—lived in the savannas of Africa, which have the most diverse large land-mammal fauna today, and even they have problems if their populations exceed the carrying capacity of the habitat.

The same goes for the prehistoric past. Among communities with large terrestrial mammals, there are no instances of more than one or two huge species, usually an elephant or mammoth, in a fauna at the same time as another huge species competing for the same resources. Even the famous "mammoth steppe," with its incredibly high diversity for an Ice Age tundra grassland, still supported no more than one species of mammoth at a given time and place. Sauropods were many times larger than elephants or mammoths.

What we are really talking about is the longstanding argument among paleontologists about "lumping" versus "splitting." Lumping puts lots of different specimens in a single highly variable species, while splitting gives a different species name to every specimen that appears slightly different. The dispute goes back to the earliest days of classification, when the pioneering collectors of the eighteenth and nineteenth centuries delighted in erecting new species willy-nilly, as sort of a mark of accomplishment, often driven by the pride of adding to their collection. All the early dinosaurs were named this way.

The splitters were dominant in the early twentieth century as well, but by the mid-twentieth century, the trend shifted. Such paleontologists as George Gaylord Simpson, who was also a pioneer in statistics in paleontology, argued that we should think of fossil samples as we think of modern populations of animals and determine how many valid species there really are based on living biological analogues. Since then, the trend has been to lump the many invalid species created by pre-1940s paleontologists and reduce the chaos of questionable species names to get at a true biological signal of diversity. The famous and powerful paleontologist Henry Fairfield Osborn was a hypersplitter who named nearly every specimen with the slightest difference from any other specimen a new species. His huge monographs on mammoths and elephants (1936) and the two-horned brontotheres (1929) are monuments of oversplit taxonomy, and both have been completely replaced by modern taxonomy that got rid of most of his invalid names. The hundreds of amazing skulls of the late Eocene brontotheres of the Badlands of South Dakota and adjacent states were once divided into many genera and dozens of species. Today, Matt Mihlbachler and colleagues recognize only one valid species, *Megacerops coloradensis*. Other famous names, among them *Titanotherium, Brontotherium, Brontops, Menodus, Allops,* and *Menops,* are no longer taken seriously, though that does not keep them from turning up in popular books today, especially for children.

When I started working on fossil rhinoceroses more than thirty-five years ago, nearly every specimen with slightly different teeth was considered to be another species. But a large quarry sample of a single population from *Trigonias* Quarry in the upper Eocene beds of Colorado showed that all those variations in the crests and cusps of the upper premolars are due to intrapopulational variability. Now all those long invalid names have been dropped. Likewise, the gigantic indricothere rhinoceroses of Asia are now all in the genus *Paraceratherium,* replacing junior names such as *Baluchitherium* and *Indricotherium,* for exactly the same reason: These huge animals would have been much like elephants with small populations roaming large distances to find enough treetops to browse on, and it is extremely unlikely that more than one species could have coexisted in the same place and time.

This is not to say that every recent study automatically leads to lumping. The early human fossil record was grossly oversplit when only a handful of fossils were known and each one got its own name. Then, during the 1960s, scientists went in for the trend toward lumping and perhaps overlumping on the grounds that only one human species lives on the planet today. But by the 1970s and 1980s, so many anatomically different fossils had appeared that anthropologists could no longer shoehorn them all into just a few species and now must concede that there are more taxa of real species of extinct humans.

Could this apparent high diversity of sauropods in the Morrison Formation also be due to oversplitting and failure to account for high intrapopulational variability? The biological and ecological arguments suggest this. To cite a similar example, Mihlbachler and colleagues did a careful study of African giraffes, long-necked, large-bodied animals somewhat like sauropods, and found that they showed huge variability not only in cranial appendages (their hornlike ossicones) but also in the proportions and shapes of the skull, features of the neck, and the like—precisely the same features that are used to justify so many different sauropod taxa. Giraffes are all one species (*Giraffa camelopardis*), with several local geographic subspecies, yet no one suggests that zoologists recognize separate species or genera for these differences. Tschopp and colleagues have apparently accounted for juveniles and changes in shape due to growth of immature individuals, which is reassuring. Another possible source of variability might be sexual dimorphism, which I do not see mentioned in their paper. That is a tough issue, since it is hard to tell whether fossils are truly male and female in most cases, except for those such as deer for which we have good modern analogues.

Some dinosaur paleontologists are aware of the problem, of course, and a number of people have speculated about so many closely related gigantic herbivores in the same place and time, when the resource base of the dry savannas of the Morrison Formation was too meager to support even one gigantic herbivore. The most recent effort, by David Button and colleagues in 2014, argues that the skulls of these fossils are just different enough in their feeding mechanics that they could have specialized in eating different types of trees and foliage. Such studies assume that the classification is valid and that there really were a large number of huge species living together, and therefore this has to be explained somehow. Maybe that is plausible, but it still does not fully address how so many different species of gigantic animals, with monstrous appetites, made a living at the same time and place on just the foliage of treetops and maybe some ferns. Remember, this is the Late Jurassic, when most of the trees were conifers and cycads with tough, fibrous, slow-growing needles and fronds, not rapidly growing nutritious leaves and fruits of flowering plants and especially grasses.

Is there any way to look at the sample of specimens from Carnegie Quarry as a single population of diplodocines, possibly some males and some females, or are the anatomical features completely incompatible with this idea? Keep the example of the extreme variability of giraffes in mind. Until someone has convincingly addressed the issue, I will continue putting the name "Brontosaurus" in quotes to indicate its uncertain status. I will ask the same questions when I read about yet another new genus or species of gigantic titanosaur from the Cretaceous of Argentina.

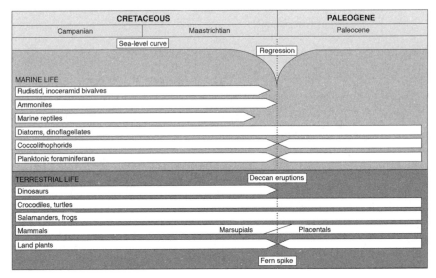

CRETACEOUS		PALEOGENE
Campanian	Maastrichtian	Paleocene

Sea-level curve

Regression

MARINE LIFE
Rudistid, inoceramid bivalves
Ammonites
Marine reptiles
Diatoms, dinoflagellates
Coccolithophorids
Planktonic foraminiferans

TERRESTRIAL LIFE

Deccan eruptions

Dinosaurs
Crocodiles, turtles
Salamanders, frogs
Mammals   Marsupials   Placentals
Land plants

Fern spike

Figure 4.1. Diagram showing the pattern of extinction of major groups of plants and animals through the Late Cretaceous. Some marine groups (rudistid and inoceramid clams, marine reptiles) were apparently long gone before the impact occurred. Only planktonic algae known as coccolithophorids and amoebalike foraminiferans showed a major crash at the end of the Cretaceous. On land, only the non-bird dinosaurs vanished completely; most reptiles sailed through with no effect, as did amphibians. There was a shift in the dominance of mammals from marsupials to placentals. (Diagram by D. R. Prothero.)

 **Demise of the Dinosaurs**

Why did the dinosaurs vanish? One popular account is a simplistic story of a colliding object from space as the only cause of extinction. The true story is much more complicated and much more interesting.

This Is the End

Dinosaurs ruled the earth at the end of the Cretaceous Period, about 66 Ma. They did so for more than 120 million years. During all this time, they were preeminently successful around the world. In North America, the Late Cretaceous dinosaurs included the most famous dinosaur, *Tyrannosaurus rex*, as well as the three-horned *Triceratops* and other horned dinosaurs, turtlelike armored ankylosaurs, and lots of different kinds of duck-billed dinosaurs—but very few long-necked sauropods, which we saw in the previous chapter. No sauropods are found in the Upper Cretaceous beds of Montana or Wyoming, and only the titanosaur *Alamosaurus* is known from the Late Cretaceous of the San Juan Basin in New Mexico.

In South America, there are numerous fossil assemblages of latest Cretaceous age, especially in Patagonia. These fossils are very similar to those of other Gondwana landmasses, such as India and Madagascar, but very different from those in North America. In contrast to North America and Asia, there were no horned dinosaurs such as *Triceratops* in South America. Instead of the rare sauropods that we see in North America, there were abundant titanosaurs in South America. Some, such as *Puertasaurus* and *Laplatasaurus*, were not much smaller that the gigantic *Argentinosaurus* from the middle part of the Cretaceous (about 93 Ma). There were also small titanosaurs such as *Neuquensaurus* and *Saltasaurus*, which were only about 13 meters (40 ft) long and weighed only 7 metric tonnes (8 tons), small for a sauropod. These titanosaurs closely resemble those found on other Gondwana continents. Instead of the tyrannosaurs found in Asia and North America, the dominant predators in South America were the horned abelisaur theropods, such as *Carnotaurus*.

Thus, most of the Argentinian dinosaurs were Southern Hemisphere groups that lived across the Gondwana continents, especially Madagascar and India as well as South America. But in the latest Cretaceous, for the first time since Pangea had begun to break up, there were also dinosaurs from the north that reached the Lost World. As in Mongolia and Canada, there were smaller predatory dinosaurs, such as the *Velociraptor* relative known as *Unquillosaurus*. In addition, latest Cretaceous beds in South America yield a diversity of both duck-billed dinosaurs and the turtlelike armored ankylosaurs, both typically found in Mongolia, China, and North America but never seen in South America until the end of the Cretaceous. From this, most scientists have concluded that there was some sort of land bridge between the Americas in the Late Cretaceous, allowing the first exchange between the continents in a very long time—and the last exchange for another 60 million years.

Out with a Bang . . . or a Whimper?

These are the creatures that ruled the earth 66 Ma. Let's look at three possible scenarios for what happened to them at the end of the Cretaceous.

Scenario I

With no warning, a giant asteroid about 10 kilometers (6 mi) across came hurtling from space at speeds greater than 100,000 miles an hour (160,000 kph). It would have an energy level equivalent to 100 million megatons of TNT. As it approached the earth's atmosphere, it formed a huge fireball in the sky, brighter than the sun, that temporarily blinded the land animals that witnessed it. Shortly after it lit up the sky, the shock wave ahead of it produced a series of incredible sonic booms. Then it slammed into the earth with the energy a billion times stronger than the Hiroshima nuclear bomb. It hit in the spot where the modern Yucatán Peninsula of Mexico is located today. The impact excavated a crater over 20 kilometers (12 mi) deep and 170 kilometers (106 mi) wide, with a flash brighter than any nuclear blast.

The impact caused giant tsunamis to crash around the coastline of the Gulf of Mexico and Caribbean, leaving huge deposits of impact debris and storm waves in places from Mexico to Texas to Cuba and Haiti. Meanwhile, the "mushroom cloud" of dust and debris shot 12,000 meters (40,000 ft) up into the stratosphere, where it created a nuclear winter effect—that is, the dust-choked deep freeze associated with the aftermath of a thermonuclear explosion. The dust circulated around the global stratospheric layer and blocked the sunlight for years, chilling the planet and cutting off photosynthesis by the plants. In one version of this scenario, sulfur from the gypsum located in the Yucatán bedrock created sulfuric acid rain around the globe. Land animals quickly died off, especially the dinosaurs.

In the oceans, the darkness caused the food pyramid based on planktonic algae to collapse, wiping out many organisms higher in the food chain. Especially prominent were the ammonites, shelled relatives of squids and octopuses that looked like the living chambered nautilus. These had survived the previous great mass extinctions in the Permian and Triassic and yet succumbed abruptly at the end of the Cretaceous to the extreme stresses. Widespread death and destruction occurred throughout the oceanic realm, wiping out marine reptiles, many of the clams and snails, and other marine creatures. The end had come with a bang, and it would take much of the next 10 million years of the Paleocene for the planet to recover.

Scenario 2

The second largest volcanic eruption in all of earth history erupted from the mantle during the latest Cretaceous, about 68 Ma, then intensified about 66 Ma. Known as the Deccan lavas, they erupted mostly in what is now western India and Pakistan, in the area centered on Mumbai (Bombay). Huge floods of red-hot lava poured from cracks in the earth and flooded the landscape for more than 500,000 square kilometers (almost 200,000 sq mi), with a volume of 512,000 cubic kilometers (123,000 cubic mi). The volcanoes erupted over and over again, building up a stack of cooled lava flows over 2,000 meters (6,500 ft) thick. Immense quantities of volcanic gases were released from these mantle-derived magmas, including carbon dioxide, sulfur dioxide, and other nasty chemicals. The stratospheric dust and gases blocked the sunlight for a time and led to a global cooling event. The global cooling and dark skies produced the same kinds of death and extinction that the postulated asteroid impact might have produced.

Scenario 3

Global sea level dropped around the world, the biggest sea level drop in the entire Age of Dinosaurs. Apparently, the mid-ocean ridges that produced new oceanic seafloor abruptly began to slow down their eruption and spreading rates, which caused the volume of the mid-ocean ridges to shrink. As the ridges shrank, they displaced less water onto the land and caused shorelines to retreat and huge areas of shallow marine habitat to be exposed to the air and to the erosion of rivers. Most impressive was the loss of the great Western Interior Seaway, which ran from the Arctic to the Gulf of Mexico during the entire Cretaceous. It once teemed with marine life, especially huge mollusks, gigantic fish, and marine reptiles such as mosasaurs, plesiosaurs, and giant sea turtles. The loss of so much shallow marine habitat was devastating to marine life and led to mass extinctions.

Meanwhile, the exposed continental shelves caused a change in the reflectivity of the earth's surface, altering global temperature. There were also big changes in ocean circulation patterns and global wind patterns as the seas retreated and the land was exposed. These complex changes in climate and temperature are still poorly understood, but they meant bad news for the dinosaurs and much of the plankton that had flourished through most of the Cretaceous.

On land, coastal plains and freshwater habitats expanded rapidly as the seas retreated. This was good for freshwater fish, which thrived, but caused mass extinction in the sharks that once swam into the realm of the dinosaurs.

> There are three different explanations for mass extinctions at the end of the Cretaceous. Most people have heard only of the first one, the impact scenario, and even many scientists have never heard of the other two, although all three of them are well documented and all three actually happened. Which was most important? What really killed off the dinosaurs?

Serendipity

Many people think that scientific research is about finding a problem and solving it. However, it turns out that most great scientific discoveries are made by accident. More often than not, scientists who discover something important were looking for something else and made their great discovery without planning to do so. We call these lucky accidents *serendipity*, from an old Persian tale named "The Three Princes of Serendip"—the old name for Sri Lanka or Ceylon—whose heroes make discoveries unexpectedly.

There are hundreds of examples of accidental discoveries. Alfred Nobel accidentally mixed nitroglycerin and collodium ("gun cotton") and discovered gelignite, the key ingredient for his development of TNT. Silly Putty, Teflon, Superglue, Scotchgard, and Rayon were all accidents, as was the discovery of the elements helium and iodine. Among drugs, penicillin, laughing gas, Minoxidil for hair loss, the birth-control pill, and LSD were all discovered by accident. Viagra was originally developed to treat blood pressure but later was discovered to be a cure for erectile dysfunction. Great accidents in physics and astronomy include the discoveries of the planet Uranus, infrared radiation, superconductivity, electromagnetism, X-rays, and many others. Two Bell Lab engineers who were trying to eliminate noise from their newly developed microwave antennas accidentally discovered the cosmic background radiation from the Big Bang in the process.

There are also many practical inventions that were stumbled upon by accident, such as inkjet printers, cornflakes, safety glass, Corningware, and the vulcanization of rubber. Percy Spencer was working on surplus magnetrons from World War II for Raytheon, which had built hundreds of them for the war effort and could no longer sell them. When he found that a candy bar in his lab coat pocket had melted, he accidentally invented microwave ovens.

Geologists have also found important things they were not expecting. In 1855, John Henry Pratt and George Biddell Airy were doing routine surveying for the British government in northern India. They noticed that the plumb line weight under the surveying tripod was not as gravitationally attracted to the Himalayas as they had expected, and they eventually discovered the evidence for the deep crustal roots of mountains. The marine geologists who mapped the magnetic anomalies on the seafloor were not looking for the crucial evidence that proved plate tectonics but were simply doing routine data collection of magnetic, bathymetric, and oceanographic data as their ships undertook regularly scheduled voyages of discovery. Maurice Ewing, the founder of Lamont-Doherty Geological Observatory (now Lamont-Doherty Earth Observatory) at Columbia University, gave a standing order that each ship take a deep-sea core at the end of the day, no matter where it was. Many of those cores turned out to have crucial evidence for the history of oceans and climates and the evolution of life.

Likewise, the arguments over the possible causes of the great Cretaceous extinction events were inconclusive until serendipity stepped in. For generations, scientists had been blaming the extinction of dinosaurs on all sorts of ideas, most of which could not be subjected to scientific testing. These included climate change (too warm or too cold), the evolution of flowering plants (except this happened at the beginning of the Cretaceous and may actually have spurred the evolution of duck-billed dinosaurs), mammals eating their eggs (except mammals and dinosaurs both appeared 200 million years ago, so why did they suddenly eat all the dinosaur eggs?), diseases and epidemics (no way to scientifically test this idea), and many other notions. The problem with all these suggestions was not only that they were not easy to test scientifically but also that they focused exclusively on dinosaurs. But the great Cretaceous extinctions also affected the food chain in the oceans, from the planktonic algae to the ammonites to the marine reptiles, and the food chain on land as well, from flowering plants to many other animals besides dinosaurs. Any explanation that focused on dinosaurs alone missed the point. Dinosaurs were a side effect. Clearly, dinosaurs would be affected by any event that disrupted the biosphere from the base of the food chain to the top.

The breakthrough came in 1978, when a young structural geologist named Walter Alvarez was working on some marine limestones in the Apennine Mountains near Gubbio, Italy. (I first met him when he was a postdoctoral student at Lamont, where I was a grad student in the late 1970s.) Walter wanted to find a way to estimate how quickly the sediments that spanned the end of the Cretaceous had been deposited, especially the distinctive clay layer found right at the top of the highest Cretaceous limestone and right below the lowest Paleocene limestones. This level is known as the "KPg" or "KT" boundary to geologists. (The Cretaceous is abbreviated "K" in geological maps, after *Kreide*, the German word for the Cretaceous chalks of the White Cliffs of Dover; "Pg" stands for "Paleogene"; and "T" is short for the now-obsolete term "Tertiary.")

Walter's father, Nobel Prize–winning physicist Luis Alvarez of the University of California, Berkeley, suggested that they might use the rate of accumulation of cosmic dust in these ocean-bottom sediments. If there was lots of cosmic dust, then the sediments had accumulated slowly, but if there was little dust, then it had been quicker. Walter took samples of the rocks all across the KPg boundary (figure 4.2), and they looked for a rare platinum-group metal called iridium as a tracer for cosmic dust. Iridium is relatively abundant in extraterrestrial rocks and in the earth's mantle but rare in the crust.

What they found shocked them. The iridium levels were much higher than anything that could be explained by the gentle rain of cosmic dust.

Figure 4.2. Close-up of the KPg boundary layer at Gubbio, Italy. The gray layers on the bottom are Cretaceous limestones, and those on top are from the Paleogene. The thin layer of clay with the coin on it is the iridium-rich deposit from the KPg impact event (courtesy Alessandro Montanari, Geological Observatory of Coldigioco, Italy).

Walter, Luis, and their collaborators Frank Asaro and Helen Michel, geochemists who had measured the iridium at Berkeley, brainstormed their puzzling results. They came up with the idea of an asteroid impact as an explanation for the iridium and extinctions. Their scientific paper finally appeared in 1980, and it has become one of the most cited papers in the history of science. It spurred a stampede of scientists into studying mass extinctions and generated thousands of other scientific papers and many books.

The paper hit the scientific community like the asteroid impact it described. At first, most geologists were skeptical, as any scientific community should be of such wild ideas. Such skepticism also was warranted because there are several ways that rare elements can be concentrated in clay layers like that at the Gubbio KPg boundary. But after finding iridium-rich layers in marine sections in Denmark and many other places, in numerous deep-sea sediment cores, and eventually even in land sections, most scientists had to agree that the Gubbio iridium spike was real and not just a bad data point. In addition, hundreds of scientists looked for additional impact evidence, and soon there were reports of quartz grains with shock features from impacts in the KPg boundary layer, plus blobs of melted crustal rock from the impact site and tsunami deposits all around the Gulf of Mexico. But throughout the controversy in the 1980s, the impact hypothesis was missing one crucial piece of data: Where was the crater?

Meanwhile, other scientists were doing detailed research on the Deccan lava flows of India and Pakistan and pointing out that they would have had many effects similar to an asteroid impact and were reliably dated to just before the KPg boundary. The controversy got to be intense and bitter as hundreds of scientific papers argued one side or another. I could see it every year as I attended the annual meeting of the Geological Society of America (GSA). The GSA meeting brings four thousand to six thousand geologists together for four days, and they give thousands of presentations. A hot topic such as the KPg extinction always guarantees dozens of intensely debated talks and posters each year.

Then, in 1990, a breakthrough occurred. The crater was found deeply buried under the jungle vegetation (and younger sediments) at a site called Chicxulub (pronounced CHICK-zoo-loob), on the tip of Yucatán. Oil geologist Glen Penfield had originally discovered it in 1978, but he did not connect it to the KPg impact idea, which had not yet been published. It took astronomer Alan Hildebrand, who was looking for just such a structure with the impact idea in mind, to track it down, and in 1990 he rediscovered the evidence buried in old oil company reports. This tipped the scales for a while, and most geologists, geophysicists, and geochemists considered the asteroid impact model the only one worth pursuing.

What Do the Fossils Say?

While some earth scientists considered the debate over, paleontologists questioned the asteroid impact model from the beginning. Paleontologists are trained not just in geology but also in biology and are accustomed to the subtle complexity of living systems, with multiple causes and effects. Even before the debate began, they knew that the pattern of extinctions at the end of the Cretaceous was complicated. The impact would produce a sharp, distinct boundary, with all the species dying out precisely at the end of the Cretaceous and not before it. But if a lot of species were declining before the impact or had vanished from the fossil record altogether before the end of the Cretaceous, then the impact model was less important, and other factors might be more influential. The gradual deterioration of the environment by the continual eruption of the Deccan lavas might prove to be more significant, as could the fall in sea level.

During the 1980s and 1990s, paleontologists continued to document the patterns of extinction in both land and marine animals and plants and to determine whether extinctions were instantaneous or followed a more complex pattern (figure 4.1). Now, four decades after the asteroid impact model was first proposed, the pattern of extinctions is far more complicated than can be explained by a single extinction event triggered by impact.

First, let's look at extinctions in the marine realm. The most important species are the plankton, which are the crucial base of the marine food chain and extremely sensitive to environmental changes. Their tiny shells can be found by the thousands in deep-sea sediment cores, so we can study their extinction in fine detail. The planktonic algae known as coccolithophorids, the algae that make chalk, did indeed have a severe crash, as would be expected if the light was dimmed by dense dust clouds, but two other kinds of algae, diatoms and silicoflagellates, which are equally sensitive to the loss of light, did not. Two groups of shelled amoebalike plankton were also studied. The group known as the foraminiferans seemed to show a crash (although some micropaleontologists argued differently), but the other group of planktonic amoebas, the radiolarians, did not. Some foraminiferans lived on the sea bottom rather than in the plankton, and they showed no extinction at all.

Moving up the food chain, we can look at the fossilized shells of the mollusks (clams, snails, and their kin) that once inhabited the Cretaceous seafloor. Some groups, such as the big, flat "dinner-plate" clams known as inoceramids (which reached 1.7 meters, or 5 feet, in diameter) and the conical reef-forming oysters known as rudistids, were extinct long before the end of the Cretaceous, so the impact is irrelevant to them. Of the remaining mollusks, 35 percent of snails and 55 percent of clams and oysters died out, but every study shows their extinction was gradual through the end of the Cretaceous.

Critical to this debate are the rapidly evolving ammonites. They had survived every previous mass extinction since the Devonian. Most studies suggested that ammonites died out slowly through the Cretaceous, with only a few species that survived to near the KPg boundary. On Seymour Island on the Antarctic Peninsula, just south of Chile and Argentina, Bill Zinsmeister has documented a long, protracted extinction in the ammonites through the Upper Cretaceous rocks there (figure 4.3).

The rest of the marine invertebrates—corals, lamp shells, bryozoans, sea lilies, brittle stars, sea urchins, and the like—show either no effect of the KPg event at all or only a gradual extinction through the interval. At the top of the food chain are the marine reptiles, especially the giant marine lizards known as mosasaurs. Their fossil record is not complete enough to show whether they were even around to witness the rock from space, but most of the data suggests that they were dying out long beforehand.

In summary, the only sea creatures that show an obvious abrupt effect consistent with the asteroid impact model are some (but not all) of the plankton. The rest of the marine realm appears to be deteriorating slowly throughout the Late Cretaceous, consistent with the effects of volcanic gases and climate change, as well as the falling sea level exposing most of the shallow marine habitat.

What about the land record? Here the answer is complex and confusing as well (figure 4.1). At the bottom of the food chain are the land plants,

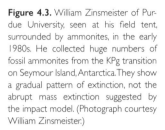

Figure 4.3. William Zinsmeister of Purdue University, seen at his field tent, surrounded by ammonites, in the early 1980s. He collected huge numbers of fossil ammonites from the KPg transition on Seymour Island, Antarctica. They show a gradual pattern of extinction, not the abrupt mass extinction suggested by the impact model. (Photograph courtesy William Zinsmeister.)

and there is certainly a striking change in the leaf fossils across the KPg boundary. In addition, the spores and pollen in these sediments suggest a high abundance of ferns growing in the dark, cool aftermath of the impact, consistent with some aspects of the nuclear winter model of the impact. But the rest of the land fauna shows a complex pattern. Sure, the non-bird dinosaurs vanished, but whether it was sudden or gradual is disputed because their fossil record is so incomplete. A study published just as this book went to press shows that the dinosaurs were declining long before the end of the Cretaceous, and only a few species remained to witness the asteroid. There are suggestions that many of the groups of Cretaceous birds vanished, but the fossil record is not good enough to tell whether it was abrupt and precisely at the KPg boundary or gradual.

The reptiles, especially the crocodilians, lizards, snakes, and turtles, sailed right through the impact event with only minimal extinction—and some of those crocodilians were bigger than smaller dinosaurs. If the entire planet was as hellish as the impact suggests, how did the large crocodiles survive while no dinosaurs of their body size did so? Unlike small animals, crocodiles cannot hide from the effects of the impact or go into hibernation with no warning. In fact, given the warm greenhouse climate of the Late Cretaceous, it's unlikely that crocodilians hibernated at all.

Although there was a minor extinction in sharks (consistent with the loss of marine seaways and expansion of freshwater habitats), more than 90 percent of the freshwater fish survived. The tiny shrew-sized mammals showed some changes in dominance. For example, the pouched opossum-like mammals known as marsupials were replaced by placentals in some places like Montana, and groups such as the squirrel-like egg-laying mammals known as multituberculates did fine in Montana but not in China. Nevertheless, there were only a few extinctions among the mammals. Nearly all of South America's peculiar Mesozoic mammals, including their Jurassic relicts such as the unique dryolestoids and gondwanatheres, survived well into the Cenozoic. In short, the land record does not strongly support the impact-only model of extinction. Only the land plants show a clear, abrupt effect, and the rest of the groups other than dinosaurs did just fine through the supposedly extreme climates of the nuclear winter and came right back in the Paleocene no worse for wear. This casts serious doubt on any model that is too extreme. In particular, any scenario that argues for a global bath of sulfuric acid rain can be discarded right away, because amphibians went through the KPg events without any extinctions. Yet they are extremely sensitive to even small amounts of acid in their habitat, and there would be no frogs or salamanders alive right now if the acid rain scenario were true.

What Is the Answer?

The debates over the Cretaceous extinctions are not just about what killed the dinosaurs. They reveal a bigger theme in the sociology of science and the nature of science communication today.

First, they are a classic demonstration of the problem of communicating science to the public. Nearly all science is reported as one-sided sound bites, with no details, doubts, caveats, or nuance, and crucial information is often left out. In addition, flashy science headlines often prove to be wrong once other scientists look closer and double-check the results. Yet the media rarely report that a sensational study covered years earlier has since been debunked. Consequently, the public learns only the spectacular headlines ("asteroids killed the dinosaurs") and never finds out that the story is more complex, with multiple possible causes.

In the scientific community, things are different. Scientists are capable of going behind the headlines, checking the data, and patiently waiting for years until all the studies have been done and the bad data abandoned and the answer starts to become clear. The KPg debate has brought out another interesting phenomenon: the contrast among different scientific communities. The impact advocates are overwhelmingly found among geologists, geochemists, geophysicists, planetary scientists, and especially those scientists who know no geology or paleontology at all. Many of them are used to plugging samples into a machine and getting simple yes-or-no answers in their science. They like clear-cut results—even if they might be too simplistic.

Paleontologists, on the other hand, are trained in biology, where the systems are typically complex, nuanced, and interrelated and very few things occur in a simple fashion. From the very beginning, they argued with other geoscientists that the pattern of extinction did not match the simplistic idea of a "rock from space" doing everything. Their argument has not abated even four decades later. When vertebrate paleontologists who study the dinosaurs and mammals were polled in 1985, only 5 percent agreed that the impact was the cause of the KPg extinctions. In 1997, a survey of twenty-two distinguished British paleontologists, specialists in each of the groups that lived in the Late Cretaceous, voted overwhelmingly against the impact being significant in the marine fossil record. In 2004, another survey of vertebrate paleontologists found that only 20 percent accepted the impact cause for the KPg extinctions, whereas 72 percent argued that it was a gradual process inconsistent with the asteroid model. In 2010, a paper was published in the eminent journal *Science* with multiple authors, few of whom were paleontologists, again pushing the impact as the sole explanation of the KPg extinctions. It was immediately rebutted by a paper authored by twenty-eight paleontologists that demonstrated that the impact was only a minor part of the story. Even Walter Alvarez, in his popular book *T. rex and the Crater of Doom*, conceded that the KPg extinctions had multiple complex causes.

You see the battles in the professional meetings as well. During the 1980s and 1990s, nearly every meeting of the GSA had several sessions devoted to the KPg debate. By the mid-1990s, it seemed like the impact advocates had won. The tide has shifted again, and during the 2014 GSA meeting in Vancouver, Canada, there was a daylong symposium emphasizing the importance of the Deccan volcanoes and how they better explained most of the KPg extinctions. These battles can be very tense and emotional, since many scientists are not just dispassionately arguing about events from 66 Ma. They have a lot at stake. They are deeply invested in their research program, which has meant years of study and writing and publication and thousands of dollars in grant money. It is not easy to back down from a position once you have defended it in print and in front of your colleagues for years. Thus, the extremists on both sides will continue to argue, and thirty-six years is not long enough for the battle to die out completely, even though neutral outside observers see a complex pattern of multiple causes for the KPg extinction, not the simplistic "rock from space" model.

We often forget that scientists are human. Sometimes individual scientists make their research a personal quest and even insult the other side. The scientific papers on the subject often contain direct attacks on scientific credibility and competence of opponents. At professional meetings, the name-calling was even worse. Careers were ruined by being on the wrong side of the debate, and others suffered enormously as the big boys battled it out. Luis Alvarez said, "I don't want to say bad things about paleontologists, but they're really not very good scientists. They're more like stamp collectors." On the opposite side, paleontologist Bob Bakker told a reporter,

> The arrogance of these people is simply unbelievable. They know next to nothing about how real animals evolve, live, and become extinct. But, despite their ignorance, the geochemists feel that all you have to do is crank up some fancy machine and you've revolutionized science. The real reasons for the dinosaur extinctions have to do with temperature and sea level changes, the spread of diseases by migration and other complex events. In effect, they're saying this: we high-tech people have all the answers, and you paleontologists are just primitive rockhounds.

Indeed, there is no simple final answer. The impact happened. So did the Deccan eruptions. So did the huge drop in sea level. Most of the evidence suggests that the world of the latest Cretaceous was already extreme and hellish from the effects of volcanic gases and climate changes, especially in the oceans. These events must have been too much for the inoceramids, the rudistids, the marine reptiles, and many other animals and plants that vanished well before the rock from space arrived—possibly even the dinosaurs.

When the impact occurred, it was more of a coup de grâce for some of the stressed-out survivors of the environmental deterioration. It definitely had an effect on the planktonic algae and foraminifera and on the land plants. But the impact could not have produced huge amounts of acid rain, or there would be no amphibians today. It could not have been as extreme as Scenario 1, mentioned earlier in the chapter, suggested, or there would have been some effect on the crocodilians, turtles, lizards, snakes, mammals, freshwater fish, and nearly everything else on land at the time.

When someone asks me, "Did an asteroid wipe out the dinosaurs?" I say, "Yes. And no."

The Aftermath

South America is not the place to study the KPg boundary on land, because most of the fossiliferous areas in Argentina and elsewhere were underwater at the end of the Cretaceous. There are no good fossiliferous terrestrial sections that span the KPg boundary anywhere on the continent, and the youngest Cretaceous dinosaur faunas, which are dominated by titanosaurs and *Carnotaurus*, plus immigrant duckbills and ankylosaurs from the north, lived long before the end of the Cretaceous.

Then there is the peculiar locality known as Laguna Umayo in southern Peru. When it was first studied in the 1970s and 1980s, it appeared to have dinosaur eggshell fragments and pollen from Cretaceous plants associated with Paleocene mammal fossils, including some primitive marsupial teeth and peculiar isolated molars of a hoofed mammal named *Perutherium*. Was it proof that dinosaurs survived into the Paleocene in South America before they finally vanished, long after they had disappeared in the Late Cretaceous elsewhere? The poor quality of the fossils and the difficulty of dating the locality left the question unresolved for many years. Finally, in 2004 a careful study of all the fragmentary fossils using the latest dating techniques showed that the locality was Paleocene after all, but the "dinosaur eggshells" and "Cretaceous pollen" had all been misidentified.

There are other, more fossiliferous early Paleocene localities across South America, and they give us the first glimpse into what survived the KPg catastrophe. The best known of these are near Tiupampa in Bolivia and Punta Peligro in southern Argentina. They are dominated by two of the three "Old Timer" groups that came to dominate South America through the rest of the Cenozoic, as we will see in chapters 7–9. Most of the fossils are of different groups of marsupials related to opossums. By the Eocene, these creatures would evolve to fill the meat-eater niche, with marsupials that resembled wolves, hyenas, and even saber-toothed cats. Other fossils are of very archaic hoofed mammals, much like the early Paleocene mammals known as mioclaenids from North America. These creatures would eventually evolve into the native hoofed mammal groups, the second group of Old Timers that dominated South America until about 2 Ma. The similarity between North and South American mioclaenid hoofed mammals suggests that the Late Cretaceous land bridge that allowed duckbills and ankylosaurs down from North America was still in operation in the earliest Paleocene.

This is further confirmed by the presence of fossils known as *Alcidedorbignya*, named after the early-nineteenth-century French paleontologist Alcide d'Orbigny. These specimens closely resemble fossils of a group of heavy-bodied, leaf-eating ground mammals known as pantodonts. They were mostly dominant in China and Mongolia and in western North America in the Paleocene, but apparently at least one lineage was able to migrate south to reach Tiupampa, probably via the land bridge that allowed the Late Cretaceous duckbills and ankylosaurs from North America and Mongolia to reach Argentina. These mammals were among the survivors of the great KPg catastrophe, and they formed the foundation for mammal evolution in South America for the next 65 million years.

They were not the only survivors. One group of dinosaurs also survived, and it dominated the mammals of South America for most of the next 50 million years—just as dinosaurs had done for the first 120 million years of their shared history with mammals. Who were these surviving dinosaurs? They are alive today. We know them as birds.

Figure 5.1. The "terror birds," or phorusrhacids, were flightless predatory birds with powerful hooked beaks for catching and tearing apart their prey. This is a selection of the many dozens of species, compared to a typical 1.75-meter (6-ft) human silhouette. (*a*) The seriema bird, the only close living relative of the phorusrhacids. (*b*) *Mesembriornis milneedwardsi.* (*c*) *Psilopterus bachmanni.* (*d*) *Andagalornis steuletti.* (*e*) *Phorusrhacos longissimus.* (*f*) *Paraphysornis brasiliensis.* (*g*) The heavy-bodied *Brontornis burmeisteri.* (Drawn by E. Brettas; courtesy Luis M. Chiappe, Natural History Museum of Los Angeles County.)

CHAPTER 5

Living Dinosaurs

Dinosaurs did not vanish from the planet 66 million years ago. They are alive and well as birds. South America had some of the most spectacular birds, including the largest bird ever to fly, and huge ground-dwelling flightless birds that preyed on mammals.

Dinosaurs Are Alive—and Have Feathers

Charles Darwin was overjoyed. In 1859, he had published his landmark book, *On the Origin of Species by Means of Natural Selection*, and a scientific and cultural revolution was born. Two years had passed since the book's publication, and although evolution was still controversial, most of the European scientific community had come to accept it.

One of the weakest spots in Darwin's original book was the lack of a good fossil record to support his case. So little was known about it in 1859 that there was just no good fossil evidence to support evolution. There was, of course, the fact that the rocks showed a long and distinct sequence of fossils through time, the faunal succession. This sequence had been discovered back in 1795 by William Smith and other avowedly Christian naturalists, who were able to accept that it pretty much ruled out the flood story of Genesis. By the 1830s, nearly all naturalists had come to regard the Noachian flood and Genesis as creation myths, and they no longer followed the Bible as a guide for science. Still, Darwin spent two chapters in *The Origin of Species* apologizing for the lack of transitional fossils known at that time and admitting the poor quality of the fossil record as it was known then. It has since gotten much better, and it now has produced hundreds of transitional fossils that are proof of evolution.

In 1861, a remarkable discovery was made. For centuries, stonemasons had been excavating the fine-grained Jurassic limestone of the Solnhofen quarries in Bavaria. These smooth, flawless stones made perfect litho-graphic plates that could be etched to print illustrations. Occasionally they would find extraordinary fossils as well: horseshoe crabs, shrimp, the first known pterodactyls, and many other creatures that died in the bottom of a stagnant Jurassic lagoon and were perfectly preserved without decay or destruction. But in 1861, they found an imprint of a feather. Shortly after that, they found a nearly complete skeleton of a fossil that had been covered in feathers. The first good specimen was bought by the British Museum in London, and soon afterward it was described as *Archaeopteryx* ("ancient wing"). In 1877, an even better and more complete specimen was found (figure 5.2), which today resides in a vault behind bulletproof glass in the Museum für Naturkunde in Berlin. These are the best of the twelve known specimens of *Archaeopteryx*. There were indeed fossils of feathered reptiles back in the Jurassic, and they were excellent transitional forms between birds and reptiles.

Darwin could not have predicted a better example of how it was pos-sible for reptiles to evolve into a completely different group, the birds. By the fourth edition of *The Origin of Species*, he would say that at one time some scientists argued "that the whole class of birds came suddenly into existence

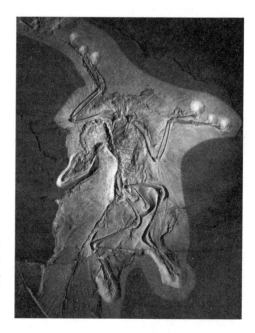

Figure 5.2. *Archaeopteryx* fossils show that birds are descended from dinosaurs, although it took a century for paleontologists to finally realize this. This is the most famous and best preserved of the twelve known specimens, discovered in 1877 and now in the Museum für Naturkunde in Berlin (courtesy Emily Willoughby/CC-BY-SA 4.0).

during the Eocene period [54–34 Ma, as we now date it]; but now we know, on the authority of Professor Owen, that a bird certainly lived during the deposition of the Upper Greensand [Late Early Cretaceous in modern terminology, about 100 Ma; this specimen turned out to be a pterosaur]; and still more recently, that strange bird, the *Archaeopteryx*, with a long lizardlike tail, bearing a pair of feathers on each joint, and with its wings furnished with two free claws, has been discovered in the oolitic slates of Solnhofen. Hardly any recent discovery shows more forcibly than this how little we as yet know of the former inhabitants of the world."

The British Museum specimen was described by Richard Owen, who had earlier taken on the task of describing Darwin's South American fossils from the *Beagle* voyage (see chapter 8). He was considered the most brilliant anatomist and paleontologist in Britain at the time, yet he was one of the few scientists who rejected Darwin's ideas of evolution. When it was his turn to describe the London *Archaeopteryx*, he deliberately downplayed the anatomical features that made it look very reptilian.

A much younger scientist, Thomas Henry Huxley, was then making a name for himself in British scientific circles. Hardworking, brilliant, and ambitious, he had risen from a lower-class upbringing to prominence through sheer effort and talent, in contrast to the majority of naturalists of the time, who were wealthy gentlemen pursuing fossils and natural history as a hobby. He was one of the first to see the importance of Darwin's ideas. When he read the final drafts of *The Origin of Species*, he said, "How stupid of me not to have thought of that!" Once the book was published, he wrote to Darwin to say,

> I trust you will not allow yourself to be in any way disgusted or annoyed by the considerable abuse and misrepresentation which, unless I greatly mistaken, is in store for you. Depend upon it, you have earned the lasting gratitude of all thoughtful men. And as to the curs which will bark and yelp, you must recollect that some of your friends, at any rate, are endowed with an amount of combativeness which (though you have often and justly rebuked it) may stand you in good stead. I am sharpening up my claws and beak in readiness.

For the next decade it was Huxley who was the primary public defender of evolution in Britain, writing about it in many places and even battling in the forum of public debate. This was something that the shy and retiring Darwin hated to do. In 1861, Huxley debated a slick public speaker, Archbishop Samuel Wilberforce, nicknamed "Soapy Sam" for his rhetorical skills. After Wilberforce (coached by Richard Owen) had given a complete distortion of what evolution was about, Huxley demolished his arguments, and a riot ensued. By contrast, Darwin preferred the quiet of his country home southeast of London, where he read and wrote and did his research and dealt with his constant illness. In public, Huxley earned the nickname "Darwin's Bulldog."

Once Owen had published his study, Huxley got his chance to study *Archaeopteryx*. Not blinded by Owen's idiosyncratic ideas or opposition to evolution, Huxley could clearly see that the specimen was an ideal transitional fossil between reptiles and birds. Moreover, Huxley realized that it was a dead ringer for the small dinosaurs that were also found at Solnhofen. Huxley himself had described a fossil of *Compsognathus*, the little bipedal dinosaur featured in the *Jurassic Park II* and *Jurassic Park III* movies, and he noticed the similarities. *Archaeopteryx* had teeth, unlike any living bird, which all have toothless beaks. It had large functional fingers and claws on its hands, something all birds lack. (The hand of the bird is fused into a solid bone where the flight feathers attach; this is the meatless bony tip of the chicken wing.) Its hind feet were built like those of dinosaurs, including the peculiar ankle joint where the first row of anklebones is fused to the shinbone. (This is the little cap of cartilage at the top of a chicken or turkey "drumstick.") It has a long dinosaurian tail composed of many bones, unlike the short, stubby, bony tail of modern birds, whose tails are mostly composed of feathers, with no bony support. Huxley concluded that birds are not just descended from reptiles, but in particular are direct descendants of predatory dinosaurs.

Yet the idea that birds are dinosaurian descendants fell out of favor for the next few decades, mostly due to the efforts of German illustrator and anatomist Gerhard Heilmann. He argued that all birds have a wishbone made up of fused collarbones, while all the dinosaur fossils known at that time appeared to lack collarbones. For decades, paleontologists sought the ancestry of birds among the more primitive Triassic reptiles, then called thecodonts, that had been ancestral to both crocodiles and dinosaurs. That name, given to a catchall group for all relatives of crocodiles and dinosaurs that are not crocodiles or dinosaurs, is no longer in use.

The turning point came in the 1960s and 1970s, when John Ostrom of Yale University discovered an amazing dinosaur with a sicklelike slashing claw and a long, straight tail. Dubbed *Deinonychus* ("terrible claw" in Greek), it was the basis for the velociraptors in the *Jurassic Park* movies. (The actual *Velociraptor* is only about the size of a turkey.) Then Ostrom began to reexamine all the known specimens of *Archaeopteryx*, only a dozen of which have ever been found, and rediscovered Huxley's evidence for their dinosaurian features. Indeed, some had been misidentified as *Compsognathus* or pterodactyls until the feather impressions were noticed.

The clincher was the details of the wrist joint. Both birds and dromaeosaurs such as *Velociraptor* and *Deinonychus* have a distinctive half-moon-shaped bone in their wrists. This allowed *Velociraptor* and *Deinonychus* to snap their hands downward and forward to grab prey. The exact same motion can be seen in the downward part of the bird's flight stroke. This unique anatomy never occurs anywhere else in the animal kingdom, and it is among the hundreds of anatomical features that prove birds are descended from dromaeosaur dinosaurs.

In the mid-1990s, a startling new set of discoveries further revolutionized our view of dinosaurs. Beautifully preserved fossils began to emerge from the Lower Cretaceous Liaoning beds of northeast China. Some were clearly very primitive birds with teeth and a bony tail, and all of them had not only their feathers preserved but often the remains of their last meals in their stomachs as well. Others were clearly nonflying dinosaurs—and they had feathers, too! This demolished the idea that feathers evolved for flight. Instead, it is now clear that feathers occurred on nearly all dinosaurs, and they were there primarily for insulation, just as the down and body feathers of birds are used. Not just *Velociraptor* and *Deinonychus* but also tyrannosaurs, huge sauropods, and even the horned dinosaurs and duckbills all had at least some feathers on them, even if only when they were juveniles.

This is one of the things that annoyed and frustrated paleontologists when the fourth *Jurassic Park* movie, *Jurassic World*, came out in 2015. The original novels and the first three movies were written by Michael Crichton and filmed before the late 1990s, when the evidence that all dinosaurs were feathered became overwhelming. Paleontologists praised the original movies for bringing dinosaurs up to date in the public eye. No longer were dinosaurs portrayed as slow and sluggish tail-dragging lizards in the swamps; now their film versions reflected the paleontological understanding of dinosaurs as intelligent and fast-moving, holding their tails straight out behind them as they ran. To many paleontologists, the 2015 movie was a big disappointment: The filmmakers "chickened out" and decided they had to keep the "look" of their outdated creations from the 1990s, rather than embrace cutting-edge science yet again and update their dinosaurs to reflect what paleontologists now know of them.

From the ideas of Huxley to Ostrom to the discovery of feathered dinosaurs, the case for birds descending from dinosaurs is now overwhelming.

Only a handful of scientists, mostly older-generation ornithologists unfamiliar with the fossils and unwilling to change their old notions, still resist this mountain of evidence.

The latest work from developmental biology has even supported it even further. Birds still have most of the genes for the dinosaurian skeleton, genes that were later suppressed. Back in 1980, scientists grafted mouse lip tissue into the mouth of a developing chicken, and it grew teeth—only they were dinosaurian teeth, not mouse teeth. In 2015, scientists were able to alter the genes of chicken development so that they could develop a dinosaurian mouth, not the beak of a bird. Other embryonic studies have managed to change the genes that form the birds' short, stumpy, bony tail and develop a long, bony tail like a dinosaur's instead. Another experiment on developing chickens has modified their feet so they look like dinosaur feet, not bird feet. Thus, birds are simply highly modified dinosaurs that happened to survive the Cretaceous extinctions. Dinosaurs did not go extinct, in other words. They are flying above you right now, maybe even singing outside your window.

Birds of Terror

When South America became isolated as a "Lost World" in the early Cenozoic, it had none of the predatory mammal groups (cats, dogs, bears, hyenas) that evolved in North America or in the Old World. The only predators were the opossumlike marsupials that grew into beasts that resembled wolves and saber-toothed cats. These creatures never became very large, nor did they evolve into animals that could exploit niches like those occupied by bears, lions, and other big predators that once lived on other continents.

This presented an opportunity for other animals to take over as the big predators. As we will see in the next chapter, the crocodiles and alligators were often huge, as were the snakes. The non-bird dinosaurs had vanished at the end of the Cretaceous, but the birds could diversify into many ecological niches that mammals did not yet occupy. And the birds rose to the challenge. They evolved into a huge group of large flightless predators known as phorusrhacids (FOR-us-RAYK-ids) (plates 5–6; figure 5.1). These birds had huge skulls with long, deep, but narrow beaks with hooked tips, ideal for catching mammalian prey and ripping it open. Their heads were proportionally the largest heads ever to evolve in a bird, which makes sense if they were taking large prey and had only their huge beaks and powerful feet to attack with. They had long necks with an S-shaped bend that could flex and strike out during a lunge after prey.

These birds had tiny vestigial wings that could not have lifted them in flight, but they had no need to fly with their fast-running, long hind legs. Like ostriches, emus, rheas, cassowaries, and numerous extinct giant birds such as the moas of New Zealand and the elephant birds (*Aepyornis*) of Madagascar, phorusrhacids surrendered the advantages of flight in order to get larger and focus on running. Their feet were powerful and robust, with sharp claws, so they undoubtedly used them to kick and slash at prey and to pin the unfortunate victim down as they ripped it open with their hooked beaks.

We can get a sense of how phorusrhacids might have lived and fed by watching their closest relatives, a South American ground bird known as the seriema (figure 5.1*a*). Seriemas act much like the reptile-hunting secretary birds of Africa. Both have long, powerful legs with a fringe of feathers so they can kick and slash at lizards and venomous snakes without fear of being bitten. Both birds grab prey with their powerful hind legs, then tear it apart with their beaks, or grab a snake or lizard in their mouth, crush it, and shake it to stun it or break its neck or back. Then they slam it to the ground before jumping on it and slashing it with their beaks. But some phorusrhacids were large enough (over 3 meters, or 10 feet, tall) that they would not have settled for just small mammals and reptiles; many could attack sheep-sized or larger mammals as well.

Phorusrhacids were a very diverse group through the entire Cenozoic in South America, with at least eighteen species in five different subfamilies (see figure 5.1). They first appeared with the meter-tall *Paleopsilopterus* from the middle Paleocene (60 Ma) and increased in diversity through the Eocene and Oligocene. The primitive Psilopterinae (figure 5.1*c*) were the lineage from which the rest evolved, and they never exceeded 1 meter (3.3 ft) in height, even though they ranged from the Paleocene to the early Pliocene (60 to 3 Ma), the entire history of the group.

By the middle Miocene, all five subfamilies had appeared, and they came in a variety of sizes and shapes. Some, such as the Mesembriornithinae (figure 5.1*b*) were relatively small phorusrhacids, reaching only 1.5 meters (5 ft) in height. At another extreme, the Phorusrhachinae (plate 6, figure 5.1*e*) were taller and more slender, reaching 3.3 meters (10 ft) in height but not weighing nearly as much. Others were huge and heavy-boned (the Brontornithinae; figure 5.1*g*) yet reached up to 2.8 meters (9.2 ft) in height and weighed as much as 400 kilograms (880 lbs).

The biggest of all the phorusrhacids was *Kelenken*, from the middle Miocene of Patagonia (figure 5.3). Discovered in 2006, it had the largest

Figure 5.3. Profiles of several of the largest phorusrhacids, showing their size compared to a human.

skull of any bird ever known: more than 71 centimeters (28 in) long, of which the beak portion was 48 centimeters (18 in) all by itself! However, instead of the massive, deep skull of some phorusrhacids, *Kelenken* had a relatively long, narrow beak with a hooked end that resembled an eagle's beak. It reached over 3.3 meters (10 ft) in height, and with its long legs, it is estimated that it could run 48 kilometers (30 mi) an hour.

Thus, the top predators in South America for most of the last 65 million years were not the doglike and hyenalike marsupials, but huge terror birds that could kill all but the largest mammals. Near the lakes and rivers, they had to contend with huge alligators and snakes as long as a bus, but on the dry land, the terror birds were the kings. No mammal could compete with them, and most had to fear them and hide or run from them—which was difficult, since some phorusrhacids could run faster than any animal at the time. The dinosaurs had not relinquished the role of top predators in South America. The phorusrhacid birds, their direct descendants, kept their spot at the top of the food chain.

Phorusrhacids ruled South America unchallenged until only 3 million years ago. Then they rapidly began to vanish in the middle Pliocene. The reason, as we will see later in the book, seems obvious: This was the time when large mammalian predators from North America, such as saber-toothed cats, jaguars, cougars, wild dogs, bears, and many other advanced predators, came down across the Panama land bridge. The last of the phorusrhacids was found in the late Ice Age deposits of Uruguay, dying out with the last of the Ice Age megamammals.

But one phorusrhacid managed to buck the trend of being overwhelmed by northern invaders. Known as *Titanis walleri* (figure 5.3), it managed to walk north up through Central America. It shows up in Texas and Florida in deposits about 5 million years old, much earlier than most of the creatures that walked across Panama. Like the other phorusrhacids, it was a huge predator that could hold its own against most mammalian carnivores. The biggest specimens were 2.5 meters (8.2 ft) tall and weighed 150 kilograms (330 lbs). *Titanis walleri* was also very fast; its speed has been estimated at 65 kilometers an hour (40 mph), faster than nearly all mammals of that time. However, it was different from many phorusrhacids in having a shorter, thicker neck, bulkier head, and overall a heavier build than the faster-running phorusrhacids that remained in the south.

For a long time, *Titanis walleri* was thought to have died out at the end of the last Ice Age with the extinction of the megamammals, but recent redating of the specimens show that *Titanis* survived in most places only until the beginning of the Ice Ages, about 2 Ma. Still, it managed to hold its own in the Gulf Coast for 3 million years, fighting back challenges from saber-toothed cats, dogs, and bears that eventually wiped out all its southern relatives.

Death from the Skies

The phorusrhacids were the largest predatory birds ever to evolve on land, since the largest ground birds (moas and elephant birds) were apparently not predators but ate fruits and seeds. Winging through the skies of South America were huge birds as well, including the largest flying bird that ever lived.

Imagine a bird the size of a small airplane soaring above you, getting ready to dive down and attack from above. That bird was *Argentavis magnificens*, the "magnificent Argentine bird," and it was probably the heaviest bird ever to fly, with one of the largest wingspans (figure 5.4). It was originally discovered in the 1970s by Argentine paleontologists Rosendo Pascual and Eduardo Tonni, working in the Miocene badlands in the eastern foothills of the Andes. They brought the specimens to Ken Campbell of the Natural History Museum of Los Angeles County, an expert on fossil birds, who had started a research program in the Amazon Basin. Although the specimens were incomplete, the less fragmentary bones showed it was a huge creature. Its upper arm bone, or humerus, was longer than the entire arm of an adult human.

In 1980, Campbell and Tonni described and published it. It was a shock to imagine a flying bird this large. Most estimates suggest that it had a wingspan of 7 meters (23 ft) and a body length of 1.26 meters (4.1 ft)

Figure 5.4. A restoration of *Argentavis* (top), the largest flying bird that ever lived, with the much smaller Andean condor (bottom), the largest living flying bird (courtesy Nobumichi Tamura).

and weighed about 72 kilograms (160 lbs). *Argentavis* was a vulturelike bird, so it invites comparison to the largest flying land bird, the Andean condor, which soars above the beds yielding *Argentavis* even today. The Andean condor has a wingspan of 3.2 meters (10 ft) and weighs 15 kilograms (33 lbs), about a fifth the size of *Argentavis*. The only heavier flying birds today are bustards, which weigh as much as 21 kilograms (46 lbs)— still less than a third the size of *Argentavis*. Only the recently described seabird *Pelagornis sandersi* has a longer wingspan at 7.4 meters (24 ft), but it was a much lighter, more slender albatrosslike bird, weighing no more than 40 kilograms (88 lbs), only about half the weight of *Argentavis*. Although *Argentavis* was the heaviest bird ever to fly, it was smaller than pterosaurs such as the Texas giant *Quetzalcoatlus*, which had a wingspan of 10–12 meters (33–40 ft), as large as that of a Piper Cub.

Many scientists have speculated about the aerodynamics of a flying animal this large. Although it is not beyond the physical limits for a flying creature, it is near the limits for birds. Its broad wings compared to seabirds' would have made its wing loading large enough for powered flight. Still, it probably flew like most eagles and vultures and condors, using rising thermal updrafts in the mountains to soar for miles without flapping its wings. Some have suggested it would have needed a headwind to get off the ground, although its powerful legs could have given it a running or jumping start. But its long wings would not have been able to flap while it was standing, and it would have needed to get a good takeoff before it could flap using a full downstroke of its wings.

The size of this bird also suggests other things about its paleobiology. Birds this big must lay large eggs, probably weighing almost a kilogram, and they tend to have only one or two per clutch each year. Large birds develop slowly, so they would have not have fledged and become independent until about sixteen months and were not fully mature until they were twelve years old. Such large birds do not fear predators, so they have a slow reproductive rate but a high survival rate and long lifespan, usually dying from accidents, disease, or old age rather than from larger predators. Based on the age spans of living birds, *Argentavis* would have lived fifty to a hundred years, barring accidents, but probably lived in small numbers, and then mostly in the mountainous regions of the Andes where the thermals provide lift.

Argentavis probably soared above huge territories of at least 500 square kilometers (193 sq mi) to find enough food for such a large body. *Argentavis* is neither an eagle nor a vulture or condor, but a member of an extinct group of birds called teratorns, which have features of both eagles and condors. Since they are extinct, we do not know exactly what *Argentavis* ate, but with their size they surely would have eaten a lot of carrion, as condors and vultures do, driving off predators from the kill when necessary. Their raptorlike beaks and their powerful legs show that they certainly were aerial predators as well, being able to grab and kill smaller prey in their talons, as eagles and hawks do. Their large skulls have structures that suggest they usually ate their prey whole, as eagles and hawks do, gulping it down without tearing it apart.

In the form of their avian descendants, the dinosaurs still ruled South America long after the Cretaceous extinctions. There were terror birds running around that could kill all but the largest mammals, and the South American skies saw some of the largest birds that ever flew. Alfred Hitchcock may have scared viewers with large, aggressive flocks of crows, seagulls, and smaller birds in his movie *The Birds*, but he had nothing on South America, where the birds truly were huge and terrifying.

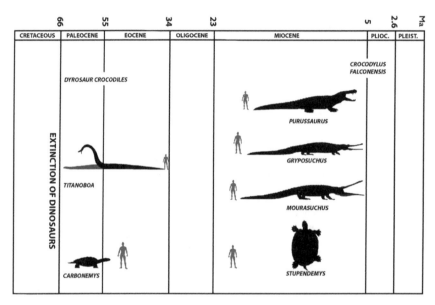

Figure 6.1. Diagram showing the occurrence of gigantic reptiles in South America through time (original art by E.T. Prothero).

6

Land of the Reptilian Monsters

Dinosaurs were not the only gigantic reptiles in prehistoric South America. There were also snakes as long as a school bus, immense crocodiles and alligators, and the largest turtles that ever lived.

The Nightmare Snake of the Colombian Swamps

People have a strange relationship with snakes. Most of us fear them, and some people are so acutely afraid of them—a condition called ophidiophobia—that they have panic attacks and break out in sweats when they even see an image of one. Many animals fear snakes as well, possibly since certain snakes are among the few creatures with venom strong enough to sicken or kill humans and large animals.

As they roamed the African savannah millions of years ago, our earliest hominid ancestors probably were hard-wired to fear and avoid snakes as a deadly threat, since cobras, mambas, vipers, and many other killers lurked in the grass. Sadly, most Americans fear snakes and kill the harmless ones unnecessarily, even though the vast majority of American snake species are not venomous.

Yet this fear of snakes is matched by fascination. Many different cultures have had snakes in their religion and mythology, some as benevolent deities and others as evil presences. The ancient Egyptians worshiped the cobra, and a sculpture of a cobra adorned the crown of the pharaoh. In Greek myths, the Gorgon Medusa had snakes on her head instead of hair, and a glance at her turned you to stone. Hercules had to kill the Lernean Hydra, a creature with nine snakelike heads, which grew a new head as soon as one of them was cut off. In Hindu, Chinese, Maya, and Hebrew traditions, among many others, snakes take a central role in important stories explaining the world and its ways.

Some cultures have imagined huge mythical snakes performing important roles in their religious traditions. But no one could imagine a monster
snake three times the size of the largest living anacondas and pythons, let
alone that such a creature once lived and roamed in South America.

The discovery of that creature, an accidental discovery at that, happened
in a giant open-pit coal mine in northwestern Colombia, about 97 kilometers (60 mi) from the coast. The mining pits are some 24 kilometers (15 mi)
across and cover an area larger than Washington, D.C. This mine is excavating thick coal seams from a geologic unit called the Cerrejón Formation,
taking 31.5 million tons of coal from the ground each year, making it the
largest coal mine in Latin America.

In 1994, local geologist Henry Garcia found what he thought was a
petrified tree branch and put it in a display case in the coal company's office.
Nine years later, a college geology student, Fabiany Herrera, found beautifully preserved fossil leaves and showed them to state geologist Carlos
Jaramillo. Jaramillo brought in Scott Wing of the Smithsonian, an expert
on Paleocene plants, and soon they had huge collections of beautiful fossil
leaves from the hot jungles of ancient Colombia. Wing took a picture of the
supposed petrified branch and showed it to paleontologist Jonathan Bloch
of the University of Florida Museum of Natural History in Gainesville.
Bloch immediately recognized it as the jaw of a group of extinct crocodiles
called dyrosaurs.

The staff at the University of Florida Museum began working on the
Cerrejón locality at an abandoned pit called La Puente in 2004. As reported
in *Smithsonian*,

> La Puente is a forbidding, naked surface of soft mudstone cut by gul-
> lies leading downslope to a lake filled with runoff and groundwater.
> The only vegetation is an occasional scraggly bush clinging to the
> scree. The pit shimmers at temperatures above 90 degrees Fahrenheit,
> while a hot wind blows constantly, with 25-mile-per-hour gusts.
> Methane fires belch periodically from the naked cliff face across the
> lake. Immense trucks can be spotted in the distance, driving loads of
> coal scooped up after blasting. The mudstone was the paleontologi-
> cal pay dirt. "Wherever you walked, you could find bone," Bloch said,
> recalling the wonder of the first trip. During that expedition, in 2004,
> the researchers grabbed everything they saw, and everything was big:
> ribs, vertebrae, parts of a pelvis, a shoulder blade, turtle shells more than
> five feet across. They found bits of dyrosaur and turtle everywhere, and

other animals as well, but the team could not sort everything immediately. They put what they could in plastic bags, then dug pits and cast the big pieces in plaster of Paris. "It's like prospecting," Bloch said. Walk along with brushes and tweezers and eyes focused on the ground until you find something you want. Put the little bits in plastic bags and label them. Mark the bigger pieces on a GPS device and come back the next day with plaster and a tarp. Wait too long, and the GPS reading is useless: The rain is a curse, washing everything down the slope, never to be seen again. But the rain is also a blessing, for when it stops, a whole new fossil field lies open for exploration.

In 2007, University of Florida graduate student Alex Hastings was unwrapping packages of fossils that had been shipped from Colombia. Among the packages was a single vertebra from the backbone of a very large reptile. Based on its size, the collectors in the field had labeled the package as a "croc." Hastings knew at once that it did not belong to one of the many crocodiles found in the locality. He showed it to fellow graduate student Jason Bourque, a reptile specialist. Bourque knew at once that it came from a snake, and a huge one (figure 6.1; plate 7*a*). They quickly walked over to the museum's reptile collections and found a box with the skeleton of an anaconda in it. Sure enough, when they compared the two specimens, the fossil was unquestionably from a large snake like an anaconda—but it was more than three times as large! The anaconda is the heaviest snake on the planet at 98 kilograms (215 lbs), as well as one of the longest, reaching 6.6 meters (22 ft).

Bourque and Hastings began going through all the miscellaneous fossil vertebrae in the Cerrejón collections that had not been clearly identified. Soon they had more than a hundred huge snake vertebrae representing at least twenty-eight different individual gigantic snakes. Then they showed their discovery to their supervisor, Jonathan Bloch. A specialist in fossil mammals, he too had collected many of the large vertebrae but not realized what they were. As he put it, "We'd had some of them for years. My only excuse for not recognizing them is that I've picked up snake vertebrae before. And I said, 'These can't be snake vertebrae.' It's like somebody handed me a mouse skull the size of a rhinoceros and told me, 'That's a mouse.' It's just not possible."

As soon as Bloch realized what they had, he called Jason Head, then at the University of Toronto. Head is one of the few people in the world who could tell him what kind of snake it was and how big it was. The two of them had met back in the early 1990s when they were both students at the University of Michigan. Bloch assembled a tray of "a whole bunch" of bones, brought them to his Florida office, and called up Head on iChat, holding the bones up to the computer camera. Thanks to modern technology, Head could see in real time what used to require weeks to photograph, process, and mail back and forth. Within seconds of viewing a few of the specimens more than 3,200 km (2,000 mi) away, Head told Bloch, "I'm buying my ticket tonight!"

As soon as he arrived in Gainesville, Head began studying the specimens and confirmed that they came from a monster snake larger than any other that has ever lived. Snakes are very rarely fossilized, since their bones are delicate and easily broken, and their long string of vertebrae and ribs tend to fall apart when they die. In addition, there is a problem with estimating the size of snakes because you seldom find the complete skeleton intact. Most often, you find a few vertebrae and not much else, since the ribs are very slender and fragile. Snakes keep adding new vertebrae to their backbones as they grow, so a large anaconda can have as many as three hundred vertebrae in its spine. By contrast, you have only thirty-three vertebrae in your spine and never add any. Most other mammals have about that many, too, not counting the tail.

For years, most scientists had just collected snake vertebrae and stopped there, since no one had figured out a method to tell which part of the spine each individual vertebra was from. But Head and Dave Polly of Indiana University had been working hard on a technique for telling exactly where in the spine each bone might come from. Each bone is distinctive to a region in the snake's back, although no one had taken the time to really notice this before. From this, Head and Polly were able to tell where most of the fossil vertebrae came from and get a more accurate estimate of the snake's length.

The skull of a snake is constructed of many thin struts of bone held together by tendons and ligaments and muscles. This allows snakes to completely unhinge their jaws, stretch their mouths around prey much larger than their heads, and still swallow it whole. Unfortunately, it also means that the skull bones are very delicate as well, very loosely attached to one another, and easily scattered when the animal dies.

In 2011, the Cerrejón team found a skull of the gigantic snake. This confirmed what they had suspected: The monster snake was a constrictor, like the anaconda, the python, and the boas (plate 7*b*).

In 2009, Head and his collaborators had published their findings and formally named the creature *Titanoboa*, or "titanic boa constrictor." Even though they did not have a complete spine, they had enough pieces to estimate its length at between 12.8 and 15 meters (42 and 49 ft) long. Scaling up its size from the known weight of anacondas and other large boas, they estimated that it weighed about 1,135 kilograms (2,500 lbs), as much as a full-grown rhinoceros.

Swamp Monsters

What kind of world did this monster snake live in? What did it eat? Why did it grow so big?

The first thing to keep in mind is that *Titanoboa* lived about 5 million years after the giant non-bird dinosaurs had vanished from the planet. During the 10 million years since that event, a period of time known to geologists as the Paleocene Epoch, the world slowly recovered from the great mass extinction that had wiped out not only the dinosaurs (other than birds) but also the giant marine reptiles in the oceans, plus about 75 percent of species on the planet. Thus, the niche that dinosaurs had occupied as large predators and herbivores was left wide open.

At first, the Paleocene world was a planet devoid of large land animals. Mammals were evolving rapidly now that their dinosaurian overlords were gone, but none was larger than a sheep even by the end of the Paleocene, 10 million years after the dinosaurs vanished. More important, no large carnivorous mammals had evolved yet. There were no wolves, bears, or saber-toothed cats, which would appear much later—only flesh eaters the size of weasels or badgers.

In their places, other survivors of the great mass extinction took over the role of top predator. In North America, South America, and Europe, the dinosaurs still ruled—as huge predatory flightless birds. There were also huge crocodiles on both continents as well, taking advantage of their head start in size as the largest land predators that had survived the great mass extinction.

There were large crocodiles in Cerrejón, too, but even more impressive is the size of the snake *Titanoboa* and the giant turtles. The biggest of these was a gigantic turtle known as *Carbonemys* ("coal turtle"), also from Cerrejón (figure 6.2). Found by North Carolina State student Edwin Cadena in 2005, it had a shell 1.72 meters (5 ft 8 in) in length. Its skull was as big as a football, compared to most turtle skulls, which are smaller than your fist. Its jaws were massive and strong, capable of crushing and eating large prey. Yet it was a member of a group of primitive turtles still living in South America today, the pelomedusoids. These turtles are called "side-necked" turtles, since they fold their necks sideways when bringing their heads under their shell. Scientists compare *Carbonemys* to the huge snapping turtles that often live in the bottom of deep lakes and ponds today. These snappers float just beneath the surface and catch any unwary prey that swims above them with their crushing jaws. *Carbonemys* could have done the same, although it could feed on nearly every smaller creature that swam in the lake, including crocodiles.

South America remained the land of gigantic turtles throughout its history. The largest turtle that ever lived was the stupendously huge *Stupendemys*, found in beds about 5 to 6 million years old in Venezuela and Brazil (figures 6.1, 6.3). It had an immense shell over 3.3 meters (11 ft) long and almost as wide. It, too, was a side-necked pelomedusoid turtle, but it does not appear to have been a monster predator. Instead, its relatively small jaws and weak limbs suggest that it was a slow swimmer and may have fed on water plants in large, quiet lakes and swamps. It was thick-shelled and heavily built, so it probably used its weight to stay submerged in the water while it fed. This is very different from modern giant turtles, such as the sea turtles, which greatly reduce the bone in their shells since they are active swimmers. *Stupendemys* was too bulky, and too weak a swimmer, so it probably avoided swift-moving streams.

The Cerrejón fossils come from a period when there was no competition from large predatory dinosaurs. Another factor was at work as well. The

Figure 6.2. Reconstruction of the gigantic Paleocene Colombian turtle *Carbonemys* (courtesy @User: AuntSpray/Wikimedia Commons/CC-BY-SA 3.0).

Figure 6.3. The shell of the largest turtle that ever lived, *Stupendemys*, from Venezuela (courtesy Open-Cage Systems/CC-BY-SA 2.5).

climate of the later Age of Dinosaurs was a "greenhouse" planet, with no ice on the poles or mountains or anywhere else on the earth. The climate was subtropical even up to the Arctic Circle and in Antarctica at that time, and it remained so for 20 million years after the dinosaurs had vanished. Based on their fossils, places such as Montana, North Dakota, and Wyoming (which today yield mammals from this Paleocene greenhouse planet) were once tropical jungles, as Colombia is today. If you go to Montana, North Dakota, or Wyoming now, of course, they are mostly harsh, dry grasslands, with extremely cold and snowy winters.

In short, the planet was still very warm, and this favored reptiles, which cannot tolerate extreme cold but do well in tropical climates. The presence of reptiles such as crocodilians, which are very temperature-sensitive, is a good indicator of ancient climate. The occurrence of crocodile fossils above the Arctic Circle in the early Eocene is one of the strongest proofs that polar climate was warm and mild during the greenhouse world. Scientists use the size of reptiles such as snakes and turtles to estimate the temperatures as well, since reptiles grow faster in warmer climates and cannot live at all if it is too cold, since they are cold-blooded. The Cerrejón team estimated the temperature in Colombia in the Paleocene at between 30 and 34°C (86 and 93°F), compared to the average from a modern tropical rainforest, which is only about 28°C (82°F). The atmosphere was also much higher in the greenhouse gas carbon dioxide, another relic of the greenhouse world of the dinosaurs. Based on the leaves and other geological evidence, scientists estimate that the coal swamps of Colombia not only were hotter than the modern rainforests but also experienced 4 meters (13 ft) of rainfall a year, higher than any modern rainforest, the wettest of which sees 250 centimeters (about 8.2 ft) of rain in a typical year!

This greenhouse of the dinosaurs was still very much in effect 20 million years after the non-bird dinosaurs had vanished, making the Paleocene the Planet of the Reptiles. There were large snakes, turtles, and crocodilians on every continent, preying on the smaller, more hapless mammals, and in some places the giant predatory birds ate the mammals as well. It was not until almost 25 million years after the Age of Dinosaurs ended that larger mammals the size of cattle or rhinos finally appeared and began to dominate the planet. But it took a major climate cooling event and mass extinction 37 million years ago, and then another one 33 million years ago, to eliminate the dominance of crocodiles and other reptiles from the Northern Hemisphere. As *Stupendemys* shows, the tropics of South America still had gigantic turtles even as recently as 5 million years ago.

Using our imaginations, we can picture the dense, humid tropical swamplands in northern Colombia 60 million years ago. The largest creatures were the monster snake *Titanoboa* and the huge turtle *Carbonemys*, but the area was also populated by large dyrosaur crocodiles and a diverse assemblage of smaller turtles, crocodiles, fish, lungfish, and amphibians— plus millions of insects, judging by the damage seen on the fossil leaves. No fossil mammals have been found yet at Cerrejón, but elsewhere in South America the Paleocene mammals were no bigger than sheep, and simple plant eaters. They would have been constantly in fear of being eaten by all the predators of this Planet of the Reptiles.

The Caiman King and Croco-Duck

Gigantic snakes and turtles were not the only monstrous reptiles in South America. The crocodilians were huge, too. Those from Cerrejón were larger than any modern crocodile. Even more impressive are the crocodilians from the Urumaco region of Venezuela, a late Miocene (5–9 Ma) locality that yields no fewer than fourteen different species. They include true crocodiles, as well as the narrow-snouted fish-catching gharials (or gavials) now found only in South Asia (figure 6.4) and several kinds of alligators. The biggest of all was a true crocodile, *Crocodylus falconensis*, which grew to over 4 meters (13 ft) long. The alligators were particularly specialized, with one of them (*Globidentosuchus brachyrostris*) evolving blunt globular teeth that could only be used to crush mollusk shells and were not sharp enough to kill other prey.

Figure 6.4. The gharial (or gavial) is a living crocodilian with a long, narrow snout suited for catching fish. Today they live mostly in the rivers of India, but during the Miocene there were huge gharials in South America (courtesy Jonathan Zander).

South America still has lots of caimans, which are a subfamily of alligators with four living species and many more fossil species and genera. Caimans look a lot like alligators, with their blunt, rounded snouts, but they have some clear differences in anatomy and tend to have longer, more slender teeth than those found in alligators. Today, caimans are restricted to Latin America and Australia, but they used to be distributed over a much wider area.

Most of the living species of caimans tend to be smaller than alligators, but not their prehistoric relatives. During the late Miocene, slightly earlier than those in Urumaco in Venezuela, some enormous caimans lived in Brazil, Colombia, and Peru. The biggest of these was *Purussaurus*, a monster caiman (plate 8*a*) that reached 12.5 meters (41 ft) in length and weighed about 8.4 metric tonnes (9.25 tons). It was larger than any other predator (reptile or mammal) at its time, so it would have eaten even the largest mammals. Its bite force would have been about 7 metric tonnes, stronger than any crocodilian ever, and stronger than most dinosaurs.

Almost as big as *Purussaurus* was another enormous caiman from the same time and place known as *Mourasuchus* (figure 6.1). Instead of the powerful bulldog bite, however, this caiman had a broad snout shaped more like a duck's bill, weak lower jaws, and rows of small conical teeth that would not have been good for a strong bite or grappling with large prey. Instead, it had a hugely expandable throat sac. Taken together, these features suggest that *Mourasuchus* fed more like a duck, pelican, or baleen whale, using its snout to disturb the water and the bottom muds, then taking a huge gulp of water and food into its throat, and finally forcing the water back out through its teeth and swallowing the food. It was truly a crocodilian trying to feed like a duck. Some creationists, unable to image how birds evolved from reptiles, cooked up a strange hybrid they call a "croco-duck" as their conception of a model of how reptiles turned into birds—though in this case, ironically, the fossil record actually demonstrates a reptile that was trying to eat like a duck.

Besides these two monstrous caimans, the late Miocene swamps also hosted a gigantic fish-eating gharial called *Gryposuchus* (plate 8*b*). In this land of giants, it was also enormous, reaching at least 10 meters (33 ft) in length, only slightly shorter than *Purussaurus*, and weighing about 1,745 kilograms (3,850 lbs). These three were the largest crocodilians ever to live on the planet since the death of the dinosaurs. Only two extinct crocodilians from the Cretaceous of Africa (*Sarcosuchus*) and North America (*Deinosuchus*) were larger. *Gryposuchus*, *Purussaurus*, and *Mourasuchus* lived in the late Miocene swamps, which also supported another huge crocodile, *Charactosuchus*, that independently evolved to resemble the narrow-snouted gharials, plus the gigantic turtle *Stupendemys*, as well as abundant freshwater animals, such as smaller turtles, lungfish, sharks, rays, bony fish, birds (including the diving anhingas), ground sloths, primitive New World monkeys (*Stirtonia*), rodents, bats, and the big terrestrial crocodile *Langstonia* and a number of South America's native hoofed mammals.

The Age of Mammals may have prevailed over most of the earth for the past 65 million years, but in South America it was still the Age of Reptiles, from the gigantic flying and running birds to the immense crocodilians and caimans, turtles, and monster anacondas. Some interesting mammals, though, lived among these reptilian overlords.

CHAPTER **The Old Timers I**

Killer Opossums

Dogs, cats, bears, and other placental predators were absent from South America during most of its history. In their place, pouched mammals related to opossums evolved into huge predators that resembled wolves, hyenas, and even saber-toothed cats.

On the Bottom of the World

On Seymour Island, no one can hear you scream—because the wind howls and gusts so loudly that it is hard to hear *anything* when you're wrapped up in your polar-grade parka. Seymour Island is a tiny place just off the east coast of the Antarctic Peninsula, not far from the southern tip of South America. During the winter it is covered in ice, but in the brief Southern Hemisphere summer, from November through February, the ice melts back and the naked rock is exposed. Still, the temperatures are barely above freezing on the sunniest days, and the wind blows almost constantly. Heavy rains or snows can fall at any time, and they cover up the rocks with a blanket of the white stuff. Scientists working there must often huddle in their tents during bad weather, losing precious days of fieldwork after spending many years planning and getting funding for their research.

Even when the sun comes out and the temperatures warm up to above freezing, working there is no picnic. The wind can be so strong it knocks you down, or it can lift a light person like a kite. When it is really howling, gusts fly at 130 kilometers per hour (70 mph) or more. If the temperatures warm up, the ground thaws and turns into a thick layer of what is called gumbo mud, which clings to your boots and clothes and is impossible to completely scrape off. Once the weather gets better, scientists use every hour of daylight to walk as far as they can, collecting as much data

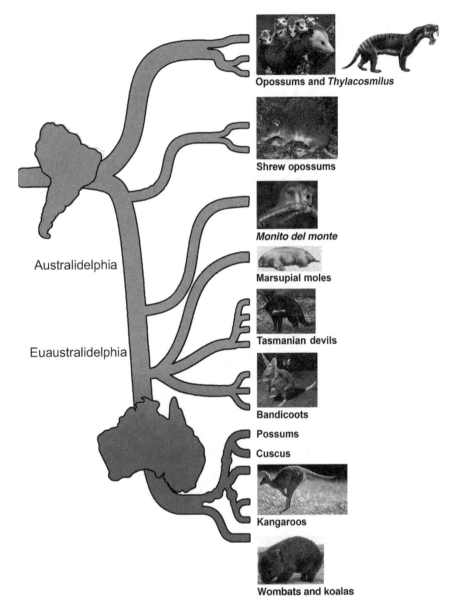

Figure 7.1. The evolutionary history of the marsupials, showing their origin from the South American groups and then their spread to Australia (art by E.T. Prothero, modified from several sources).

and as many fossils and rocks as they can, because their time is short and expensive.

There are compensations, however. The view is breathtaking, from the amazing ice floes on the water to the weirdly sculpted landscape (plate 9). The beaches are home to roving penguins as well as elephant seals and Weddell seals. The midnight sun never goes down but creates spectacular skies and amazing "sunsets" as it travels in a circle around the horizon. Most important, Seymour Island is the key to understanding many essential things about the geologic past, because it is one of the few places with exposed rocks and fossils of the right age to tell us what happened on the bottom of the earth over the past 70 million years.

Fossils have been recovered from there ever since the 1882 Norwegian expedition of Carl Anton Larsen. But exploration can be dangerous. During Larsen's Swedish Antarctic expedition of 1901–04, his ship was crushed and sunk by the ice. Larsen's crew was stranded on one of the nearby islands for fourteen months, living by eating penguins and seals. Later expeditions by Argentinian geologists were commissioned to study Seymour Island, which they called Marambio, since Argentina claimed it as their territory. Argentina still maintains the Marambio military base there today for that reason, even though there are no hostile powers in the area, and Seymour Island, like most of Antarctica, is an international zone free of political conflicts.

The oldest rocks there, called the Lopez de Bertodano Formation, are from the end of the Age of Dinosaurs, the Late Cretaceous, and yield not only a variety of dinosaurs but also a number of primitive birds. Most of the sequence, however, is marine rocks that yield an incredible array of fossil ammonites, shelled, squidlike creatures distantly related to the modern nautilus (see figure 4.3). Above these beds is the Eocene La Meseta Formation, and this has been the focus of a lot of research since the 1980s and 1990s, since it tells climate researchers about the critical time when Antarctica was not glaciated but instead green and forested.

In February 1982, exactly a century after the island was first discovered, Mike Woodburne, a former professor of mine, and Bill Daily of the University of California, Riverside, were on Seymour Island collecting fossils (figure 7.2). Woodburne was particularly interested in the extinct marsupials of Australia, ancestors of modern kangaroos, koalas, wombats, and Tasmanian devils. He knew that the only other place to yield a large variety of these pouched mammals, living and extinct, was South America. In those days, though, it was not clear how these animals had traveled between

Figure 7.2. Bill Zinsmeister, Mike Woodburne, and Bill Daily on Seymour Island, 1982 (photograph courtesy Michael O. Woodburne).

the continents or how they were related. Did they start on South America and then colonize Australia, or was it the other way around? Would the fossil record prove that they had actually lived in Antarctica?

By the 1970s, it was clear that during the Late Cretaceous, Australia, Antarctica, and South America were all connected as parts of Gondwana; these continents had not yet split apart completely. We also knew from the fossil record that marsupials had originated in the Early Cretaceous, about 120 Ma, but the split between the modern families in the two continents had not yet happened. The biggest missing piece in the puzzle was Antarctica. No fossil land mammals had ever been recovered from there. Any fossils would go a long way toward showing whether the marsupials also lived near the South Pole and spread toward South America or Australia, or spread in both directions.

You might wonder how any land mammal could live there at all, but during the Cretaceous and Eocene, the earth was a greenhouse planet. There was no ice anywhere, and both the north and south polar regions had cool temperate climates and forests, even though they experienced many months of darkness during the winter. Crocodiles and alligators lived above the Arctic Circle. So did numerous dinosaurs recovered not only from polar Canada and Alaska but also from Antarctica and Australia, which were both near the South Pole in the Late Cretaceous. By the middle Eocene, Australia was getting farther and farther away from Antarctica, with a widening gulf of water between them that had started in the Late Cretaceous. South America had also begun its separation from Antarctica by then, although the dating on when the Drake Passage opened between the two continents is still unsettled.

So what kinds of land organisms were living in Antarctica in the middle Eocene? Woodburne and his lab preparator, Bill Daily, plus paleobotanists Rosemary Askin and Farley Fleming, went there in 1982 to find out. They were aided by Bill Zinsmeister, now retired from Purdue University. He had worked in Antarctica for many years and knew of good outcrops of the right age that had produced Eocene fossil penguins, so he was able to arrange for Woodburne and his crew to visit a place where the odds were good for finding Eocene land mammal fossils.

Woodburne and crew spent a week or two prospecting without finding anything other than fish bones. Their time on Antarctica was nearly up when on March 5, 1982, they went to a locality where, Zinsmeister said, penguin bones had been found (figure 7.3). Almost as soon as he took off his backpack, Woodburne saw the tiny jaw of a rat-sized fossil mammal (figure 7.4). He and Daily collected the entire area carefully and managed

Figure 7.3. The mammal locality on Seymour Island. Bill Daily and Mike Woodburne crawl on hands and knees for hours, bundled up against the cold, looking for tiny mammal jaws and teeth (photograph courtesy Michael O. Woodburne).

to find a few more teeth before they had to pack up and return to civilization. Woodburne carefully wrapped up the precious specimens and kept them in his pocket during the trip home. As the first fossil mammals ever found in Antarctica, these were a groundbreaking discovery. The finding was published in *Science*, one of the most prestigious scientific journals in the world, just a few months after they got back. The fossil was formally named *Antarctodolops dailyi* because it is a member of an extinct South American group of rodentlike marsupials known as polydolopids. The species name honors Bill Daily.

Since this original brief visit in 1982, numerous scientists have been back to Seymour Island to collect more specimens. There are now many different kinds of marsupial fossils from there, most of which resemble those from the middle Eocene of Argentina. There are also fossils of the native South American hoofed mammals known as litopterns, as well as a group of peculiar South American Cretaceous mammals known as gondwanatheres. In addition to lots of different penguin fossils, Seymour Island yields bones of the giant "terror birds," or phorusrhacids, and of sea turtles.

Marine mollusk fossils are common, as are sea stars and brittle stars. The chemistry of their shells shows that the waters in the area 47 Ma were as warm as those off coastal Southern California, with big beds of sea grasses that protected many of the creatures (especially brittle stars and lamp shells) from predators. At the very top of the Seymour Island sequence, in the youngest rocks preserved there, is the first evidence of Antarctic glaciers in the early

Figure 7.4. The tiny lower jaw of *Antarctodolops dailyi*, the first fossil mammal ever found in Antarctica (photograph courtesy Michael O. Woodburne).

Oligocene, the proof that the greenhouse planet of the Cretaceous and early Cenozoic was vanishing and the icehouse planet of today was beginning.

The discovery of extinct groups of Eocene marsupials in Antarctica connects this region to South America at the same time. But what kinds of marsupials lived in South America?

Possums, Yapoks, and Little Mountain Monkeys

Most of us are familiar with the North American opossum, *Didelphis virginianus*. It is found all over the continent, and it is a tough survivor. It roams mainly at night and feeds on just about anything from meat and insects to fruit and nuts to pet food to garbage. The creatures are famous for "playing possum," faking a death pose, complete with their tongues lolling out of their mouths, when they are injured or cornered by a predator. They can also fight viciously when they need to protect themselves. Although they manage to survive most natural threats, they are especially prone to being hit by cars.

Like all marsupials, opossums give birth to young prematurely. The babies are about the size of a honeybee when they are born, and they have only a functional set of front limbs and a mouth; the rest of the body is not yet developed. The babies must climb up the belly hair of the female from the uterus to clamp onto a nipple in the mother's pouch, where they finish their development. Unlike most other marsupials, such as kangaroos, opossums can give birth to as many as fifty tiny babies at once. However, they can nurse only thirteen babies at a time, each clamped to a separate nipple on the mother's belly. As they grow, they ride piggyback on the mother until they are old enough to forage for themselves. Opossums are also famous for having a prehensile tail that can grab branches and allow them to hang upside down. Only a few other groups of mammals, including the South American monkeys, have evolved this capability.

South America has more than ninety species of opossumlike marsupials, including bushy-tailed opossums, mouse opossums, water opossums, four-eyed opossums, and many more. Most are about the size of the North American opossum, although some are tiny, such as the mouse opossum. They live widely all over South America, especially in the Amazonian rainforest and in the forests of the Andes Mountains. Some are really odd looking. The four-eyed opossum has two white spots just above its eyes, which look like an extra set of eyes and confuse predators. The thick-tailed opossums are built much like otters and live in the same way, swimming and diving for their food.

The oddest of all is the yapok, or water opossum. It lives in holes on the banks of streams from tropical southern Mexico to northern Argentina, especially in the headwaters of the Amazon. It has short, dense, water-repellent fur, long sensory bristles on its face for feeling its way in murky water, webbing on its hind feet, and a strong tail that aids in swimming as it catches its prey: aquatic animals such as fish, frogs, crustaceans, and other denizens of fresh water. Because they swim so much, the female yapok can close her pouch tightly to prevent the young inside from drowning while she is swimming and hunting. The male has a similar pouch, which protects his genitals.

In addition to those ninety-plus species of opossum, the other large group of South America marsupials is known as the shrew opossums, or caenolestids (figure 7.1). These archaic creatures are living relics of the evolutionary past of South American marsupials. They have an extensive fossil record going back to the Paleocene, although only seven species remain today.

The third and strangest living group of modern South American marsupials is the "little mountain monkeys," or *monitos del monte*, known in scientific parlance as microbiotheres. They are about the size of a mouse but look something like a cross between an opossum and a monkey (figure 7.1). Found in the temperate rainforests of the Andes in Chile, they have large eyes for their nocturnal wanderings, grasping hands for catching insects, and a long prehensile tail with a naked underside to help them get traction when they grasp a branch.

Only one species of this relict of the early Cenozoic lives today, mostly in the forests of the Andes. However, the microbiotheres have a long fossil record in South America, and they occur in the earliest Paleocene localities (Tiupampa) as well as in the Eocene of Seymour Island. More important, there are fossils from the Eocene of Australia that are possibly relatives of these South American marsupials, so they were widely distributed across all of South America, Antarctica, and Australia by the middle Eocene.

This suggests that microbiotheres might be the link between the marsupials of Australia and Antarctica. Indeed, when a detailed genetic analysis of all the living marsupials was performed in 2010, this is exactly what it showed. The family tree of marsupials begins with the opossums and their relatives (figure 7.1), which were widely spread all over Pangea in the Late Cretaceous, occurring from Asia and North America to South America. During the latest Cretaceous, however, marsupials were greatly diminished in the northern continents, and only a few opossums persisted in the

Cenozoic of North America and Eurasia. By contrast, marsupials evolved rapidly and diversified in South America. By some point in the early Paleocene, relatives of the microbiotheres had spread across Antarctica to Australia, and they became the ancestors of all the huge evolutionary diversification of Australian marsupials, from kangaroos and koalas to wombats and bandicoots to Tasmanian devils. Thus, by the Eocene, marsupials dominated in at least three of the former Gondwana continents—Australia, Antarctica, and South America—while the placental mammals were dominant elsewhere and only a handful of species of opossums remained.

Saber-Toothed Opossums and Pouched Hyenas

Opossums feed on almost anything, but they eat lots of meat and insects. They were the only carnivorous mammals left in South America when its isolation began in the Paleocene. True carnivorans (relatives of dogs, cats, bears, raccoons, and so on) were just beginning to evolve in North America and Eurasia, but they could no longer reach South America, since the Lost World was now fully isolated. The only other mammals in South America at the dawn of the Age of Mammals were the other two groups of Old Timers: the sloths and anteaters and armadillos and their kin, which feed on ants and termites or on leaves, and the native hoofed mammals of South America, which were all herbivores. Thus, there was a tremendous opportunity for the opossumlike marsupials to evolve into large body forms and take over niches occupied by dogs, cats, hyenas, and even saber-tooths on the northern continents.

Sure enough, marsupials took advantage and soon evolved into large predators, known as sparassodonts. In the early Paleocene, sparassodonts resembled weasels with long prehensile tails, suggesting that they were tree-climbing predators that ate small birds and mammals. One of the later sparassodonts, *Cladosictis*, had a long body, snout, and tail like an otter or mongoose and apparently fed on a variety of prey in trees and in the water. But soon they evolved into creatures that closely mimicked wolves, hyenas, cats, and even saber-tooths (plates 10–12). The most impressive and remarkable of these were called borhyaenids, since they vaguely resembled true hyenas, which occurred only in Africa and Eurasia and briefly in North America. Many of them even developed big, crushing teeth for breaking bones, just as hyenas did. This is an example of convergent evolution: Sparassodonts were completely unrelated to true hyenas, since they were descended from relatives of the opossums and were pouched mammals like kangaroos and koalas.

The biggest and most fearsome of these was *Proborhyaena*, a wolf-sized nightmare with huge fangs and wicked teeth for slicing up meat and breaking bones (figure 7.5, plate 10). It was about 1.5 meters (5 ft) long and weighed up to 75 kilograms (165 lbs). It had a remarkably large skull and a powerful set of jaws, with a heavily muscled neck, suggesting that it could crush almost any prey it caught, as well as break the bones of carcasses as hyenas do. The skeleton of *Proborhyaena* had a heavy build, with short, stocky limbs and flat feet, so it was no swift runner. Instead, it must have relied on ambushing its prey from a hiding place along a game trail, leaping out from concealment, then ripping out the victim's throat with its sharp teeth and powerful jaws and gorging itself on the carcass.

Perhaps the most remarkable carnivorous marsupial of all was *Thylacosmilus*, the "saber-toothed opossum." Just like the famous saber-toothed cat, it sported a set of long, saberlike canines in its mouth that could slash through the neck or the hide on the belly of even larger prey animals (plates 10–11, 12*a*). It had other similarities to saber-toothed cats as well. It had relatively weak jaw muscles because it killed by slashing its prey, not crushing its windpipe as lions and most large cats do. Like saber-toothed cats (plate 12*d*), it had powerful neck and shoulder and arm muscles for tackling its prey after an ambush and stabbing down with its head while slashing with its saberlike teeth. But its legs were not particularly long, so it must have leaped out at prey from ambush and could not outrun them if they got up to full speed. It was about 120 kilograms (260 lbs) in weight,

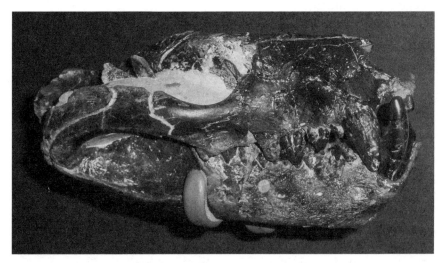

Figure 7.5. The skull and wicked teeth and jaws of *Proborhyaena*, the marsupial that evolved to mimic a wolf or hyena (courtesy @User: Ghedoghedo/Wikimedia Commons/CC-BY-SA 3.0).

or the size of a big jaguar, and pretty close to the size of the saber-toothed cat as well. This made it one of the largest predatory marsupials ever to evolve.

As we have noted, this entire suite of similarities between saber-toothed opossums and saber-toothed cats is entirely due to convergent evolution from very different ancestors. *Thylacosmilus* was a marsupial, not a cat, no matter how much it looked like a cat. It probably had a pouch and carried its joeys around like a kangaroo or like a Tasmanian devil, a pouched predator still living in Australia. If you look closely at the skull, you can see it is shaped in a very different way from the saber-toothed cat's, and the only real similarities are due to the saberlike canine teeth. In the details of the rest of their teeth, the anatomy of their skulls, and much of their skeleton, they are as different as an opossum and a cat are today. The most obvious difference is the extremely long bony flanges hanging down from their lower jaws, which acted as sheaths around the sabers when the mouth was closed. The sheaths on *Thylacosmilus* were much longer and broader than those on any saber-toothed cat.

This is not the only time that such amazing convergent evolution has occurred. One example is the archaic predators known as creodonts, which were the dominant flesh-eaters in North America and Eurasia during the early and middle Eocene, until they were pushed out by the dogs and other true carnivorans in the late Eocene. There were at least two cases of saber-toothed predators in the creodonts: *Machaeroides* (plate 12*b*) and *Apataelurus*. Their sabers are not as long and curved as those of saber-toothed cats or opossums, but they are clearly saber-toothed.

The independent evolution of sabers occurred in another extinct group, known as the nimravids or "false cats" (plate 12*c*). Even though they looked much like cats in their general shape, detailed analysis of their skull and bones show they were not cats at all but on a different branch of the Carnivora, possibly closer to dogs. Yet creatures such as *Hoplophoneus*, from the Oligocene beds of the Big Badlands of South Dakota, are remarkably similar to the true saber-toothed cat (plate 12*d*), even though they are not descended from cats, creodonts, or opossums.

Nature has experimented with the saber-tooth body form in at least four entirely unrelated groups at different times and places. This suggests that it was a highly successful ecology that was rediscovered many times by whatever predatory groups happened to live in an area. The saber-toothed creodonts discovered it first in North America and Eurasia in the early and middle Eocene, then went extinct. They were followed by the saber-toothed nimravids in the late Eocene and Oligocene of Eurasia and North America, which also vanished by the late Miocene, about the time that true cats were taking over.

The marsupials also found a way to evolve a saber-toothed predator in the Miocene and Pliocene of South America, which vanished in the late Pliocene (about 3 Ma), long before true saber-toothed cats arrived in the middle Pleistocene (about 500,000 years ago), with a gap of 2.5 million years between their time spans. There is no evidence that saber-toothed cats had anything to do with the extinction of saber-toothed opossums.

Why did saber-toothed mammals vanish? Since they were so successful in many places for much of earth history, today's world, without saber-toothed predators, is unusual. Nature always seems to be eager to push some new group to grow large, stabbing canine teeth and the suite of adaptations that goes with them. No one knows for sure, of course, but a possibility is that saber-toothed predators are specialists on big game, killing large prey that no other predator can touch. It is thought that the saber-toothed cats could slash the throat or belly of large Ice Age animals like ground sloths, bison, horses, camels, and possibly even young mastodons or mammoths. Likewise, the saber-toothed opossum lived in a world with many kinds of large hoofed mammal prey in South America. If so, then the extinction of the megamammals at the end of the Ice Ages may have doomed their specialized predators. *Thylacosmilus* vanished at a time when many native South American prey animals were vanishing as new competition came from North America.

That is our best guess. The real answer has been lost to time, and we will probably never know for sure.

8

The Old Timers II

Pseudo-Elephants, Pseudo-Hippos, and Pseudo-Horses

Large hoofed mammals such as horses, rhinos, elephants, hippos, and camels could not reach South America during most of the Age of Mammals. In their place, several groups of South American natives evolved to fill their ecological niches, resulting in remarkable examples of convergent evolution.

Darwin the Dropout

Charles Darwin was a failure.

His family had held high hopes for him, their younger son. After all, he came from a distinguished background. His grandfather Erasmus had once been the king's personal doctor, and a distinguished naturalist and poet as well. His father, Robert, was a successful and wealthy doctor. Charles was expected to take up a career in medicine, too.

In 1825, when Charles was sixteen, his father sent him to the medical school at the University of Edinburgh in Scotland, one of the best in the world. But young Charles could not stomach dissecting stinking, rotting corpses that had been stolen from graves. He could not watch as doctors conducted surgery without anesthetics, with the patients screaming in agony while their limbs were sawn off. He spent more time collecting insects, shooting birds to make stuffed mounts with his taxidermy skills, and collecting marine life from the local tide pools. Within two years, he dropped out.

Exasperated, his father sent him to Cambridge University in 1828 in the hope that he might earn a divinity degree and become a country parson. In that role, he could still be useful to society while indulging his love of collecting natural history objects. Once again, Charles paid little attention to what he was supposed to be studying. Instead, he hung out

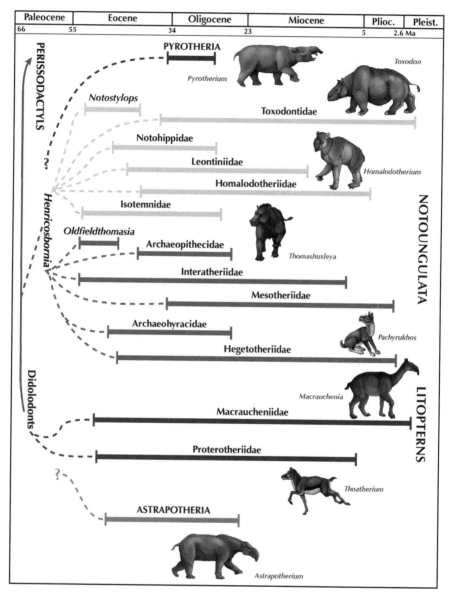

Paleocene	Eocene	Oligocene	Miocene	Plioc.	Pleist.
66	55	34	23	5	2.6 Ma

PERISSODACTYLS

PYROTHERIA

Pyrotherium

Toxodon

Notostylops

Toxodontidae

Notohippidae

Leontiniidae

Homalodotheriidae

Homalodotherium

Isotemnidae

Henricosbornia

Oldfieldthomasia

Archaeopithecidae

Thomashuxleya

Interatheriidae

Mesotheriidae

Archaeohyracidae

Hegetotheriidae

Pachyrukhos

NOTOUNGULATA

Macrauchenia

Macraucheniidae

Proterotheriidae

LITOPTERNS

Didolodonts

?

Thoatherium

ASTRAPOTHERIA

Astrapotherium

Figure 8.1. Schematic family tree of the extinct native South American hoofed mammals. The largest group was the Notoungulata, with a variety of hippolike, rhinolike, piglike, and even rabbitlike forms. The second large group was the litopterns, with the camel-like macraucheniids, and the proterotheres, which resembled horses. Based on their protein biochemistry, these two groups appear to be distantly related to the odd-toed hoofed mammals, or Perissodactyla (rhinos, tapirs, and horses). Two other long-extinct groups are also known: the mastodonlike pyrotheres and tapirlike astrapotheres. (Drawing by Mary P. Williams.)

Figure 8.2. Charles Darwin as a young man, shortly after returning from the *Beagle* voyage.

with some of the prominent natural historians at Cambridge. Professor John Stevens Henslow introduced him to collecting plants; a cousin got him hooked on collecting beetles. Darwin went into the field with Adam Sedgwick, the first person ever to bear the title Professor of Geology. From him Darwin learned just about all there was to know about geology at that time. By 1831, he had gotten a degree from Cambridge but was no closer to settling on a career—and he was clearly not interested in his father's plan to make him a country cleric.

His father had just about given up on him when an extraordinary opportunity came his way. Henslow sent Darwin a letter telling him about an opportunity onboard HMS *Beagle* (figures 8.2–8.3), a British naval ship that was getting ready to make a voyage to South America to survey the coast of Brazil and Argentina and produce navigational charts for the Royal Navy. The ship's captain, Robert FitzRoy, was a gentleman and aristocrat, and he needed a self-financing passenger of the same social class just to talk to during dinners on the long voyage. In the British Navy, the captains were not allowed to socialize with any of the lower-class crew they commanded, and they spoke to the crew only when they gave orders. It was not uncommon for sea captains to go crazy from the months or years of loneliness and isolation, as they could not talk to a peer. Indeed, *Beagle*'s previous captain

Figure 8.3. HMS *Beagle* as it passed by the southern part of South America.

had shot himself, and FitzRoy's own uncle had slit his throat. Later in life, FitzRoy himself would suffer insanity, too. After Darwin pleaded and got support from Henslow and his uncle Josiah Wedgwood (of Wedgwood pottery fame), his father relented.

The Dropout Makes Good

Two days after Christmas 1831, *Beagle* sailed from Portsmouth harbor with twenty-two-year-old Charles on board. Initially, his only duty was to have meals with the captain, but he also collected specimens and made notes every time he got the chance. At the second stop, the official ship's naturalist and surgeon, Robert McCormick, left the expedition, and Charles took over the former role. As a civilian with no shipboard duties, Charles could spend a lot more time collecting specimens than could an official ship's surgeon, who had to tend to the crew.

Charles Darwin made amazing discoveries every time *Beagle* put him ashore to do exploring and collecting. He saw the tropical rainforests of Brazil, which amazed him, and witnessed the horrors of slavery on the plantations in Brazil, which sickened him. The voyage continued down the coast of Argentina, where on September 22, 1832, the *Beagle* reached Punta Alta in Argentina, about 725 kilometers (450 mi) southwest of Buenos Aires. Darwin, FitzRoy, and a crew of sailors rowed out to the rocky outcrops just above the water level. Despite the name, Punta Alta ("high point") is not that high, but only about 6 meters (20 ft) above sea level. The outcrops were full of large bones. Darwin and a crewman worked hard on the soft sandstone and excavated skulls, jaws, and many large limb bones. By the time they had finished collecting there, they had the fossils of nine huge mammals that were previously unknown to science.

Darwin made brief notes on these specimens, but they were quickly packed into crates and loaded onto *Beagle* for future study by qualified specialists. When Darwin returned to London in 1836, he invited the leading paleontologist in Britain at that time, Sir Richard Owen of the Natural History Museum, to study and publish his fossils.

The Bow Tooth

Richard Owen studied Darwin's fossils of the giant ground sloth and was able to relate them to modern tree sloths, and the fossil glyptodonts to armadillos. But some creatures were complete puzzles to him. In 1833, Darwin had found a number of "large cutting teeth" in several localities along the Argentine coast. On November 26, 1833, he purchased a large, nearly complete skull from a farmer in what is now Uruguay. As Darwin wrote,

> I set out on my return in a direct line for Monte Video. Having heard of some giant's bones at a neighbouring farmhouse on the Sarandis, a small stream entering the Rio Negro, I rode there accompanied by my host, and purchased for the value of eighteen pence the head of an animal equalling in size that of the hippopotamus. Mr Owen in a paper read before the Geological Society, has called this very extraordinary animal, *Toxodon*, from the curvature of its teeth.

When Owen looked at the specimens a few years later, he was equally confused. Darwin described the quandary in *The Voyage of the Beagle*:

> Lastly, the *Toxodon*, perhaps one of the strangest animals ever discovered: in size it equalled an elephant or megatherium, but the structure of its teeth, as Mr Owen states, proves indisputably that it was intimately related to the Gnawers, the order which, at the present day, includes most of the smallest quadrupeds: in many details it is allied to the Pachydermata: judging from the position of its eyes, ears, and nostrils, it was probably aquatic, like the Dugong and Manatee, to which it is also allied. How wonderfully are the different Orders, at the present

time so well separated, blended together in different points of the structure of the *Toxodon*!

Here Owen was justifiably confused, because he was looking at the very first specimen ever found of one of South America's unique radiation of hoofed mammals, the notoungulates, which evolved to look like mammals from other continents. *Toxodon* was particularly puzzling (figure 8.4; plates 11 and 13). In its body shape, it looked vaguely like a hippopotamus or a rhinoceros. It was about 2.7–3 meters (8–10 ft) long and weighed about 1,500 kilograms (3,300 lbs), with a high hump over its shoulder about 1.5 meters (5 ft) above the ground. The skeleton was heavy and massive, like that of a hippo or rhino, with robust, stumpy legs and short, stubby toes for bearing the great weight.

Owen coined the name *Toxodon*, which means "bow tooth," because the broad molars have crests shaped like a bow. The molars are massive for eating huge amounts of gritty vegetation. However, *Toxodon* is odd for a hoofed mammal in that it had a pair of chisel-like teeth in the front, similar to the gnawing teeth in rodents. As the quote above demonstrates, these chisel-like front teeth fooled Owen into thinking that this creature, which resembled a hippopotamus, was a rodent! Instead, *Toxodon* was performing the role of a large, rhinoceroslike herbivore in South America, a region

Figure 8.4. The skeleton of the rhinolike Ice Age notoungulate *Toxodon*, one of the last of its lineage (courtesy @User:WereSpielChequers/Wikimedia Commons/CC-BY-SA 3.0).

that never had native rhinos or hippos. Although early paleontologists thought it might have lived like a modern hippo, its body posture and the wear on its teeth argue against that. In addition, it is found not in river or stream sediments but in the dryland pampas deposits, as were most of the other animals Darwin found. Thus, its analogue is more likely to be a rhino than a hippo.

The Brothers Ameghino

Darwin was an early pioneer in South American paleontology, collecting just a few specimens during his brief land excursions from the *Beagle*. In 1832, about the time Darwin passed through, the Danish naturalist Peter Wilhelm Lund arrived in Brazil, and in 1835 he began to collect and describe almost twenty thousand fossils from Ice Age Brazilian caves, including bones of mastodonts and ground sloths. Then he discovered human fossils in these caves and realized that humans had lived alongside Ice Age mammals, something that Georges Cuvier and other devout naturalists said was impossible. This produced a crisis in his faith, and he abruptly retired in 1848. His collections were sent to the Zoological Museum in Copenhagen, where they reside today. Lund's fossils were eventually studied and described by a younger Danish naturalist, Herluf Winge.

Europeans had studied and described nearly all the early South American fossils when the bones were brought back from South America, where there were few homegrown naturalists with the training to study the fossils of the Lost World. The first such native-born paleontologists were two brothers named Carlos and Florentino Ameghino (figure 8.5). Children of Italian immigrants, both were born in Luján, about 100 kilometers (60 mi) west of Buenos Aires, Florentino in 1854 and Carlos in 1865. This is the place where the very first South American fossil mammals, ground sloths, were found. Darwin had recovered many of his specimens from their localities in the Luján Formation as well. Today, the Lujanian South American land mammal age, based on the fossils from the Luján Formation near their birthplace, ranges from 800,000 to 11,000 years and represents the late Pleistocene.

Both of the Ameghino brothers were self-taught, since there were few universities in Argentina at that time, and none had instruction in paleontology. They began to collect spectacular mammal fossils eroding from the dry, desolate badlands of the Patagonian pampas, and soon they had built up a huge collection. Carlos eventually focused on doing the fossil

Figure 8.5. The Ameghino brothers, (a) Florentino and (b) Carlos.

collecting, spending sixteen lonely years under harsh, primitive conditions, while Florentino stayed in Buenos Aires and wrote up descriptions of the fossils for the scientific literature. Their brother Juan did not have the fossil bug, so he maintained the family bookstore, helped by Florentino, which supported their work on fossils until Florentino earned a museum job.

By the time the explorer and anthropologist Francisco Moreno established the Museo de la Plata in 1888, thirty-five-year-old Florentino was well known in the region. Moreno hired him as deputy director, secretary, and head of the paleontology department of the new museum. The Ameghinos transferred their collections to the new museum, and their efforts became better supported and more professional. A year later, Florentino's 1,028-page volume, *Mammalian Fossils in the Argentine Republic*, appeared in the *Proceedings of the National Academy of Sciences* and won the bronze medal at the 1889 Exposition Universelle in Paris. It brought all their amazing discoveries to the attention of scientists worldwide. The Ameghinos were now the world's experts on South American fossil mammals, and they became the first important homegrown paleontologists in South America.

While Carlos kept on finding new localities and new fossils, Florentino was a research dynamo, publishing more than two dozen stout volumes describing more than nine thousand species of extinct animals before he died at age fifty-six in 1911. He and Carlos not only described fossils but also worked out the sequence of fossils in Argentina, and they described the patterns of evolution in mammals through the entire Age of Mammals. Carlos lived on for another twenty-five years after Florentino, dying at age seventy-one in 1936. Today they are considered the founders of paleontology in South America.

Unfortunately, Florentino's work was hampered by his geographic and intellectual isolation from paleontologists in Europe and North America and by lack of specimens from other continents to compare his finds to. He had no real way to establish the age of Argentinian fossils with respect to those from elsewhere. Consequently, he believed they were older than they really were and argued that South American fossils were the ancestors of groups found elsewhere in the world. He was also continually fooled by the amazing examples of evolutionary and ecological convergence that the South American mammals evolved. Thus, he often mistook his fossils for mammals found in the northern continents, when in fact they were members of groups that were unique to South America. Some of this was also motivated by a bit of regional pride. In the nineteenth century, South America was still a scientific backwater, but Florentino wanted to put it on the map and make it the homeland of every group of mammals found elsewhere. Later paleontologists, such as John Bell Hatcher, William Berryman Scott, and George Gaylord Simpson, spent much of the twentieth century correcting these mistakes, but in the process they established just how amazing these South American fossils were in their own right.

The Greek and Latin roots of many of Florentino's scientific names for these fossils suggest that they are horses, hyraxes, primates, or other animals, when in fact they were not closely related to these creatures. Eventually, Florentino had described so many new fossils that he was running out of ideas for names. He began naming his new specimens after famous scientists from around the world, so there are genera such as *Carolodarwinia* (after Charles Darwin), *Thomashuxleya* (after Thomas Henry Huxley), *Ricardowenia* (for Richard Owen), *Asmithwoodwardia* (after British paleontologist A. Smith Woodward), *Oldfieldthomasia* (after British anatomist Oldfield Thomas), *Ricardolydekkeria* (after British mammalogist Richard Lydekker), and *Guilielmofloweria* (after British anatomist William Flower), plus *Henricosbornia, Guilielmoscottia, Edvardocopeia, Josepholeidya,* and *Othnielmarshia* (after the pioneers of American paleontology Henry

Fairfield Osborn, William Berryman Scott, Edward Drinker Cope, Joseph Leidy, and Othniel C. Marsh). There were names based on six French and three German paleontologists as well; more than twenty were published. He even named *Carloameghinia* in honor of his brother and *Leontinia* in honor of his wife, Leontine Ameghino. Not many later paleontologists outside South America have followed this peculiar practice. However, there is a fossil named *Florentinoameghinia*. It was an Eocene manatee relative found in Patagonia, which George Gaylord Simpson named in 1932 as a tribute to Florentino.

The Notoungulates

If *Toxodon* was not related to rhinos or hippos or rodents, as Owen and Florentino thought, what was it? *Toxodon* is just one of the most extreme examples of the largest group of native South American hoofed mammals, the notoungulates (which means "southern hoofed mammals" in Greek and Latin). They were extremely diverse, with at least fourteen families and several hundred species over the past 65 million years in South America (figure 8.1). Not only was *Toxodon* a good rhino mimic, but there was also an even better pseudo-rhino known as *Trigodon*, a toxodont that had a short bony horn on its forehead (plate 13), as did the sheep-sized *Adinotherium*. Another peculiar notoungulate, *Homalodotherium*, was built like the extinct chalicotheres, a group of clawed, horselike, hoofed mammals from the Northern Hemisphere. Like chalicotheres and ground sloths, *Homalodotherium* probably used its long arms and hooked claws to drag down branches so it could feed on leaves. Another was a pseudo-horse called *Rhynchippus*, which Florentino Ameghino thought was a real horse (*hippos* is the Greek word for "horse"). *Rhynchippus* closely resembled some of the primitive three-toed horses found in North America in the Miocene, except that the teeth and other skeletal details show that it is a notoungulate, not a real horse. Yet another fossil, *Thomashuxleya*, was an ecological equivalent of a warthog, except it had teeth nothing like those of a pig.

All of these animals belong in the same group of notoungulates known as the toxodonts (named after *Toxodon*, of course). Yet another group of notoungulates was the typotheres, which were just as clever as the toxodonts in mimicking the body forms of mammals found elsewhere. There were the strange, sheeplike interatheres. The mesotheres had chisel-like front teeth, like those of a rodent. The archaeohyracids, as their name suggests, vaguely resembled the hyraxes of Africa and the Middle East. The hegetotheres were remarkably convergent on rodents and rabbits. One of them, *Propachyrukhos*, even had large ears, long legs for hopping, and large eyes for nocturnal vision (figure 8.6).

Pseudo-Camels and Pseudo-Horses: The Litopterns

On February 9, 1834, at Port Julian, farther south on the coast of southern Patagonia, Charles Darwin found the bones of yet another creature that reminded him of a camel. Even though South America does have camel relatives—the llama, alpaca, vicuña, and guanaco—this creature would prove to be a case of extraordinary convergent evolution. Indeed, the name that Owen gave it was *Macrauchenia* ("big llama" in Greek). As Darwin wrote, "a tooth of a Pachydermatous animal, probably the same with the Macrauchenia, a huge beast with a long neck like a camel, which I shall also refer to again."

The only fossils that Owen had to work with were several neck bones, plus leg bones, some teeth, and other bone fragments. The neck bones look much like camel neck vertebrae, so it was no wonder that Owen was confused. Once most of the skeleton was found, it was apparent that

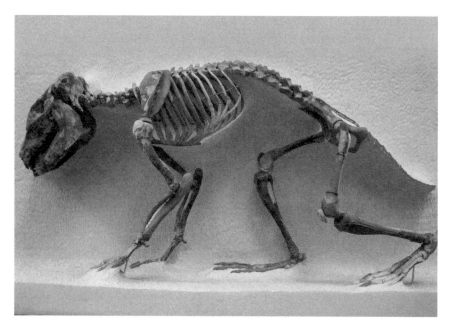

Figure 8.6. The skeleton of *Propachyrukhos*, a notoungulate that evolved into a rabbitlike shape. Even though the details of the skull and teeth are notoungulate and look nothing like a true rabbit's, it has long rabbitlike jumping hindlimbs, rabbitlike body proportions, chisel-like front teeth, and ear openings high on the skull, suggesting large rabbitlike ears (courtesy @User: Ghedoghedo/ Wikimedia Commons/CC-BY-SA 3.0).

Macrauchenia was not related to any group of mammals (camel or otherwise) from any other continent. Instead, it was a member of a uniquely South American group, the litopterns. It was a classic case of convergent evolution by an unrelated South American hoofed mammal trying to *look* like a camel.

This is apparent once you look at the entire animal (plate 11), not just the neck bones. It was a big animal, about 3 meters (10 ft) long and weighing about 1,000 kilograms (1 ton), more the size of a giraffe than a camel. Its head was large, with a prominent snout, and the fact that its nostrils are high on the top of its skull suggests that it had a snout or proboscis, much like that of a tapir or mastodont. Even though its neck was long and slender, it had a massive body, with feet more like those of a rhinoceros, not the delicate two-toed feet seen in modern camels such as llamas and guanacos. Yet research into its feet and ankles suggests that it had unusually high mobility and was able to change directions quickly, much like certain living antelopes do to avoid predators. It had a full set of forty-four teeth with a crown pattern unique to litopterns and not found in any group of non–South American mammals, including camels, antelope, giraffes, rhinos, or tapirs. Analysis of the wear on its teeth, and the carbon chemistry in them, suggests that it fed on a mixture of grasses and leaves and was not a specialist in either. In short, *Macrauchenia* is a bizarre composite of a camel, a tapir, a rhino, and an antelope or giraffe—a creature designed by a committee.

Macrauchenia is just the tip of the iceberg. It is just one extreme example of a second group of uniquely South American hoofed mammals, known as litopterns (LITT-top-terns). Just like notoungulates, they were very diverse over the past 65 million years, with at least five families and dozens of species (figure 8.1). Many were sheep-sized hoofed mammals with a variety of adaptations for different kinds of diets.

One of the most distinctive types of litopterns was the proterotheres, including the three-toed *Diadaphorus*, which resembled three-toed horses of North America, and the one-toed *Thoatherium* (figure 8.7; plate 13). In body form, *Thoatherium* closely resembled the Late Miocene horses that lived in North America, but it was an even more specialized runner than any true horse. While even living horses still have tiny splints of their reduced side toes alongside their main toe, *Thoatherium* had only one central toe on each foot, with no trace of side toes. Once again, South American hoofed mammals demonstrate amazing convergence on unrelated mammals from other continents. In this case, *Thoatherium* has reduced its side toes even

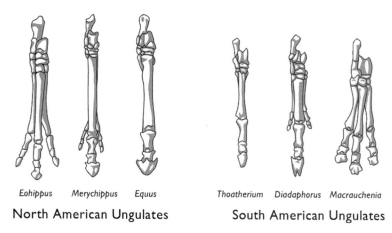

| Eohippus | Merychippus | Equus | | Thoatherium | Diadaphorus | Macrauchenia |

North American Ungulates   **South American Ungulates**

Figure 8.7. Convergent evolution of the feet of horses and litopterns. Horses began with three toes (*Eohippus*), then reduced the side toes in *Merychippus*, and today have only one central toe, with tiny splints remaining of their side toes in *Equus*. Litopterns mostly had three toes (*Macrauchenia*), but side toe reduction occurred in the proterothere lineage leading to *Diadaphorus* and culminated with *Thoatherium*, which had no traces of its side toes. It was more one-toed that any modern horse. (Redrawn by Mary P. Williams from several sources.)

more than has the living horse, so it was a better one-toed horse than any living horse.

Lightning and Fire

Notoungulates and litopterns make up most of the diversity of South America's native hoofed mammals. But there are two other peculiar creatures that are placed in their own groups, and whose relationships to other mammals are controversial (figure 8.1). In many ways, they appear to be South American imitations of the mastodonts, or maybe tapirs, found on the rest of the continents, but in detail they are clearly not related to any other kind of mammal.

The first of these were the pyrotheres, whose name means "fire beasts." Pyrotheres were about the size and build of a rhinoceros or mastodont, with short, slender legs, a long, barrel-shaped body, and a skull with short upper and lower tusks (plate 13). The bones on top of the snout are shifted backward, suggesting that it also had a short trunk like that of a tapir or mastodont as well. Pyrothere molars have well-developed cross-crests like those of tapirs and some mastodonts, suggesting a leaf browsing diet. Only six genera of pyrotheres are known, scattered from the Paleocene to the Oligocene, and their relationships are controversial. Despite the tusks and proboscis that fooled Ameghino and other early scientists, they are not related to mastodonts. They have anatomical features that resemble a wide range of extinct mammals from other continents, although some paleontologists consider them to close relatives of the notoungulates. Unfortunately, there are not enough good anatomical characters in the fossils, so we have yet to answer this question.

Even more peculiar than the pyrotheres were the astrapotheres, whose name means "lightning beasts." About thirteen genera of astrapotheres are known. The strangest of all of them was *Astrapotherium* itself, which was the size of a rhino or mastodont (about 3 meters or 10 feet long), with a very long trunk and spindly legs, features that suggest it was amphibious (plate 13). Its skull is truly amazing, with large hippolike or mastodont-like curved upper and lower tusks protruding from its mouth, and large openings in the snout region around the nostrils, suggesting a longer proboscis or trunk. Once again, we have an example of a South American hoofed mammal mimicking tapirs or mastodonts, complete with the trunk and tusks.

Jurassic Park Redux

What are all these peculiar creatures related to? Since they are all extinct, scientists have done their best with the bones and teeth to figure out what they might be related to among more familiar mammals, but with limited success. Then, in 2015, a startling piece of science was published that seemed to finally solve at least part of the puzzle. It smacks of *Jurassic Park*, but this is an example of molecular paleontology that gives long-sought answers, not monsters out to eat you.

Scientists have been trying to extract the sequence of the genomes of extinct animals for a long time, mostly to see if they could recognize and decipher their genes and see how they differ from living animals. However, contrary to *Jurassic Park*, DNA is very fragile and decays very rapidly once an animal dies. There is no possibility that the DNA of dinosaurs that are 65 million years old or older could survive intact, so *Jurassic Park* and all its sequels are pure fiction. Instead, scientists have focused on very young specimens less than 100,000 years ago from the last Ice Age, which have the best chance that their DNA is still intact.

Even with this limited goal, the problem turned out to be much harder than anyone expected. Nearly all the early announcements of the genomes of mammoths, saber-toothed cats, dire wolves, and early humans turned out to be false alarms, because there are so many ways modern DNA (even from the dust in a normal lab) can contaminate the specimens. While the fossils lie in the permafrost, the tar pits, the soil, or museum drawers, not only does the original DNA break down and disappear, but the DNA from bacteria and many other contaminants gets into the sample, and this is what fooled all the early studies.

Now that the research procedures and protocols are extremely strict, checked and rechecked many times, most of these false alarms can be ruled out and the truly ancient genetic sequences determined. In the past decade, certain labs have successfully determined the genomes of not only mammoths but also several kinds of extinct humans, such as Neanderthals, and possibly a previously unrecognized species of humans known as Denisovans that lived in Siberia during the last Ice Age.

The South American hoofed mammals have been extinct for long time, so the chance of getting their DNA seemed unlikely. However, there are a few well-preserved specimens of *Toxodon* and *Macrauchenia* that date from the end of the last Ice Age, and their preservation is as good as any notoungulate or litoptern we have. Instead of DNA, a group of scientists looked at the sequences of the proteins in these fossils, and compared them to the proteins of living hoofed mammals. Proteins are much more durable and long lasting than DNA, so there is a better chance of preservation. From this method, they found that at least one notoungulate (*Toxodon*) and one litoptern (*Macrauchenia*) both seem to be related to the perissodactyls, the group of odd-toed hoofed mammals that includes horses, rhinos, and tapirs. It would be nice to have data from more specimens of other notoungulates and litopterns, but for the moment, these are the only choices because these two species were the last survivors of their lineages and vanished at the end of the Ice Ages.

This does not definitively prove that *all* South American hoofed mammals are very distantly related to horses and rhinos, but it is a start. What about the other two groups? So far, there are no fossils of astrapotheres or pyrotheres that are young enough—both groups were gone by the end of the Miocene—so protein analyses are unlikely to solve that mystery. The protein data are consistent, however, with the strong similarity of an early Paleocene South American fossil group, the didolodonts, which are considered primitive litopterns but also resemble some types of extinct Paleocene hoofed mammals from North America known as mioclaenids. Indeed, there are some mioclaenids in the Paleocene rocks of South America, showing that they were able to walk from North America on the remnants of the land bridge that brought duck-billed dinosaurs and ankylosaurs down in the latest Cretaceous and was apparently still connected in the Paleocene.

As scientists since Florentino Ameghino have shown, the details of teeth and skull bones show that these are uniquely South American groups only distantly related to any groups of hoofed mammals from other continents. Like the rest of the Old Timers, they got into South America early, before it was isolated, probably during the latest Cretaceous or Paleocene, based on the earliest fossils, and they never had a genetic link with other groups of mammals afterward. Once they were established, they had no competition from the more familiar mammals found on the northern continents and Africa, since South America was completely isolated. Without any true mastodonts, horses, rhinos, hippos, or rabbits around, South America's native hoofed mammals evolved to fill the same ecological niches those creatures occupied in other places—just as the opossumlike marsupials evolved to fill the niches of wolves, hyenas, and saber-tooths. This is one of the most extraordinary examples of evolutionary convergence ever demonstrated. It is all due to the isolation of South America—and to the power of evolution and ecology.

Plate 1. The bull-horned, snub-nosed predatory dinosaur *Carnotaurus* from the latest Cretaceous of Argentina. (*a*) Complete skeleton (photograph by D. R. Prothero). (*b*) Reconstruction of *Carnotaurus* in life (courtesy Nobumichi Tamura).

Plate 2. The largest predator ever known, the dinosaur called *Giganotosaurus*. Skeleton in the Museo Municipal Carmen Funes in Plaza Huincul, Argentina (courtesy R. Coria).

Plate 3. The mounted skeleton of the largest land animal that ever lived, the sauropod *Argentinosaurus*, in the Museo Municipal Carmen Funes (courtesy R. Coria).

Plate 4. The strange, spike-backed sauropod *Amargasaurus*. (*a*) The mounted skeleton (courtesy R. Coria). (*b*) A reconstruction of *Amargasaurus* (courtesy Nobumichi Tamura).

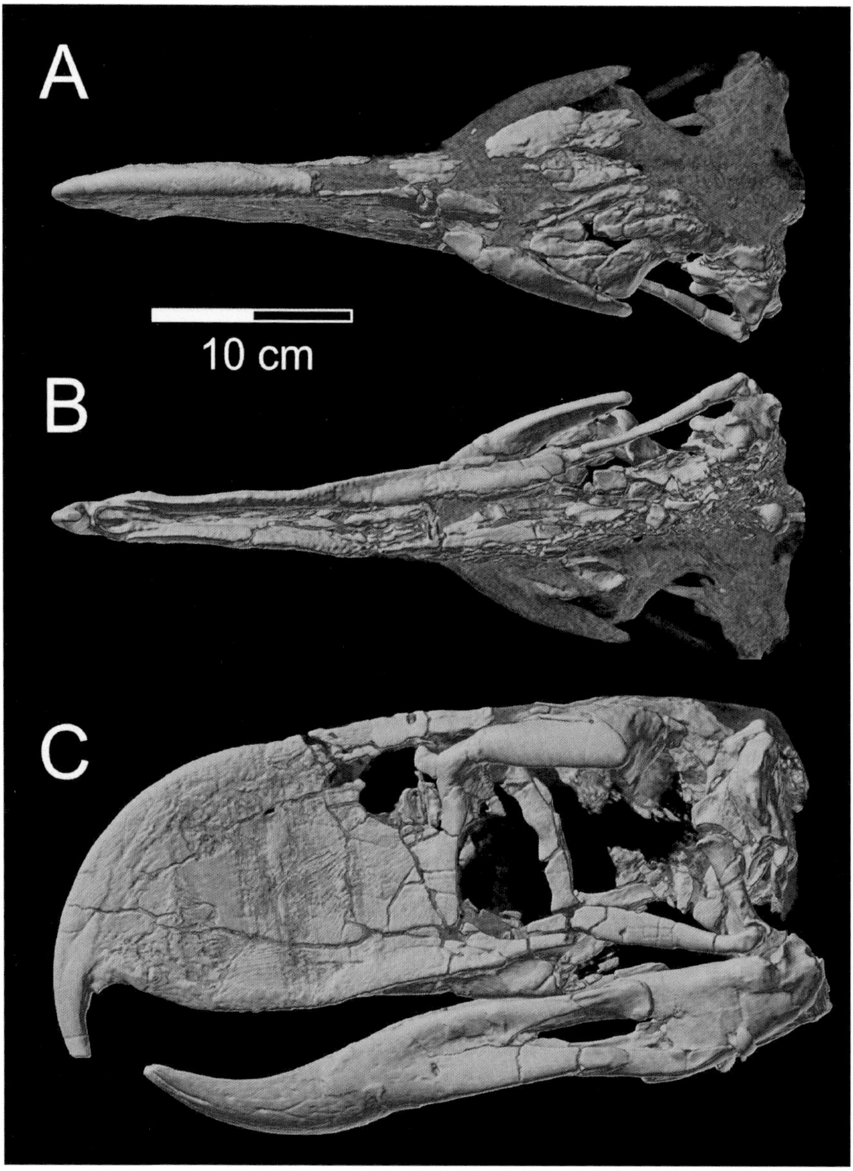

Plate 5. Phorusrhacids were huge, flightless predatory birds with deep, hooked beaks for catching and tearing apart their prey. This image shows details of the skull of the phorusrhacid *Andagalornis* (courtesy WitmerLab at Ohio University.).

Plate 6. (*a*) The large phorusrhacid *Paraphysornis*, known from an almost complete skeleton (courtesy Luis Chiappe, Natural History Museum of Los Angeles County). (*b*) Restoration of *Paraphysornis* (courtesy Nobumichi Tamura).

Plate 7. *Titanoboa*, the snake the size of a school bus. (*a*) A single vertebra of *Titanoboa* (right) compared to a modern anaconda's (left), with the photographer's hands for scale (photograph by Jeff Gage/Florida Museum of Natural History). (*b*) Life-sized reconstruction of *Titanoboa* eating a crocodile (courtesy K. Beck).

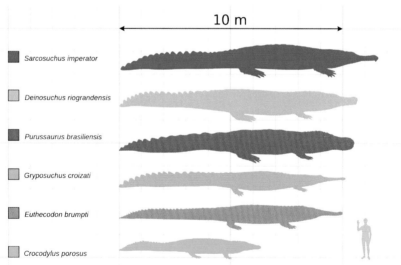

Plate 8. (*a*) The skull of the enormous caiman *Purussaurus* from the late Miocene of South America, with paleontologist Ashley Fragomeni Hall for scale (photograph by D. R. Prothero). (*b*) Size comparisons of two Cretaceous crocodilians, *Sarcosuchus* and *Deinosuchus*, plus Miocene fossils from South America (the caiman *Purussaurus* and the gharial *Gryposuchus*) and the living *Crocodylus porosus*, the largest crocodilian alive today (courtesy ©Smokeybjb/ Wikimedia Commons/CC-BY-SA-3.0).

Plate 9. The barren rock and ice sculptures of Seymour Island, Antarctica, make it an eerily beautiful place (photograph by Linda Ivany).

Plate 10. Two of the most extreme examples of carnivorous marsupials from the Cenozoic of South America, the wolflike *Proborhyaena* (left) and the saber-toothed opossum *Thylacosmilus* (drawing by Mary P. Williams).

Plate 11. Skeletons of the major groups of Old Timers that dominated South America after the dinosaurs had vanished. In the background is the elephant-sized ground sloth *Megatherium*; the other xenarthran, the armored glyptodont, is in the left foreground. In the right center are the rhinolike notoungulate *Toxodon* and the giraffe-like litoptern *Macrauchenia*. In the lower right corner are the skulls of the carnivorous marsupials, including the saber-toothed marsupial *Thylacosmilus*. A skull of a predatory phorusrhacid bird is in the front center.

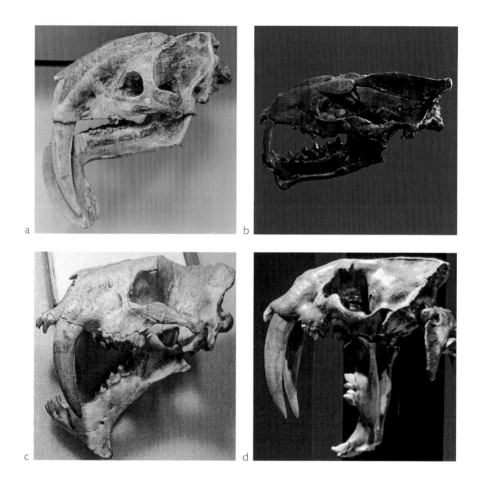

Plate 12. Convergent evolution on the saber-toothed skull shape has independently happened at least four or five times in fossil mammals. Even though they look superficially similar, with their large, stabbing canines, the details of the skull make it clear that they are not closely related but independently evolved the saber-toothed shape from different types of ancestors. (*a*) The saber-toothed marsupial *Thylacosmilus*. (*b*) The saber-toothed oxyaenid creodont *Machaeroides*. (*c*) The "false cat" (nimravid) *Hoplophoneus*. (*d*) The true saber-toothed cat *Smilodon* (*a* courtesy John Cummings/CC-BY-SA 3.0; *c* and *d* by D. R. Prothero).

Plate 13. The spectrum of South American hoofed mammals. The notoungulates include the huge, hippolike *Toxodon* in the right rear and the horned *Trigodon* in the left foreground, as well as the piglike *Thomashuxleya* (right foreground), the rabbitlike *Propachyrukhos* (right foreground), and the clawed *Homalodotherium* (right, behind the human silhouette). Litopterns include the camel-like *Macrauchenia* (left background) and the one-toed, horselike *Thoatherium* (left foreground). Between *Trigodon* and *Macrauchenia* on the left is the mastodonlike *Pyrotherium*; in front of *Toxodon* is *Astrapotherium*. (Drawing by Mary P. Williams.)

Plate 14. Some of the largest of the extinct xenathrans, including the giant ground sloths *Megatherium* (behind the human), *Eremotherium* (right background), and *Mylodon* (left background). The giant relatives of armadillos include *Doedicurus* (with the spiky tail), *Panochthus* (right foreground), and *Holmesina* (left foreground). (Drawing by Mary P. Williams.)

Plate 15. Rodents come in many shapes and sizes, and some extinct rodents were huge. In the left foreground are the beaver and the capybara, the largest living rodents. In the right foreground is the bear-sized Ice Age beaver, *Castoroides*. The rodent in the right background is *Josephoartigasia*, an immense pacarana from South America. In front of it on the right is the giant capybara *Neochoerus*, and on the left is *Telicomys*. (Drawing by Mary P. Williams.)

Plate 16. Gigantic Ice Age marsupials of Australia. In the right background is the rhinoceros-sized wombat relative known as a diprotodont. On the left are the enormous short-faced kangaroo *Procoptodon* and the slothlike marsupial *Palorchestes*. In front of the diprotodont is the marsupial equivalent of a lion, *Thylacoleo*. (Drawing by Mary P. Williams.)

9

The Old Timers III

The Slow Folk

In addition to predatory marsupials and native hoofed mammals, xenarthans made up South America's third group of native "Old Timers": sloths, armadillos, and anteaters. Some were gigantic, including ground sloths the size of elephants and armadillo relatives the size of small cars.

The Baron and the Monster Sloth

Baron Jean Leopold Frederic Georges Cuvier was an impressive man. Tall of stature, he had a massive head crowned by a mane of hair (figure 9.2). One admirer wrote that his head "gave to his entire person an undeniable cachet of majesty and to his face an expression of profound meditation." After his death, scientists weighed his brain and found that it was 1,830 grams (65 oz), more than 400 grams above average and 200 grams heavier than any brain ever measured at that time.

Cuvier was one of the most brilliant men of his time, with a command of many subjects, some of which he invented. Before Cuvier, natural history resembled stamp collecting, with many different amateur naturalists compiling long lists and descriptions of new species without seeing the similarities in their anatomy. Cuvier almost single-handedly revolutionized natural history by dissecting many different animals and discovering their underlying similarities and differences. This became the foundation of comparative anatomy, a subject that has been fundamental to biology ever since. In the process, many naturalists and explorers sent him their fossil bones, and he was the first to correctly describe many types of extinct animals for the first time. Cuvier solved the mystery of the puzzling fossil teeth called the "Great Incognitum"; he recognized them as the teeth of

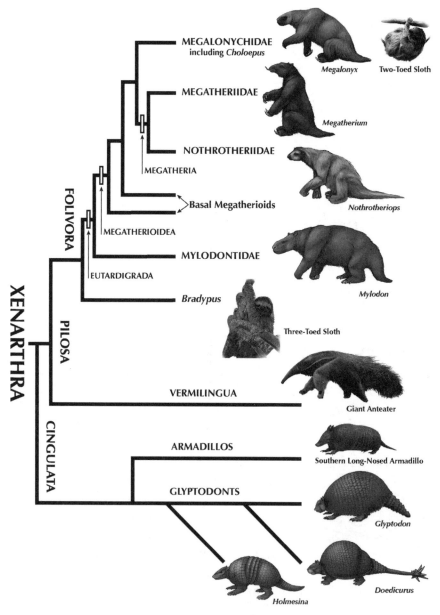

Figure 9.1. Family tree of xenarthrans. One branch is the sloths, or the Folivora, represented by four different extinct families of giant ground sloths. The two living sloths are not closely related to each other. Instead, the two-toed sloth *Choloepus* is a survivor of the megalonychid ground sloths, which became small and arboreal. The three-toed sloth *Bradypus* is more primitive than any ground sloth and evolved the tree-hanging lifestyle independently. The other main branch is the Pilosa, which includes the anteaters (Vermilingua) and the armadillos and their relatives (Cingulata), including the huge extinct glyptodonts (*Glyptodon, Doedicurus*) and the big extinct pampatheres (*Holmesina*). (Drawing by Mary P. Williams.)

Figure 9.2. Baron Georges Cuvier, founder of vertebrate paleontology and comparative anatomy.

the elephantlike mastodonts. He also correctly identified the huge marine lizards we now know as mosasaurs. For this reason, he is also considered the founder of vertebrate paleontology.

Cuvier is most famous for his law of correlation of parts, where he discovered that certain types of anatomical features tend to be associated. If you are a flesh eater, you have sharp teeth and claws; if you are a plant eater, you have grinding teeth and hooves, and so on. From this, paleontologists have been able to reconstruct whole animals from just a few key bones, because the other parts of the anatomy are so predictable. A famous legend about Cuvier claims that a prankster broke into his bedchamber one night, dressed as the Devil, and threatened to eat Cuvier. He calmly replied, "You have hooves and horns, so you only eat plants."

Cuvier was not only a scientific genius, but also a politically astute person. He was born of humble bourgeois origins in the Jura Mountains of southeast France, yet he was brilliant in school. He easily mastered all his subjects at a young age, including history, geography, mathematics, law, chemistry, mineralogy, zoology, botany, mining, police work, diplomacy, commerce, finance, economics, geometry, and Latin and Greek. Then he studied in Germany, where he quickly became fluent in German as well. During the horrors of the French Revolution, he was a tutor for a noble family in Normandy and thus avoided the Reign of Terror and the guillotine in Paris.

In 1795, the great French naturalist Étienne Geoffroy Saint-Hilaire invited the twenty-six-year-old Cuvier to come to Paris and work at the newly established Musée National d'Histoire Naturelle. It had originally been the Jardin du Roi (royal garden), but it lost its royal title when the king lost his head. Cuvier quickly rose through the ranks and kept his position (or improved it) when Napoleon overthrew the revolutionary government. Napoleon also appointed him inspector general of public education and state counselor. When Napoleon was exiled and the Bourbon monarchy was restored, Cuvier kept his status under three successive kings of France—a remarkable feat, considering that many aristocrats and scholars of the time, such as the great chemist Antoine Lavoisier, lost their heads on the guillotine, unfortunate victims of the Terror.

Among the very first fossils sent from South America to Europe were gigantic bones of a bizarre beast. The first specimens of this huge creature we now know as *Megatherium* were discovered in 1788 on the banks of the Luján River in Argentina by Manuel Torres. These bones were shipped to the Museo Nacional de Ciencias Naturales in Madrid, where museum employee Juan Baptista Bru described and illustrated them but clearly did not understand what they were.

With his vast knowledge of animal anatomy, Cuvier could understand and interpret them. He never saw the fossils themselves but based his entire description and name on Bru's sketches. Based on its huge size, he called it *Megatherium* ("great beast" in Greek). Cuvier correctly guessed that it was a gigantic sloth that lived on the ground, rather than in trees like modern sloths (plates 11, 14; figure 9.3). He first suggested they used their limbs for climbing trees, but then later suggested that the huge claws were for digging tunnels. But since it weighed up to 4 metric tonnes (about 4 tons) and was over 6 meters (20 ft) long, it was larger than almost any land mammal known except for the largest mammoths. Climbing trees seemed ludicrous. As Darwin wrote in *The Voyage of the Beagle*,

> The great size of the bones of the Megatheroid animals, including the *Megatherium*, *Megalonyx*, *Scelidotherium*, and *Mylodon*, is truly wonderful. The habits of life of these animals were a complete puzzle to naturalists, until Professor Owen solved the problem with remarkable ingenuity. The teeth indicate, by their simple structure, that these Megatheroid animals lived on vegetable food, and probably on the leaves and small twigs of trees; their ponderous forms and great strong curved claws seem so little adapted for locomotion, that some eminent

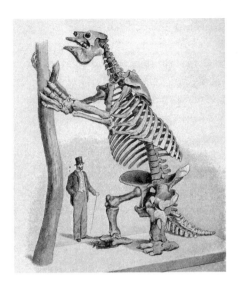

Figure 9.3. The skeleton of the giant ground sloth *Megatherium*, with a human for scale.

naturalists have actually believed that, like the sloths, to which they are intimately related, they subsisted by climbing back downwards on trees, and feeding on the leaves. It was a bold, not to say preposterous, idea to conceive even antediluvian trees, with branches strong enough to bear animals as large as elephants. Professor Owen, with far more probability, believes that, instead of climbing on the trees, they pulled the branches down to them, and tore up the smaller ones by the roots, and so fed on the leaves. The colossal breadth and weight of their hinder quarters, which can hardly be imagined without having been seen, become, on this view, of obvious service, instead of being an encumbrance: their apparent clumsiness disappears. With their great tails and their huge heels firmly fixed like a tripod on the ground, they could freely exert the full force of their most powerful arms and great claws. Strongly rooted, indeed, must that tree have been, which could have resisted such force! The *Mylodon*, moreover, was furnished with a long extensile tongue like that of the giraffe, which, by one of those beautiful provisions of nature, thus reaches with the aid of its long neck its leafy food. I may remark, that in Abyssinia the elephant, according to Bruce, when it cannot reach with its proboscis the branches, deeply scores with its tusks the trunk of the tree, up and down and all round, till it is sufficiently weakened to be broken down.

The immense size of *Megatherium* made it a popular creature in the imagination of Europeans in the early 1800s, as one of the first of the great prehistoric creatures to be discovered. In fact, several museums displayed these incredible skeletons to draw big crowds. By the 1830s and 1840s, however, the discovery of dinosaurs and giant marine reptiles had captured the imagination of the public, since they were not only huge but also fearsome reptiles.

Strange Joints

Many of the specimens that Darwin sent to Owen were xenarthrans (zee-NARTH-rans), members of the group that today includes sloths, anteaters, and armadillos. The name "Xenarthra" means "strange joints" and refers to the odd extra connections between the complex vertebrae in their backbones, a feature not seen in any other group of mammals. Xenarthrans have often been called "edentates" (which means toothless), although only anteaters are really toothless; sloths and armadillos have simple teeth with no enamel. The name edentates has been abandoned and replaced by xenarthrans, because edentates used to include aardvarks and the scaly pangolins, a group of Asian and African ant-eating creatures not closely related to xenarthrans.

Along with the predatory marsupials and the native hoofed mammals of South America, xenarthrans were the third group of Old Timers (plates 11, 14). They are among the most primitive and earliest branches of placental mammals to evolve in the late Mesozoic on Pangea, and were stranded in South America before it broke away from the rest of the Pangea supercontinent. By the Ice Ages, the xenarthrans were enormous. They included huge ground sloths such as *Megatherium, Mylodon, Scelidotherium,* and *Megalonyx* and a group of armadillolike animals called glyptodonts, including *Glyptodon.*

As Darwin described the fossils he found in his book *The Voyage of the Beagle,*

> First, parts of three heads and other bones of the Megatherium, the huge dimensions of which are expressed by its name. Secondly, the Megalonyx, a great allied animal. Thirdly, the Scelidotherium, also an allied animal, of which I obtained a nearly perfect skeleton. It must have been as large as a rhinoceros: in the structure of its head it comes, according to Mr. Owen, nearest to the Cape Ant-eater, but in some other respects it approaches to the armadilloes. Fourthly, the Mylodon Darwinii, a closely related genus of little inferior size. Fifthly, another

gigantic edental quadruped. Sixthly, a large animal, with an osseous coat in compartments, very like that of an armadillo.

By the time Darwin's fossils from the *Beagle* voyage were identified by Richard Owen in 1836 and later years, *Megalonyx* was the name given to any medium-sized ground sloths smaller than *Megatherium*; a large *Megalonyx* weighed about 1,000 kilograms (2,200 lbs) and was about 2.5–3 meters (8–10 ft) in length, about half as big as *Megatherium* but still towering over a human. The name, which means "giant claw," owes, as it happens, to Thomas Jefferson, an amateur paleontologist among his many other pursuits. While he was still vice president under John Adams in 1796, Jefferson received some fossilized bones from a cave in what is now West Virginia. They were mostly foot bones, but they had enormous claws on them (figure 9.4). Jefferson thought that the claws belonged to a giant lion that was still roaming the western United States. When he sent Lewis and Clark to explore the new territories of the American West, he asked them to be on the lookout for this lion, since scholars at that time did not accept that any creature could go extinct. In fact, it was none other than Cuvier himself who established that creatures could become extinct when he argued that creatures as large as the mastodont and the mammoth would have been discovered by then if they were still alive.

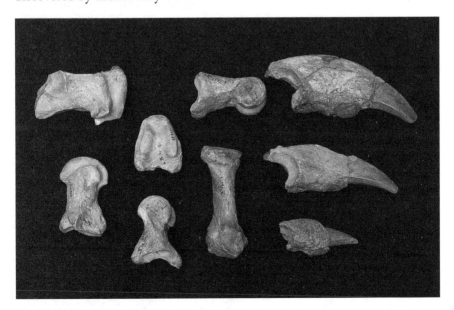

Figure 9.4. Jefferson's fossils of the claws of *Megalonyx*, which he thought belonged to an enormous American lion still roaming the West (photo © Academy of Natural Sciences of Drexel University/Fred Mullison).

Since Jefferson's discovery, *Megalonyx* has been found in many Ice Age sites all over North America, including many caves in the eastern United States, the La Brea tar pits in Los Angeles, and localities ranging from Alaska to Central America.

Armadillo Tanks

Among the fossils that Darwin brought back to Owen were fragments of "a large animal, with an osseous coat in compartments, very like that of an armadillo." All that Darwin found were tile-shaped pieces of armor from the shell, or "osseous coat," of an armadillolike creature, and a few isolated bones and teeth. Owen gave the name *Glyptodon* (carved tooth) to the fragments he had available, but he could tell only that it resembled a huge armadillo. Later specimens gave us a much better concept of glyptodonts.

From complete fossils, we now know that some glyptodonts were the size of a Volkswagen Beetle (figure 9.5; plates 11, 14). They were over 3.3 meters (10 ft) in length and weighed about 2 metric tonnes (2.2 tons). Their most striking feature was the domed bony shell, made out of more than a thousand small polygonal plates that were over an inch thick. Their head could not be pulled back for protection into their shell, as a turtle can do, but stuck out in front, so it was covered by another bony armor plate on the top of the skull.

The long, tapering tail was also wrapped in rings of armor, so that it was flexible but completely protected. *Glyptodon* had nothing extra on the tip of its tail, but other glyptodonts such as *Doedicurus* had a bony spike "mace" on the end of its tail, and *Panochthus* and *Hoplophorus*, also found by Darwin, had a bony club on the end of their tails.

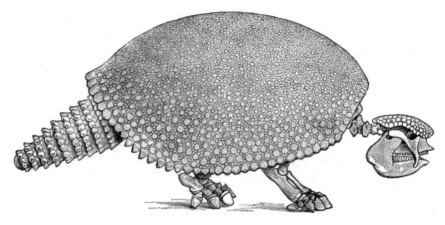

Figure 9.5. The skeleton, skull, and shell of a glyptodont.

Most of the time, these monsters probably had no reason to fear predators, especially once they were fully grown. With their short, stumpy legs and body completely wrapped in armor down to the belly and along the tail, there was almost no place for a predator to attack. All they had to do was squat down on the ground and swing their armored tail, and the predator could not harm them. Nevertheless, glyptodonts did have some predators, because the fossilized skullcap of one young glyptodont shows the twin holes made by a bite with the canines of a saber-toothed cat.

The skulls of glyptodonts are truly strange. They are very short and very deep, with large areas of attachment for very strong jaw muscles. Even though their teeth were just simple cylinders of dentin without enamel on the crowns, they must have chewed enormous amounts of coarse, fibrous vegetation based on the wear on their teeth. In addition, the nasal region is very short and has many muscular attachment sites around it. This has led to more than one paleontologist suggesting that glyptodonts might have had a short trunk or proboscis.

Despite their short, stumpy legs, glyptodonts were surprisingly widespread, mobile, and successful. We find pieces of their distinctive mosaic armor in Ice Age localities throughout the Americas. Most of them remained in South America, but *Glyptodon* reached as far north as Guatemala, and the similar *Glyptotherium* reached the United States about 2.5 Ma. However, it apparently preferred the warm subtropical and tropical regions during the Ice Ages, because it was restricted to Florida, South Carolina, and across the desert southwest states from Texas to Arizona.

All the large armored glyptodonts vanished from both North and South America at the end of the last Ice Age. Today, only much smaller armadillos are left. There are about twenty species alive today, from the living giant armadillo that is 1.5 meters (60 in) long and weighs up to 54 kilograms (120 lbs) down to the pink fairy armadillo, which is only 13 centimeters (5 in) long. Most are restricted to South America, but the nine-banded armadillo is common in the southwestern United States, and it is expanding its range northward as the climate warms. Their armor is protection against most predators, although they also use it to plunge into thorny undergrowth where predators with sensitive skin cannot follow. Some dig down quickly to protect themselves, leaving only their armored backs exposed to predators. The nine-banded armadillos have a habit of jumping straight up when startled, which often means they are killed by the bumpers or undercarriages of cars when they collide.

Wormtongue

Sloths and armadillos and their kin are the two most familiar families of the Xenarthra. The third are the anteaters, which are placed in the group Vermilingua, which means "worm tongue" in Latin. (There is no known connection to the villainous Grima Wormtongue in J. R. R. Tolkien's *Lord of the Rings*.) There are only four living species of anteaters alive in Latin America today, although there were many more in the South American fossil record.

As their name implies, anteaters have a long, wormlike tongue because they are specialists in eating ants and termites. They use their powerful front claws to rip open the anthill or termite nest, and then lap up hundreds of insects with 2-foot-long tongues covered with sticky saliva. Thus equipped, they can eat as many as thirty thousand ants in a day. The four living species of anteater include the tree-climbing tamanduas and the silky anteater, whose long fur gives it its name. The most impressive of all, however, is the giant anteater (figure 9.6). It is the largest of its kind, reaching 2.2 meters (7 ft) in length and weighing up to 45 kilograms (100 lbs).

Like the two other groups of Old Timers (plates 11, 14), the opossums and the South American hoofed mammals, the xenarthrans were established in South America possibly as early as the Cretaceous, and certainly before all land connections with the outside world ended in the Paleocene. For the next 20 million years, the Old Timers ruled South America with no interference from mammals from the rest of the world.

Figure 9.6. The giant anteater (courtesy @User: Anagoria/Wikimedia Commons/CC-BY-SA 3.0).

As we saw in the last two chapters, many of them evolved into niches occupied by dogs, hyenas, saber-tooths, hippos, rhinos, rabbits, mastodonts, and many other mammals found in the outside world.

None of them managed to evolve to fill the niches occupied by two groups: the tree-dwelling primates and the gnawing rodents. It would take lucky accidents for castaways from Africa to fill those unoccupied niches.

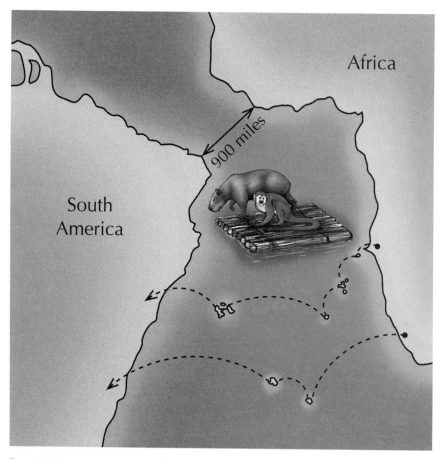

Figure 10.1. Cartoon showing the concept of New World monkeys and caviomorph rodents rafting from Africa to South America during the Eocene across a much narrower South Atlantic, possibly by island hopping (drawing by Mary P. Williams).

CHAPTER 10   The Castaways

Two of South America's signature groups of mammals, the New World monkeys (such as spider monkeys, howler monkeys, marmosets, capuchins, squirrel monkeys, and their kin) and the caviomorph rodents (chinchillas, guinea pigs, capybaras, cavies, agoutis, and their kin), were not always native to the Lost World. Both arrived much later in the Age of Mammals from a surprising direction and in a surprising manner.

Monkey Business

Charles Darwin was only twenty-two when the HMS *Beagle* first reached South America. He was used to cool, dreary, wet weather and to encountering just a handful of wild animals in the largely domesticated landscape of England. His first stop in South America was on February 28, 1832, when he disembarked in Salvador, Bahia, Brazil, at the edge of the Amazon rainforest. Immediately, he was captivated and overwhelmed by the richness of the wildlife and the intensity of the tropical jungle foliage, the stifling heat and humidity, and the numerous biting insects he encountered. As he wrote later, he was rapturous over "the elegance of the grasses, the novelty of the parasitic plants, the beauty of the flowers." He walked around half-dazed, barely able to process all the new sights, sounds, smells, and thoughts. "To a person fond of natural history," he recalled, "such a day as this brings with it deeper pleasure than he can ever hope to experience again."

Each stop in the Brazilian rainforest was ecstasy to the hardcore naturalist and collector. One day, he collected no fewer than sixty-nine different species of beetle, all new to science. Darwin wrote, "It is enough to disturb the composure of the entomologist's mind to contemplate the future dimension of a complete catalogue."

On April 3, *Beagle* reached Rio de Janeiro, where he rode with a party of British visitors to a coffee plantation about a hundred miles inland. It was a difficult journey, what with the blazing heat, poor accommodations, and vampire bats that bit their horses at night. But Darwin was still rapturous in his amazement. Brilliant birds and butterflies were everywhere, and hummingbirds darted from flower to flower. Cabbage palms towered 15 meters (50 ft) overhead, and long lianas hung down from them. Some forests looked positively prehistoric, with their enormous tree ferns, relicts of the time before the dinosaurs. The giant tree canopy towering overhead reminded one of a huge, high-ceilinged cathedral, with just small shafts of light penetrating through the thick covering of leaves.

Darwin continued to be staggered by the beauty and abundance of the Brazilian jungle. As he wrote later, "It was impossible to wish for any thing more delightful than thus to spend some weeks in so magnificent a country. In England any person fond of natural history enjoys in his walks a great advantage, by always having something to attract his attention; but in these fertile climates, teeming with life, the attractions are so numerous, that he is scarcely able to walk at all."

On June 4, Darwin awoke at four in the morning and joined a hunting party headed into the jungle. Although they were all there to catch specimens for his natural history collections to bring back to England (plus a little food), he soon became distracted by the trees. In Darwin's words:

I soon found this very stupid & began to hunt my own peculiar game. — The wood contained by far the largest trees I have yet seen. — the average I should think was double of what I have before seen, being about 6 feet in circumference, of course as before there are many larger & smaller trees. — Perhaps in consequence of the greater size this one was much less impenetrable than the generality & might easily be traversed in all directions.

Darwin added, "A most paradoxical mixture of sound and silence pervades the shady parts of the forest." One of the most amazing sounds and sights of the Amazon rainforest is the din of the howler monkeys, one of the noisiest creatures in existence. Although one can rarely see them high up in the forest canopy, their hoots and howls can be heard for miles. They have an expanded throat pouch that serves as a resonating chamber and amplifier.

Visibility in the forest canopy is poor, but sound carries well in the dense tropical air. Howlers keep in touch with the rest of their tribe with a variety of hoots and calls, letting each member of the group know where the others are. They make a "dinner" call when a rich food source such as a tree full of ripe fruit is found. They give out warning cries when one of them spots a predator such as a jaguar or especially their nemesis, the harpy eagle. Darwin heard them many times in his jungle wanderings, but he had yet to see one up close, since they lived so high up in the tree canopy. Finally, he encountered them in a decidedly unglamorous way:

> The day before this young man had shot 2 large bearded monkeys & had left another dead in the tree: these monkeys have prehensile tails, which when dead by the very tip will support the whole weight of the animal. — He took with him a mulatto with an axe & to my surprise proceeded in order to get the monkey, to cut down an enormous tree; they soon affected this & as it fell with an awful crash it tore up the earth & broke other trees & itself.

The New World monkeys are now known as the Platyrrhini, or "flat-nosed monkeys," a term the famous French naturalist Étienne Geoffroy St. Hilaire coined in 1812. They are also known as ceboid monkeys. They include Darwin's noisy howler monkeys, along with the agile spider monkeys; the woolly monkeys; the tiny marmosets, capuchins, and squirrel monkeys; and the owl monkeys, uakaris, and sakis. There are about fifty-three species of New World monkeys, about a third of all the known species of primates, divided into five different families. Most are medium-sized primates in a diversity known nowhere else.

New World monkeys are distinct from all other primates (figure 10.2). Unlike the Old World monkeys and apes (Catarrhini), platyrrhines have no snout, and their nostrils face sideways. In addition, they are the only monkeys to have prehensile tails that allow them to grasp branches as if they had a fifth arm. Most species have thumbs that are so short that they are not really opposable, which makes this prehensile tail very helpful indeed, since all platyrrhines are tree dwellers and rarely come down to the ground; there are no purely ground-dwelling species, such as the baboons and mandrills of the Old World. Consequently, New World monkeys depend mostly on fruit, nuts, sap, or leaves for their food, although some will catch birds or small mammals and eat them.

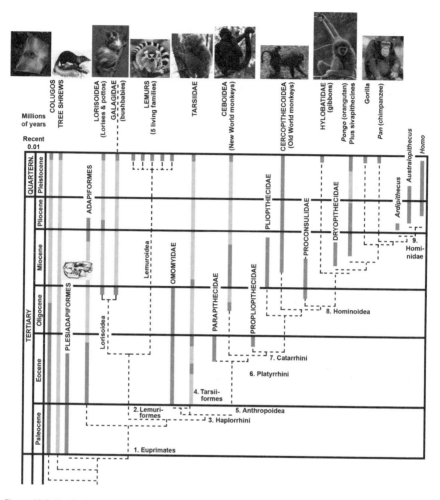

Figure 10.2. The family tree of the different groups of primates and their nearest relatives (diagram by E.T. Prothero, based on several sources).

Whence Monkeys?

Monkeys are such fixtures of the jungles of the New World that we think of them as a permanent part of the landscape. But they are not. As we saw in previous chapters, only three groups of mammals formed what we have been calling the Old Timers that lived in South America since the end of the Age of Dinosaurs: the carnivorous marsupials, the xenarthrans, and the native hoofed mammals. Yet today monkeys are among the most conspicuous and diverse members of the New World mammals. Where did they come from?

The first New World monkey fossils were discovered by Carlos Ameghino in Patagonia and described by his brother Florentino as *Homunculus patagonicus* in 1891. The name *Homunculus* (little man) is also a sly reference to old ideas about embryology. In the Middle Ages, naturalists and alchemists thought that our sperm or eggs actually contained a miniaturized human or "homunculus" inside, which grew larger as the embryo developed. Not until the invention of the microscope could scientists see that sperm and egg cells did not contain tiny humans but were simple cells that divided to form primitive balls of cells. Even today, the idea of a homunculus occurs widely in literature and science fiction. Ameghino's fossil monkey *H. patagonicus* consisted of a partial skull and jaws and some skeletal bones from the lower Miocene Santa Cruz beds of Patagonia, so it shows that New World monkeys were rapidly evolving by 18 Ma.

Since the discovery of *H. patagonicus,* more and more platyrrhine fossils have been found in South America. However, primate fossils are not particularly common, since monkeys tend to live in tropical rainforests, where the potential for their bones to be preserved without being destroyed by decay or scavengers is low. For the longest time, the oldest known primate fossil in South America was *Branisella,* from the upper Oligocene Salla beds in Bolivia, about 26 Ma. It was found by Bolivian paleontologist Leonardo Branisa, so when French paleontologist Robert Hoffstetter described it in 1969, he named it in honor of Branisa. *Branisella* has such primitive features that it cannot be assigned to any of the living families of ceboids, but it might be ancestral to any of them. It is mostly known from teeth and jaws that show a lot of wear; these suggest that it had an abrasive diet. The small portion of skull that was preserved had a small eye socket, so it was probably a daytime primate, not a nocturnal creature that would have had much larger eyeballs.

Before *Branisella,* there was a big gap in the fossil record. It appeared that no primates lived in South America before 26 Ma. *Branisella* was extremely similar to *Proteopithecus,* a very primitive primate from the late Eocene of Egypt, about 37 Ma. This suggested that New World monkeys came over from Africa some time between 26 and 37 million years ago. But when did they do it? And how?

Ken Campbell of the Natural History Museum of Los Angeles County and C. David Frailey of Johnson City College in Kansas, whom we met earlier, have been collecting in the headwaters of the Peruvian Amazon since the late 1970s. Among the amazing discoveries they have made is a series of tiny teeth found in upper Eocene or lower Oligocene beds in Peru. First recovered in 2010, at first they were not recognized for what they were because they were so unusual and odd-looking. When certain paleontologists saw the teeth, they recognized their similarities to New World monkeys right away. The fossils were finally published in April 2015 after a five-year delay and named *Perupithecus*. These teeth pushed the origins of New World monkeys back to at least 36 Ma, so they are roughly the same age as their close relatives from the late Eocene of Egypt.

The time difference between these fossils vanished, but still this points to an amazing voyage to get descendants of *Proteopithecus* across the Atlantic Ocean about 36 Ma (figure 10.1). When I was a graduate student in paleontology in the 1970s, there were still scientists who could not accept this idea. They argued that New World monkeys were somehow descended from the last of the lemurlike primates that had once dominated the jungles of North America during the Paleocene and early Eocene (figure 10.2). There were three big problems with this: somehow they crossed from North America despite the evidence that the land bridge was absent after the early Paleocene, and no other North American groups managed to cross since then. Second, none of the lemurlike primates were very close to any kind of New World monkey, and we knew of the early African monkey fossils, which were much more similar to New World monkeys. Third, the lemurlike primates vanished from North America by the middle Eocene, and none were known from the late Eocene, so there was no American source still surviving from which the New World monkeys could have evolved. This problem was more acute when we thought the oldest South American primate was from only 26 Ma.

The last of those "North American origin" arguments has died out long ago, and now primatologists agree that New World monkeys came from Africa. New research on the molecular similarity between Old World monkeys and New World monkeys (figure 10.2) further confirms that they are close relatives and never had much to do with lemurs or their ancestral lemurlike fossils.

It seems amazing that monkeys could sail across the Atlantic Ocean, but there are several things to keep in mind. First, during the Eocene the Atlantic Ocean was about half as wide as it is now during the time in question (figure 10.1). Thanks to plate tectonics and seafloor spreading, the Atlantic Ocean widens by about 6 centimeters (2 in) every year, about the rate that your fingernails grow. This may not seem like much, but over 37 million years it adds up. In the late Eocene, the distance was probably only 1,440 kilometers (900 mi) at its narrowest point. There were islands along the way poking up along the mid-Atlantic Ridge that might have served as stepping-stones for small animals to cross, just as Iceland, the Azores, Ascension Island, and many other mid-Atlantic Ridge islands rise above the Atlantic today.

Finally, scientists have seen just such examples of animals far out at sea being carried by rafts of floating vegetation, usually washed out into the ocean by huge river floods. More than 1,200 species are known to have used rafts to reach their present locations, mostly on remote islands. On a number of occasions, scientists have documented huge floating chunks of jungle turf almost an acre in area, including trees and soil, washed down rivers in floods. These would be capable of sustaining quite a few animals for a long time. In 1955, scientists found a floating mat of uprooted trees from the mainland that had floated to the island of Anguilla in the Caribbean. A dozen green iguanas were witnessed swimming ashore to an island that previously had none.

Marine creatures can get around this way, too. Most of the time, their tiny planktonic larvae can spread across huge distances, but they have other ways of getting around, including rafting. After the March 11, 2011, tsunami in Japan, a floating piece of Japanese dock drifted 8,000 kilometers (5,000 mi) for over a year and landed on June 5, 2012, on Agate Beach in Oregon, having crossed the entire Pacific Ocean with over two tons of its marine life intact and alive. They included mollusks, anemones, sponges, oysters, crabs, barnacles, worms, sea stars, mussels, and sea urchins. There were also some serious invaders, such as the European blue mussel (itself an invader of Japan), the Asian brown seaweed, an Asian shore crab, and a Japanese sea star. These creatures were already implicated as potentially dangerous invasive species, but many others had never been seen before on U.S. shores.

Monkeys were not the only colonists to reach South America by rafting from Africa. It turns out that there are lots of animals that did the same thing: geckos, skinks, tortoises, the blind burrowing reptiles known as amphisbaenids, and even the peculiar birds known as hoatzins. And then there were the rodents.

Rodents of Unusual Size

On October 19, 1832, the *Beagle* was about 48 kilometers (30 mi) up the coast from Punta Alta, at another sea cliff that rose 37 meters (120 ft) above the water level. Known to the locals as Monte Hermoso, it was rich in fossil rodents, especially large fossils that resembled the living capybaras and agoutis still roaming South America today.

As Darwin later wrote in *The Voyage of the Beagle*,

> The remains of these nine great quadrupeds and many detached bones were found embedded on the beach, within the space of about 200 yards square. It is a remarkable circumstance that so many different species should be found together; and it proves how numerous in kind the ancient inhabitants of this country must have been. At the distance of about thirty miles from Punta Alta, in a cliff of red earth, I found several fragments of bones, some of large size. Among them were the teeth of a gnawer, equalling in size and closely resembling those of the Capybara, whose habits have been described; and therefore, probably, an aquatic animal. There was also part of the head of a *Ctenomys*; the species being different from the Tucutuco, but with a close general resemblance. The red earth, like that of the Pampas, in which these remains were embedded, contains, according to Professor Ehrenberg, eight fresh-water and one salt-water infusorial animalcule; therefore, probably, it was an estuary deposit.

A characteristically South American group are these caviomorph rodents. The caviomorphs include everything from the pig-sized capybaras, the largest rodents alive, to the chinchillas with their soft fur, to the guinea pigs found in pet shops and kindergarten classrooms everywhere. There are many others that are less familiar to us, including gopherlike forms such as the *tuco tuco*, tree-dwelling forms such as the porcupine and spiny rats, fast grassland runners such as the maras, jungle runners such as the pacas and agoutis and cavies, mountain dwellers such as the chinchilla rats, and large grazing swimming herbivores such as the nutrias and capybaras (figure 10.3). Nutrias or coypus have been ranched in many parts of the world for their soft, waterproof fur.

The caviomorph rodents include fourteen different families, dozens of genera, and hundreds of species. Indeed, the rodents are not only the most diverse group of mammals in South America, but also the most diverse group of mammals worldwide. As suggested by their wide range of body shapes and habitats, the caviomorph rodents are highly adaptable. They live

Figure 10.3. The pig-sized caviomorph known as the capybara is the largest rodent alive today.

in nearly every habitat imaginable for a mammal, from trees to burrows underground, rock piles in the high Andes, and grasslands. Some, such as capybaras and nutrias, are great swimmers and spend time in water, as rodents such as the beaver and muskrat do. Since South America has never had large native herds of deer or cattle or other grazers, the larger rodents such as the capybara perform the job of grazers. Almost all of their evolution took place in South America.

The fossil record of rodents, especially in places such as Argentina and the basins of the Andes Mountains, is excellent. South America had no native mammals to occupy most niches that rodents can inhabit, so rodents evolved rapidly to fill this void. Eventually they were diversified into many ecologies and body plans early in their evolution. They also evolved some truly remarkable monsters, bigger even than the "rodents of unusual size" featured in the movie *The Princess Bride*. There was the extinct rhinoceros-sized Plio-Pleistocene pacarana, *Josephoartigasia* (plate 15), which was 3 meters (10 ft) long and weighed as much as 1,500 kilograms (3,382 lbs). It was discovered only a few years ago. The previous record-holders were the bison-sized Miocene pacarana *Phoberomys*, whose name means "terror mouse," which was 3 meters (10 ft) long and weighed about 700 kilograms (1,500 lbs), and the slightly smaller late Miocene-Pleistocene cow-sized fossil *Telicomys*, which was about 2.7 meters (7 ft) long. These monster rodents probably evolved to occupy the role of large grazers (such as cows and sheep and deer) found on other continents, since no cows, sheep, or deer reached South America until late in the Cenozoic.

A few of the caviomorphs successfully went northward when the Panama land bridge formed in the Pliocene, including North American porcupines and the gigantic Ice Age capybara *Phugatherium* (also known as *Neochoerus*), which at 113 kilograms (250 lbs) was the size of a sheep. Today, the only caviomorph found north of the U.S.-Mexican border is the porcupine, which has many relatives in South America and even in Africa.

Once again, we find South America dominated by a unique group that, like the New World monkeys, were not among the Old Timers that began their history there. The caviomorphs were widely established across the continent by the Miocene. Like New World monkeys, there were controversies about where they came from, and when. When I was a student in the 1970s, prominent rodent paleontologists such as the venerable Albert E. Wood held that South American caviomorphs somehow evolved from North American fossil rodents. Most paleontologists realized the anatomy of these rodents was wrong, though. The caviomorphs were not that closely related to any North American group, and there was no land route for them to get to South America until the Pliocene.

As early as 1969, French paleontologist Rene Lavocat made a strong case that caviomorphs came from Africa (figure 10.1). He pointed out that their closest relatives were all African rodents, including the crested porcupines, the naked mole rats, and a variety of other groups, some of which have since been found as fossils in Asia as well. Since that time, molecular analyses have clearly shown that all the caviomorphs are very closely related, especially to their African kin, and only distantly related to other living rodent groups.

Once again, Africa is the only possible source for these creatures. Like the New World monkeys, rodents are good candidates for crossing a much narrower Atlantic Ocean on a raft of floating vegetation, since we know that they have done this many times. This is how they colonized the islands of the Caribbean, for example.

When did they do it? For the longest time, the oldest fossils were from the late Oligocene, not only on the South American mainland, but also in the Caribbean. In 1993, their record was extended back to the early Oligocene, about 32 Ma, from fossils found in Chile. In 2004, even more primitive rodents were described from the same Santa Rosa fauna in the Peruvian Amazon that produced the oldest known New World monkey, so both groups go back at least to the late Eocene (36–37 Ma) or early Oligocene (30–34 Ma). Finally, in 2012, very primitive rodents were described from another locality in Peru from more than 41 Ma, so rodents may have rafted to the New World 4–5 million years before the monkeys did.

Once rodents appeared, they soon evolved body forms that crowded out many of the competing small-bodied marsupials, such as the polydolopoids we met in chapter 7. By the late Oligocene, as many as twenty-four species in seven families are known. Today, there are hundreds of species occupying nearly all the niches for small-bodied mammals available on the continent.

After the monkeys and rodents came, South America resumed its isolation for about 26 million years, with no further instances of immigrants breaking through what George Gaylord Simpson called its "splendid isolation." Ten million years ago, though, a flood of creatures arrived, this time from the north.

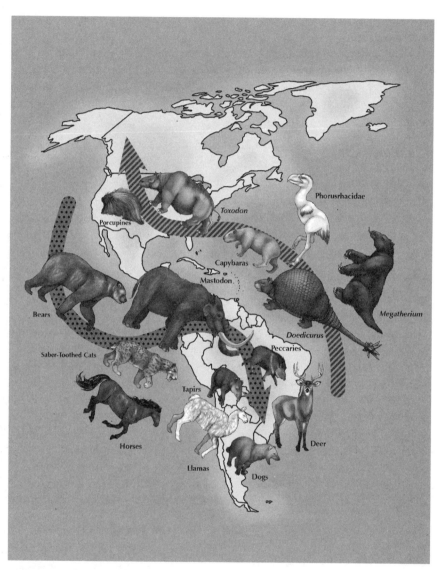

Figure 11.1. The Great American Biotic Interchange (GABI) occurred as the Panama land bridge gradually closed between 10 and 3 Ma. Most of the mammals we think of as typical of South America, such as the jaguars and other cats, the llamas and other camels, the dogs, deer, tapirs, peccaries, and bears, were all immigrants from North America, along with mastodonts, saber-toothed cats, and horses that died out at the end of the last Ice Age. Only a few South American native groups managed to cross to Mexico and the United States, including rodents such as porcupines and capybaras, xenarthrans such as ground sloths and glyptodonts, the terror bird *Titanis walleri*, and the native notoungulates known as toxodonts (*Mixotoxodon*). (Illustration by Mary P. Williams.)

11 Invasion!

South America was a Lost World from the beginning of the Age of Mammals, with no creatures from the outside world except for the monkeys, rodents, and a few other animals that rafted across huge expanses of water. This isolation ended 10 million years ago, when Central America rose out of the water. Over the next 7 million years, invaders from the north changed the Lost World forever.

Shipwrecked

Alfred Russel Wallace (figure 11.2) was both sick and exhilarated. Barely twenty-five, he had undertaken a dangerous and risky expedition to the Amazon rainforest to collect animal specimens for the growing market of rich British gentlemen who paid many pounds for exotic specimens to grace their mansions. Joining him was his friend Henry Walter Bates, also an avid collector of animals who also wanted to make money in the jungles of South America. Both Wallace and Bates were self-taught naturalists who compensated for their lack of wealth, social status, and top-drawer education by hard work and talent. They were also avid readers, especially of Alexander von Humboldt and Charles Darwin.

When Wallace arrived in Pará, at the mouth of the Amazon, in May 1848, he was just as overwhelmed by the incredible diversity of creatures as Darwin had been seventeen years earlier (figure 11.3). As he recounted in 1849:

> There is, however, one natural feature of this country, the interest and grandeur of which may be fully appreciated in a single walk: it is the "virgin forest." Here no one who has any feeling of the magnificent and

Figure 11.2. Alfred Russel Wallace as a young man, about the time of his Amazonian expeditions.

the sublime can be disappointed; the sombre shade, scarce illumined by a single direct ray even of the tropical sun, the enormous size and height of the trees, most of which rise like huge columns a hundred feet or more without throwing out a single branch, the strange buttresses around the base of some, the spiny or furrowed stems of others, the curious and even extraordinary creepers and climbers which wind around them, hanging in long festoons from branch to branch, sometimes curling and twisting on the ground like great serpents, then mounting to the very tops of the trees, thence throwing down roots and fibres which hang waving in the air, or twisting round each other form ropes and cables of every variety of size and often of the most perfect regularity. These, and many other novel features — the parasitic plants growing on the trunks and branches, the wonderful variety of the foliage, the strange fruits and seeds that lie rotting on the ground — taken altogether surpass description, and produce feelings in the beholder of admiration and awe. It is here, too, that the rarest birds, the most lovely insects, and the most interesting mammals and reptiles are to be found. Here lurk the jaguar and the boa-constrictor, and here amid the densest shade the bell-bird tolls his peal.

After two years, Bates and Wallace split up and began to explore different regions. Wallace followed the Amazon River for many miles before reaching the major tributary called the Rio Negro, which had never been traveled by European explorers. By 1852, after four years of the harsh conditions of the Amazon jungle, Wallace was desperately sick, having survived many bouts of malaria, dysentery, and yellow fever. He could no longer push himself any further, even though he had survived numerous close calls in those dangerous jungles. He slowly made his way back down the Rio Negro and the Amazon until he reached the coastal ports again. He loaded his collections onto the British brig *Helen* and on July 12, 1852, departed for England, hoping to make some decent money from four hard years of dangerous work. Twenty-six days into the voyage home, the ship caught fire. As he described it in 1853:

> The flames very soon caught the shrouds and sails, making a most magnificent conflagration up to the very peak. . . . The decks were now a mass of fire, and the bulwarks partly burnt away. Many of the parrots, monkeys, and other animals we had on board, were already burnt or suffocated; but several had retreated to the bowsprit out of reach of the flames, appearing to wonder what was going on, and quite unconscious of the fate that awaited them. We tried to get some of them into the boats, by going as near as we could venture; but they did not seem at all aware of the danger they were in, and would not make any attempt to reach us. As the flames caught the base of the bowsprit, some of them ran back and jumped into the midst of the fire. Only one parrot

Figure 11.3. An illustration of the dense Amazonian rainforest from Wallace's book *Travels on the Amazon and Rio Negro* (1889).

escaped: he was sitting on a rope hanging from the bowsprit, and this burning above him let him fall into the water, where, after floating a little way, we picked him up. . . .

The next day, the 8th, was fine, gulf-weed still floated plentifully by us, and there were numerous flying-fish, some of which fell into our boats, and others flew an immense distance over the waves. I now found my hands and face very much blistered by the sun, and exceedingly sore and painful. At night two boobies, large dusky sea-birds with very long wings, flew about us. During the night I saw several meteors, and in fact could not be in a better position for observing them, than lying on my back in a small boat in the middle of the Atlantic.

Wallace and the crew spent ten harrowing days in open lifeboats in the middle of the Atlantic, blistered by the sun and trying to survive on limited fresh water and provisions. Finally, they were spotted and rescued by the brig *Jordeson*, and Wallace finally reached London on October 1, 1852. All that remained of four years of work were a few notes he had managed to save, plus specimens he had shipped to England years earlier. As he wrote later:

It was now, when the danger appeared past, that I began to feel fully the greatness of my loss. With what pleasure had I looked upon every rare and curious insect I had added to my collection! How many times, when almost overcome by the ague, had I crawled into the forest and been rewarded by some unknown and beautiful species! How many places, which no European foot but my own had trodden, would have been recalled to my memory by the rare birds and insects they had fur-nished to my collection! How many weary days and weeks had I passed, upheld only by the fond hope of bringing home many new and beautiful forms from those wild regions; every one of which would be endeared to me by the recollections they would call up, — which should prove that I had not wasted the advantages I had enjoyed, and would give me occupation and amusement for many years to come! And now every-thing was gone, and I had not one specimen to illustrate the unknown lands I had trod, or to call back the recollection of the wild scenes I had beheld!

Wallace managed to salvage some compensation for his experiences by writing several scientific papers and two books about his expedition in 1853, selling the specimens that had arrived earlier and living off the insurance payments from his disaster. After eighteen months in London, the money was running out, so he embarked on another dangerous collecting trip, this time to what is now Indonesia, Malaysia, and Singapore. There he spent another eight years, from 1854 to 1862, almost his entire thirties, building up more collections of more than 125,000 specimens, many from species new to science, and making key observations about nature and the people of the region.

In 1857, he was again struck with malaria. While he was recovering on the island of Ternate, in the Molucca Islands just west of New Guinea, he had to lie in his hut to recuperate and read, often interrupted by bouts of fever. There he had the inspiration about natural selection and evolution that would later make him famous. In one of history's strangest twists of fate, he wrote down his ideas in a letter and mailed it to none other than Charles Darwin. Unbeknownst to Wallace, Darwin had come up with the same ideas some twenty years earlier, but had been afraid to publish them. When he received the letter, Darwin was mortified, but his friends arranged for both Darwin's short papers of 1838 and Wallace's 1857 letter to be read at the meeting of the Linnaean Society in 1858 so that each would get appropriate credit. The president of the Linnean Society, Thomas Bell, while summarizing the discoveries for the year 1858, wrote: "The year which has passed has not, indeed, been marked by any of those striking discoveries which at once revolutionize, so to speak, the department of science on which they bear."

Afraid of being scooped, Darwin ended his twenty years of fearful procrastination and hurried out a "short version" of his long-planned book on evolution. It was entitled *On the Origin of Species by Means of Natural Selection*, and it sold out the day it was published in November 1859. Wallace knew nothing of this until he returned three years later, but he was able to sell his thousands of Malay Archipelago specimens, and he wrote his own best-selling book *The Malay Archipelago*, which has never gone out of print.

The Great American Interchange

Wallace never achieved Darwin's level of fame as the joint discoverer of natural selection. Instead, he became better known as the founder of the modern science of biogeography, or the study of the geographical distribution of organisms. Thanks to his years of fieldwork in both South America and Southeast Asia, he had tremendous knowledge of the creatures of exotic regions outside Europe, and he made many discoveries that were fundamental to the field.

All the early European explorers, from the original Spanish and Portuguese colonials to Von Humboldt, Darwin, and Wallace, noticed that Latin America was populated by an interesting mix of animals not seen anywhere else. Wallace had also noticed that most of them had North American relatives. He wrote in *The Geographical Distribution of Animals* in 1876, "The sudden appearance of numerous forms of Edentata in temperate North America in post-Tertiary times . . . together with such facts as the occurrence of a considerable number of identical species of sea fish on the two sides of the Central American isthmus, render it almost certain that the union of North and South America is comparatively a recent occurrence, and during the Miocene and Pliocene periods, they were separated by a wide arm of the sea."

Before Wallace, the early naturalists had no reason to suppose that these unusual animals and plants had not always ruled South America. Indeed, when Darwin collected fossil mammals from the coast of Argentina, they included not only the native South American hoofed mammals but also some fossil horse teeth. This mixture of specimens demonstrated that members of modern groups found around the world, such as horses, coexisted with the peculiar fossils of South America. It took a brilliant deduction by Wallace to recognize that South America had once been isolated from the rest of the world.

After 1887, the Ameghino brothers collected even older fossil mammals from Eocene and Oligocene beds in Argentina. These fossil assemblages only contained unique and peculiar extinct mammals, but no true cats related to jaguars, no camel relatives like llamas, or rhinoceros relatives like tapirs. The distinction was not as obvious then as it is now, because, as we saw in chapter 8, Florentino Ameghino often was confused by convergent evolution and interpreted some of his fossils as ancestral mastodons, hippos, horses, and other creatures from the Old World. Nevertheless, Ameghino correctly regarded most of his fossils as members of native South American groups. Then the question arose: exactly *when* in the Miocene or Pliocene—as Wallace had suggested—did these native mammal assemblages began to mix with those from North America, so that by the Ice Ages, there were North America–derived horses mixing with South American native hoofed mammals?

Through the twentieth century, decades of fossil collecting and detailed geological work by paleontologists such as William Diller Matthew and George Gaylord Simpson of the American Museum of Natural History in New York, John Bell Hatcher and William Berryman Scott of Princeton

University, Bryan Patterson of Harvard University, and S. David Webb of the University of Florida, as well as South American paleontologists such as Rosendo Pascual and Carlos de Paulo Couto, documented the details of South American mammal history through time. It soon became clear that the biggest change occurred about 3 to 4 million years ago, near the middle of the Pliocene Epoch.

By the 1950s and 1960s, the details of this big migration event, called the Great American Biotic Interchange (GABI), were well documented. It was often found in textbooks as an example of what Simpson called a "filter bridge"—a land bridge that lets some creatures through but blocks others. It was a strikingly asymmetric filter, too. Only a handful of South American natives made it as far as North America, although more of them reached Central America and stopped there. These few successful northward immigrants included ground sloths, glyptodonts, anteaters, and armadillos; southern rodents like porcupines and capybaras; the notoungulate hoofed mammals; and the gigantic "terror birds," or phorusrhachids.

By contrast, the "Legions of the North" flooded south and overwhelmed the natives. They include many of the animals we associate with modern Latin America. Among these are camels like the llamas, alpacas, vicuñas, and guanacos, which originally evolved in isolation in North America through most of their history over at least 45 million years. South America is home to many kinds of native deer, which soon evolved into a radiation of uniquely South American creatures such as the pudu, marsh deer, brocket deer, and many others. Latin America is also characterized by its peccaries, which look like pigs but are a uniquely New World group that evolved in isolation in North America for the past 40 million years. No list of Latin American mammals is complete without tapirs, which underwent most of their evolution in North America and Eurasia before arriving late in Latin America, where they are mostly found today. When we think of the American predators, we think of cats like the jaguar, ocelot, and cougar, as well as Ice Age saber-toothed cats, all of which came from North America. Even more impressive were the dogs, which evolved into a big diversity of native South American canines, including the maned wolf, bush dog, and several different species of foxes. Other immigrant predators include the bears, resulting in the South American spectacled bear, plus the weasels, skunks, and otters, including the Amazon giant otter. Besides the hoofed mammals and predators, there are also South American shrews, rabbits, and numerous northern rodent groups, including squirrels, kangaroo rats, voles, and pocket gophers.

Add to these living members of the Neotropical jungle a menagerie of Pleistocene mammals that evolved their own unique South American species before vanishing at the end of the Ice Ages, including mastodonts, horses, and several others. Today, when you think of "typical" South American mammals, from jaguars to tapirs to llamas to peccaries, you are thinking almost entirely of groups that are late arrivals from North America.

Why was this exchange so unbalanced? Some paleontologists have argued that the *norteamericanos* were competitively superior to their South American counterparts. There is some evidence to support this in a few cases. Some of the South American carnivorous marsupials (plate 10) that we met in chapter 7 vanished at about the time North American carnivores (plate 12*d*) appeared, although other predatory marsupials, the Borhyaenidae, vanished before the flood of northern competition began. Likewise, the appearance of all these new, more efficient predators—not only cats, but also the dogs and bears—would not only have outcompeted the native marsupial predators but blitzed through the native prey animals of South America, such as the notoungulates and litopterns, that had no previous experience with something as terrifying as a saber-toothed cat or a bear or a pack of wild dogs. In addition to dealing with new predators, the native southern hoofed mammals also had to cope with ecological competition from all sorts of immigrant hoofed mammals, from peccaries and tapirs to deer and horses and camels.

But is that the entire story? Other scientists have pointed out that there were lots of niches in South America that were unoccupied until the northerners arrived. South America had no bearlike creatures until true bears appeared to fill that niche, nor did it have many doglike mammals. Likewise, there were no native southern counterparts for otters, horses, tapirs, and mastodonts. Scientists call these creatures the "insinuators," working their way into the open niches in the food web of South America where no native had been before, and taking advantage of an underexploited habitat.

South American mammals moving north had to contend with geography and climate. For South American plains and desert animals of Argentina to reach the North American plains, they would first have had to cross the Amazon Basin rainforest or trek through the Andes Mountains. Rainforest animals would be fine in Central America up to Guatemala and the Yucatán, but crossing much of Mexico's desert would block most of them. The handful of creatures that did successfully invade North America, such as the ground sloths, giant armored glyptodonts, and predatory terror birds, had no counterpart or competition in North America and would insinuate themselves into unoccupied niches.

Still others have argued that the Great American Biotic Interchange is a reflection of theoretical equilibrium dynamics in ecology. The number of species that can live in a given area is controlled by the area of the landmass itself, so large islands can support more species than small ones can. North and Central America have a much larger area than South America does, so according to equilibrium theory, it should be able to support more species than the smaller continent. If a large number of northern creatures flood south to a region already at maximum capacity, like South America, then some creatures *must* be pushed out because South America has no more room for additional species. If the immigrants are superior to the natives and outcompete them, then the noncompetitive natives would be the first to lose. In fact, this dynamic of hardy, successful, opportunistic, "weedy" invading species pushing out their native competition is a common tale in biology.

Whatever the reason, by the Ice Ages all but a handful of South America's native mammals were gone. What we think of as "typical" South American animals—jaguars, tapirs, llamas, peccaries, maned wolves, and so on—are nearly all North American invaders that came late to the party, crashed it, and now rule the roost.

Waiting at the Gates

The Panama Canal is truly a marvel of engineering. Built by the United States from 1904 to 1914, it is 77 kilometers (48 mi) long. Most ships take twenty to thirty hours to pass through it. It greatly reduces the time a ship takes to pass between the Pacific Ocean and the Caribbean Sea and Atlantic Ocean, eliminating as well the dangers of traveling through the stormy seas around the southern tip of South America. When it was completed, it gave a huge boost to the world economy via reduced shipping costs and dangers. It also helped make the United States a world power, since its navy could travel around the world and between oceans with greater speed. About a thousand ships passed through in the year it opened, but more than 14,700 vessels travel through it each year now, adding up to over 815,000 vessels over its first century. Today, the American Society of Civil Engineers ranks it as one of the seven wonders of the modern world, along with the Empire State Building, the Golden Gate Bridge, and the Channel Tunnel.

After a century of heavy use, however, the Panama Canal was no longer big enough to handle all the traffic passing through it, especially the gigantic supertankers that now travel the world's oceans. In 2006, Panama voted to fund construction for a huge project to widen the canal and build new navigational locks, to be begun in 2010 and completed in 2016. It planned to blast over 100 million tons of rock to make it wider, creating a new set of fresh exposures in the bedrock of the canal. These precious exposures of rocks would soon be covered up with vegetation from the jungle, washed away by the tropical rains, or flooded by the canal. Colombian geologist Carlos Jaramillo, an expert on the geology of Panama, realized that this opportunity was too important to science to pass up. He arranged a collaboration with scientists from four American and three Panamanian institutions, especially the Smithsonian Tropical Research Institute and the University of Florida, which have longstanding research interests in Central America and the Caribbean. Over years of work, Jaramillo and colleagues obtained several million dollars in grant funding and all the necessary permits from the Panamanian government to study and collect these rare outcrops of bedrock before they vanished forever.

This type of research was particularly important because fossiliferous exposures of naked rock are extremely rare in the tropical jungles of Central America. Almost no fossil mammals were known from anywhere in the jungles of Central America, despite a century of looking. The only good collections of fossil mammals from the region come from the desert areas of Mexico, and they are much closer to the United States than they are to South America or most of Central America. Thus, the entire region was a geological and paleontological mystery for a long time. Did the fossils of Central America look more like those of Mexico or the United States, or did they resemble those of nearby South America? No one knew.

As the canal exposures were scraped bare, the scientists and the field crews collected fossils, studied the rocks, and took numerous samples for many different types of analyses. More than a hundred scientists and interns spent a collective six thousand or more hours from 2010 to 2015 (figure 11.4). They found hundreds of fossil leaves that gave precise estimates of the temperature and rainfall in Panama 18–20 Ma. They collected thousands of crocodile teeth and other reptiles, fish bones and scales, and more than two dozen species of fossil mammals from eight different orders. Only four had been known before, and they were scrappy specimens collected in the early 1960s at Gaillard Cut, an earlier excavation for the canal. The new finds included camels, rhinos, peccaries, dogs, beardogs, bats, extinct even-toed hoofed mammals known as protoceratids, anthracotheres, and oreodonts, plus squirrels and several other kinds of rodents. There were

Figure 11.4. Field crews collecting fossils from the new excavations of the Panama Canal performed in 2012 and 2013, as a ship passes silently behind them (photo courtesy S. Lukowski).

also fossil whales and sea cows in the marine rocks. The specimens were precisely dated as early Miocene, about 17 to 20 million years old, by both potassium-argon dating on the volcanic ashes in the beds and by analyzing the changes in the earth's magnetic field as recorded in the sediments.

Although the thousands of fossils are still being studied and published, a preliminary picture has already emerged. Just as the original mammal fossils found in the 1960s suggested, all the specimens are from groups from North America, especially from the humid Gulf Coast and Florida region at the same time. Some are even the same species as those found in the early Miocene of Florida and coastal Texas. These include some strange camels known as floridatragulines, which have extraordinarily long snouts that make their skulls look almost crocodilian. As their name suggests, they were first found in the 19-million-year-old Thomas Farm locality in northern Florida. There are odd-looking horned beasts known as proto-ceratids, which may be distantly related to camels but vanished about 5 Ma. The pony-sized rhinoceroses known as *Menoceras* were among the earliest horned rhinoceroses on the planet; skulls of males bore a pair of small horns on the tips of their noses. The long, snouted anthracothere *Arretotherium* is a member of a lineage that was ancestral to the hippos and whales, but the Panama species of *Arretotherium* mostly resembles similar fossils found in early Miocene beds of Nebraska and South Dakota, as do the beardogs, the dogs, the oreodonts, and the peccary specimens. Then, in 2016, as this book was going to press, the first teeth of New World monkeys were found, showing that some creatures indeed were able to cross over from South America.

These discoveries show that by at least 20 Ma, North American mammals were widespread through all of Central America, ready to invade South America. All that prevented this was the impassable water barrier through Panama and Colombia, which no *norteamericano* had managed to cross since the Paleocene. They appeared to have waited at the gates for more than 15 million years before there was a route south. Or did they?

Leakage

The Amazon jungle is a difficult place to find fossils or even do geology. The dense jungle grows over nearly every exposure of bedrock. The only exposures are in the cutbanks of rivers, and they often collapse or grow over if the river floods do not continually undercut them. None are more than a few tens of meters high, so it is impossible to get long, thick, continuous exposed sections of rock like the Grand Canyon, where you can see the sequence of events through millions of years. Thus, most of the fossils of South America have come from the dry badlands in the Andean foothills of Argentina, coal mines in Venezuela, or high, dry valleys in Peru, Ecuador, Bolivia, and Chile.

Fossil collecting in the Amazon Basin has other challenges as well. You can work only during the limited dry season, when the river drops to its lowest levels, and if there are big rains up in the Andes or over the rainforest, the river rises and your field season is over. The temperatures are uncomfortably hot year-round, and the humidity is like a steam bath, without any relief of cooler, drier air. Even in the dry season, it rains a lot. About the only way to travel in the region is by boat up the rivers or its tributaries, which can be shallow and treacherous in the dry season. Much of the time, you must haul your boat out of the water and portage it around rapids, or cut paths through the jungle with machetes, to make any progress at all. As paleontologist George Gaylord Simpson wrote about his expedition in 1956:

> We worked hard under trying conditions, but saw many marvels in compensation. We collected some fossils, although fewer than we had

hoped. We mapped and remapped. We made many geological sections of river banks. We spend a great deal of our time running around and getting off again, cutting our way through *pauzadas* (log jams), repairing the motor. When the going was too hard for the *batelão* (shallow motor launch) we took to a dugout canoe of even shallower draft and much narrower beam.

There were also many other hazards, from venomous snakes to predators like jaguars, anacondas, and caiman alligators, huge spiders, bloodsucking leeches, ponds full of piranhas, and hordes of army ants that can strip any victim to the bone in minutes. Deadliest of all were the tiniest: mosquitoes, which carry numerous diseases. Not so long ago, it was routine for many people to die on these expeditions. Many of Alfred Russel Wallace's companions died, as did three of the nineteen who went with Theodore Roosevelt to the Amazon. Roosevelt barely survived himself. Simpson was nearly killed on his expedition when a tree fell on him. Gravely injured with a concussion, broken shoulder, and two broken legs, Simpson only survived because a friend of mine, American Museum lab technician George Whittaker, paddled him downriver in a canoe for a week to get him to a place where he could be flown to a modern hospital.

Thus, for many good reasons, the prehistoric life of the tropical heart of South America has long been a mystery. Just a handful of fossil localities are known, but they are few and mostly represent specimens of Ice Age mammals recovered from the young sediments in the riverbanks. In 1995, Ken Campbell Jr. and C. David Frailey discovered the peculiar Santa Rosa fauna in Amazonian Peru, the first mammal fauna older than the Ice Ages; it may date back to the late Eocene, and it produces the oldest primates known from South America.

In the 1970s, Campbell and Frailey began to find localities that produced what appeared to be late Miocene mammals. At first, the fossils were of primates closely related to the New World monkeys known from Miocene localities in the high valleys of the Andes of Bolivia, or the badlands of Argentina. Other discoveries included rodents and notoungulates. But by the 1990s, they were finding more and more fossils of mammals that were not supposed to be in South America before the Great American Biotic Interchange of three million years ago. In 1996, Campbell, Frailey, and Lidia Romero-Pittman discovered and described a mastodont skull they named *Amahuacatherium*. The mastodont itself was not that peculiar, but its age was: it came from late Miocene beds dated at least 9.5 million years in age, securely dated by volcanic ash dates in the beds just above the skull found in the bedrock (not based on some loose tooth floating about, which could be any age). It was also dated by research that I conducted, using the reversals of the earth's magnetic field to match the rocks of the outcrops with the global timescale.

If all this information was right, then mastodonts did not wait until the Panama land bridge appeared to cross from North America but were there at least 6 or 7 million years earlier than previously supposed. Apparently, they stayed in the Amazon Basin and did not show up in Argentina until much later. Since then, Ken and Dave have discovered fossils of North American groups such as tapirs and peccaries from these same beds, showing that they too had crossed much earlier than expected, but had not spread outside the Amazon Basin for at least 7 million years.

Several years ago, Ken showed me an innocuous-looking lower jaw (figure 11.5), misidentified as a deer jaw. I took one look at it and at once realized it was no deer at all. Deer did not make it from Eurasia to North America until 5 Ma, and not into South America until 3 Ma. But what was it? I had suspicions, but I had no good fossils to compare it with at home.

Several months later, in December 2011, I managed to find time and money for a trip to the American Museum of Natural History in New York. I brought the jaw with me to compare it to the best collection of extinct ruminant fossils in the world. My colleague Brian Lee Beatty and I went through drawer after drawer of fossils, comparing them to the Amazon jaw. We ruled out deer, antelopes, pronghorns, giraffes, and many other groups, one step at a time.

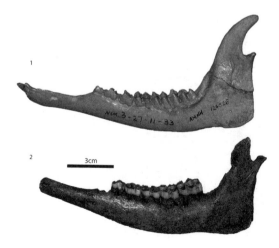

Figure 11.5. The only known specimen of the *Surameryx* (bottom), compared to the jawbone of the very similar palaeomerycid *Barbouromeryx* (top), known from rocks about 23 million years old in western Nebraska (photograph by D. R. Prothero).

Finally, we found a great match. The jaw belonged to an extinct Eurasian–North American group of deerlike mammals called the palaeomerycids or dromomerycines. I had already worked on and published the definitive studies of them in 2007 and 2008. The jaw itself was a pretty close match for the most primitive of the palaeomerycids, known as *Barbouromeryx*, which were otherwise only found in beds of western Nebraska dated at 23 million years. Brian and I finished writing up our descriptions and took our measurements and photos that same day in the museum, then over the course of the next three years we wrote it up, submitted it for publication, got rejected, battled reviewers and editors, and resubmitted it elsewhere. In 2014 it was published in the prestigious *Journal of Paleontology*. We named it *Surameryx*, "southern ruminant," in reference to its being the southernmost representative of this important ruminant group.

This is the clincher. Critics of Ken's and Dave's work have argued that the mastodonts, peccaries, and tapirs might be from Ice Age deposits. These scientists reject all the careful geologic dating work we have done and claim that these fossils are not proof of an early migration of these groups at 9.5 Ma or earlier. The presence of *Surameryx* cannot be explained as some sort of Ice Age specimen from the last 2 million years, since palaeomerycids vanished before 5 Ma from both North America and Eurasia. To me, it looks much older than the 9.5-million-year minimum age of the beds. Based on its similarity to *Barbouromeryx*, I would say that it—and the rest of the fossils, like the mastodon, tapirs, and peccaries—might be even older than the oldest date we have. I think they are close to 20 to 23 million years old. There are still no other dates to test this, so we have to stick with the minimum age for these fossils. I am waiting until my friends who are going through the collections from the Panama Canal dig find some more fossils of palaeomerycids in their deposits of 18–20 Ma. The recently announced discovery of monkey fossils in the Panama deposits shows that some mammals were able to migrate north out of South America at this time, and I would bet that that is when the ancestors of *Surameryx* crossed into South America. I bet the palaeomerycids, like the rest of the early Miocene Panamanian mammals, were also waiting at the gate, and some of them did manage to cross earlier than once supposed and make it at least as far as the Peruvian Amazon.

The Not-So-Great Great American Biotic Interchange

In retrospect, this "leakage" of mammals across the supposedly impassable water barrier of Central America before 3 Ma should not have been a surprise. The first relatives of raccoons and coatimundis in South America came from beds about 7.3 million years old, so coatis managed cross shortly after the mastodonts, peccaries, tapirs, and palaeomerycids (figure 11.6).

In addition, for years paleontologists had been finding fossils in Central and North America that showed numerous groups of South Americans had found a way to cross the barrier much earlier than 3 Ma, when the floodgates opened. In beds from Texas and Florida about 9 Ma, about the same age as our Amazon fossils, there are fossils of ground sloths *Pliometanastes* and *Thinobadistes*. Around 6 Ma, the sigmodontine rodents, a South American group, show up in Texas and Florida.

Around 5 Ma, fossils of the huge "terror bird" known as *Titanis walleri*, a South American phorusrhachid bird, occurs in beds in Florida and Texas.

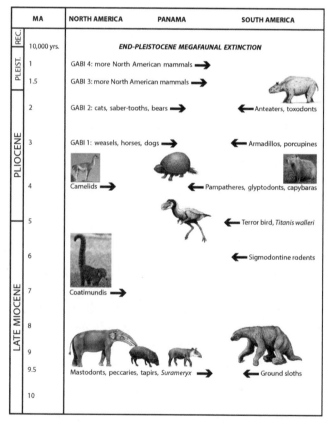

Figure 11.6. The timing of different migration events of South American mammals to the north (right) and North American mammals to the south (left). Scientists now recognize four separate GABI events in the Pliocene and Pleistocene. (Drawn by E. T. Prothero.)

Since it was flightless and could not swim, its only way to reach Florida or Texas from South America was to walk.

And the beat goes on. At 4 Ma, we see a number of mammals crossing from South America and showing up in Mexico, including the huge armadillo relatives known as pampatheres and glyptodonts (figure 11.6). They certainly did not swim huge distances in all that armor, but instead must have walked. Likewise, we find fossils of capybaras in South Carolina and Florida and Texas at that time, another creature that could not have swum long distances. Meanwhile, camels show up in South America about a million years before the Interchange, so the travel was going both ways.

In short, the Great American Biotic Interchange was not a single event, nor was it as great as once suggested. The fossil record is clear that mastodonts, tapirs, peccaries, palaeomerycids, camels, and coatimundi relatives all made it over the water barrier to South America long before the land bridge opened to the Legions of the North 3 Ma. Likewise, ground sloths, glyptodonts, pampatheres, capybaras, and terror birds were all crossing to the north. It is not hard to imagine some of these, like the sloths and mastodonts and tapirs and peccaries, doing some swimming, but the heavily armored glyptodonts and pampatheres and the terror birds could not have done anything but walked.

Then, at 3 Ma, we see what Mike Woodburne called the "Great American Biotic Interchange 1" (GABI 1): weasels, dogs, and horses heading south, while an array of armadillo relatives, plus more ground sloths and even porcupines, headed north (figure 11.6). About 2 Ma, GABI 2 released a slew of *norteamericanos* to the south, including saber-tooths, bears, deer, and additional peccaries, camels, and tapirs, while anteaters and the notoungulate *Mixtotoxodon* made it north. Two additional events, GABI 3 and GABI 4, brought additional immigrants in both directions and completed the final waves of interchange and extinction during the Ice Ages.

Panamanian Complications

How did all these creatures make the crossing before the completion of the Panamanian land bridge? A number of scientists have argued that there might have been an incomplete bridge, with chains of islands and short water barriers between them. This would have made it possible for good swimmers like mastodonts, tapirs, peccaries, and sloths to island-hop their way across, while many other mammals apparently found the water barrier impassable. Ken Campbell proposed the "Baudo pathway," a series of mountain ranges and island connections that would have provided passage from Panama to Colombia and thence down into the Amazon Basin, which would get the mastodonts, tapirs, peccaries, and *Surameryx* into the Amazon without showing up in the Andes or in Argentina until much later.

Meanwhile, geologists have begun to rethink the entire idea of a water gap across Panama. Colombian geologists such as Carlos Jaramillo and Camilo Montes have been publishing what is now called the "new model." The geological data show the tectonics of Central America was very complicated. There were numerous blocks of crustal rock that were rotating and sliding back and forth in what would eventually become Panama, and all sorts of geological evidence that there was not much of a water barrier between them—something Ken Campbell has been arguing for twenty years and more.

This flies in the face of what marine geologists and paleontologists have thought for years. When they look at the fossils of the plankton or of marine snails or clams, there is clear evidence that normal marine water flowed easily between the Caribbean and Pacific before 3 Ma. The species of plankton, snails, and clams between the two ancient oceans are nearly identical during this time, so there was no land barrier preventing them from swimming or floating between the two oceans. Only after about 3 Ma do the clams and snails and plankton of the Caribbean and Pacific begin to show evolutionary divergence, indicating there is no longer any exchange between their two populations. In a way, this is the reverse of the Great American Biotic Interchange: What is a barrier for land animals is an open door for marine life. Once the land bridge closed, it allowed mammals and birds to walk back and forth but closed the door for marine animals.

How do we resolve these complications? Tony Coates and Bob Stallard have argued that you do not need a very wide gap between landmasses to get complete exchange of marine life between oceans. They point to the modern example of the Indonesian Archipelago as an example (figure 11.7). In 1845, Alfred Russel Wallace discovered what is now called the Wallace Line in the islands of Indonesia. The animals west of the line are almost all Asian in origin, from the tapirs and rhinos to the monkeys and rodents and birds and the rest. When the sea level was lower during the last Ice Age, about twenty thousand years ago, these islands were all connected to one another by the exposed land of the Sunda Shelf (figure 11.7*a*). Somewhere east of Java and Borneo, and west of Celebes and Lombok, however, the islands begin to have animals typical of Australia and New Guinea, such as tree kangaroos, egg-laying echidnas, and the amazing birds of paradise. Between the two regions is a deep-water passage that is not very wide, yet it prevents most Asian animals from crossing to the east,

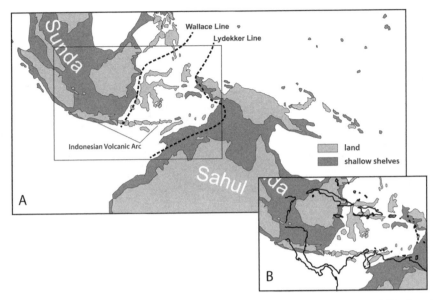

Figure 11.7. (*a*) The Indonesian Archipelago, show-ing the islands (light gray) and the shallow shelf region (dark gray). Nearly all the animals west of the Wallace Line are typical of Southeast Asia, while nearly all the animals to the east of the Lydekker Line have affinities with those of New Guinea and Australia. The zone of islands between them is surrounded by channels of deep water, which are impossible for animals to cross from one side to the other. In this zone, deep-water currents flow between the Pacific and Indian Oceans, allowing marine life to travel both ways. (*b*) The Central American isthmus region superimposed on the Indone-sian Archipelago at the same scale. A handful of narrow deep-water passages in Panama or Nicaragua could have allowed Caribbean and Pacific marine life to pass through, but the distance between islands would have been so narrow that many mammals could have crossed easily (from Anthony G. Coates and Robert F. Stallard, "How Old Is the Isthmus of Panama?" *Bulletin of Marine Science* 89, no. 4 [October 2013]).

and Australian and New Guinean animals from crossing to the west. This narrow deep-water passage, especially the Lombok Strait between Bali and Lombok, is deep enough that the snails, clams, and other marine life float freely through it and all around the Indonesian Archipelago, so there is no isolation whatever. Thus, Coates and Stallard argue, the narrow water gaps between the islands in the Panama region could have allowed some mammals to cross, while not blocking marine life from floating between the Caribbean and Pacific.

This suggests another complication in our common explanation about earth history. For decades, geologists have argued that the appearance of the Arctic ice cap at the same time as the GABI, about 3 million years ago, was no coincidence—one caused the other. Oceanographers and climate modelers suggest that if Panama closed 3 Ma and shut off water flow-ing from the Caribbean to the Pacific, that warm tropical water would be diverted north into the Atlantic to form the Gulf Stream (figure 11.8).

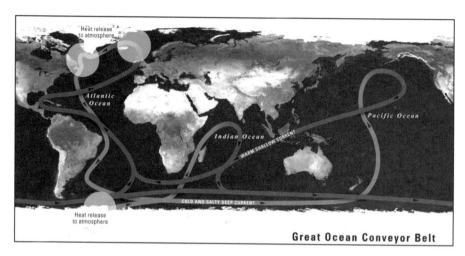

Great Ocean Conveyor Belt

Figure 11.8. The global oceanic conveyor belt of deep-water currents, which exchanges the waters of all the oceans. The Gulf Stream segment in the North Atlantic brings warm, moist conditions to the British Isles and provides moisture to the North Pole to create the Arctic ice cap. Closure of the Panamanian gap would have prevented any further warm Caribbean water from flowing to the Pacific and diverted it all toward the Gulf Stream, triggering the formation of the Arctic ice cap. (Image courtesy NASA.)

As my former Columbia professor Wally Broecker established back in the 1970s and 1980s, the flow of the Gulf Stream is part of what he called the "global oceanic conveyer belt," which transports deep-ocean water in a big loop around the globe. The closure of Panama stopped the leakage of Caribbean water into the Pacific and brought the full force of the warm tropical waters of the Gulf Stream up into the North Atlantic, where they provide not only warmth, but also moisture for the atmosphere. As the warm water washes past the British Isles, it gives that region a relatively wet but mild climate with little snow or ice—yet England is at the same latitude as frozen Labrador, and Scotland is at about the same latitude as the south tip of Greenland.

The Gulf Stream is also important because it supplies moisture to the Arctic, which is naturally cold due to the low amount of solar radiation it gets all year. Remember, above the Arctic Circle, it is dark through much of the winter. All the North Pole needs to have an ice cap is a source of moist clouds that can form snow and ice. The geologic evidence from cores in the Arctic Ocean shows this occurred about 3 Ma, coincident with the supposed closure of the Panama gateway and the diversion of Caribbean waters from the Pacific to the Atlantic.

Now that we have established that the land bridge was closed much earlier than 3 Ma, or had only narrow water gaps like those in Indonesia, is the

Panama–Gulf Stream model for the birth of the Arctic ice cap dead, too? Not necessarily. If the water gaps between the islands in Central America were as narrow as those in Indonesia, most deep-water currents would have been able to leak through (figure 11.7*b*). A land barrier does not have to be complete to block deep-water currents from going through. It only has to be very narrow and relatively shallow.

We have come the full circle, from Wallace's early thoughts about the Great American Interchange to one of his other great discoveries, the biogeographic barriers of the Indonesian Archipelago. Somehow I think Wallace would be pleased to see how far biogeography, paleontology, and climate science have come—and how his discoveries were more interconnected than he would ever realize.

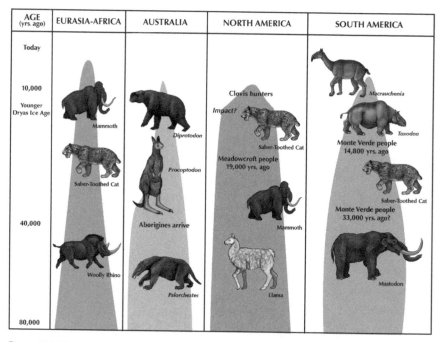

Figure 12.1. The pattern of extinction of large mammals during the end of the last Ice Age. Large mammals gradually vanished in Eurasia until about 10,000 years ago, when the climate changed dramatically and the ice sheets retreated. Mastodonts survived in North America until about 4,000 years ago. Ground sloths persisted on Caribbean islands until 4,700 years ago. Large mammals gradually vanished from Australia after the arrival of Aborigines and their dingoes about 40,000 years ago. Large mammals were thriving in North America until about 13,000 to 10,000 years ago, when the climate changed and hunters using Clovis points arrived. South American large mammals went through pulses of extinction (the "zigzag" model), with the last megamammals vanishing 9,000 years ago, later than on most other continents. (Drawing by Mary P. Williams.)

CHAPTER 12

Where Have All the Mammals Gone?

Just 10,000 years ago, South America was home to a huge menagerie of prehistoric beasts, from mastodonts, horses, and saber-toothed cats to gigantic armadillos and ground sloths and even native hoofed mammals. All of these beasts are now extinct. What happened to them?

A Horse Tooth—and a Mystery

While on the voyage of the *Beagle*, Charles Darwin found several badly broken molars of what was clearly a mastodont as well as an unquestioned horse tooth. These creatures were the survivors of the Great American Biotic Interchange from North America, and they were eventually discovered to have evolved mainly north of the border before arriving late in South America's history.

Darwin was puzzled. What were creatures known from the Old World, like horses and mastodonts, doing in South America, when most of its fossils were peculiar creatures not found anywhere else? More to the point, why were there no native horses or mastodonts roaming South America in Darwin's time—or today? Were they truly extinct? If so, why?

In the early 1800s, natural historians were still trying to reconcile the ever-improving fossil record with the book of Genesis. The first discoveries of fossils were attributed to giant humans drowned in Noah's flood or considered slight variants of animals now alive. Even as late as 1810, natural historians could not stomach the idea that animals could go extinct. It seemed to be a violation of God's Providence and His love of His handiwork. If God knew when the sparrow fell, how could He allow His creations to become extinct? As the great poet Alexander Pope wrote in "Essay on Man" (1733),

Who sees with equal eye, as God of all,
A hero perish, or a sparrow fall.

But about 1796, Baron Georges Cuvier, the most famous paleontologist and anatomist of his time, clearly showed that in fact some creatures, such as the mastodont teeth found in Big Bone Lick, Kentucky, and the huge-toothed beasts called mammoths, were similar to elephants. They were so large that if they were still alive, explorers would have found them by then.

By the 1820s and 1830s, numerous large marine reptiles, including ichthyosaurs and plesiosaurs, had been found in the sea cliffs of Lyme Regis, in southwestern England, by the first woman to attain renown as a fossil collector, Mary Anning. These, too, were clearly no longer swimming in the seas and must be extinct. Soon Cuvier was writing about a dark, dangerous "antediluvian" ("before the Flood") world not mentioned in the Bible and inhabited by these scary creatures. By the late 1830s and 1840s, the first dinosaurs had been described in England, and Richard Owen himself coined the word *Dinosauria*. No one could imagine such huge, terrible reptiles still roaming even the most remote and unexplored regions of the world today. According to Cuvier, they had all become extinct before the Creation events mentioned in the Bible, so they did not violate the biblical chronology.

As more and more fossils were found, "Cuvier's compromise" began to crumble. The first problem was the dogma that the terrible extinct creatures in the fossil record had all lived before humans or any modern animal formed by the biblical Creation week. Yet, the horse tooth in Darwin's collections clearly showed three startling things: that horses had lived in the New World long before Columbus reintroduced them on his second voyage in 1493; that horses had vanished from South America, even though they had long been successful there; and that modern-looking horses lived side by side with extinct beasts that were supposed to have died out in the dark, frightening antediluvian world that Cuvier had imagined.

Darwin's South American fossil horse only confirmed what other evidence had suggested: that the large extinct animals thought to have lived before the Creation were not extinct when humans walked the earth. In 1822, the prominent British natural historian William Buckland analyzed the bones of Ice Age mammoths, rhinos, hippopotamus, and other mammals found in Kirkdale Cave in England. They had not been washed there by Noah's flood, but instead had been dragged into the den of a group of extinct English hyenas. Apparently, these creatures were not of the antediluvian world no longer found in England, but they were similar to animals living today in Africa—a mixture of modern animals and extinct ones, like the mammoth.

This, and many later discoveries, blurred Cuvier's distinction between the antediluvian world of beasts that had become extinct and the post-Creation world of animals that were still alive today. By the late 1830s and 1840s, the complexity of the fossil record, with distinctive assemblages of animals in every layer, made the entire idea of a single Noah's flood obsolete. A few geologists, such as Alcide d'Orbigny in France, suggested twenty-nine separate creation events and mass extinctions not mentioned in the Bible. But by 1840, even this compromise was absurd. Quietly, geologists and paleontologists stopped using the Bible as a scientific work and no longer took the idea of Noah's flood seriously.

Almost twenty years later, Darwin published his most important book, *On the Origin of Species*, and forever ended efforts to explain nature with the legends of Bronze Age shepherds found in Genesis. The seeds of that book started with his observations on the *Beagle* voyage, especially his thoughts about the fossils he had found, the mixture of strange extinct beasts trying to imitate camels and rhinos, and the many other incredible sights to which the trip had exposed him. When Darwin returned from his five-year trans-global voyage in 1836, his father said, "Why, even the shape of his head had changed." What he did not know was how much the *inside* of his head had changed as well. Those ideas and thoughts from the *Beagle* expedition changed not only Darwin, but also the world.

Megamammals

The specimens that Darwin and later scientists found clearly demonstrated that there was an incredible mixture of large animals by the end of the last Ice Age in South America. Some were among the last of the "Old Timers" (xenarthrans, marsupial carnivores, and native hoofed mammals; see plate 11) that originally settled South America around the end of the Age of Dinosaurs. Others were the "Castaways" that rafted over from Africa during the Eocene. But the majority of the mammals that ruled South America during the last Ice Age (and still do today) were what I have been calling the Legions of the North: North American and even Eurasian mammals that had come down via Central America starting in the late Miocene.

By the end of the last Ice Age, South America hosted a huge diversity of medium-sized and large mammals. There were at least six elephant-sized species of ground sloths (*Megatherium, Eremotherium*), plus many other, smaller ground sloths (*Glossotherium, Lestodon, Megalonyx, Nothropus, Ocnopus,*

Mylodon, Nothrotherium). There were many different kinds of huge armadillos, glyptodonts, and pampatheres, some the size of a Smart Car (*Doedicurus, Glyptodon, Panochthus, Parapanochthus, Scelidotherium, Scelidodon, Pampatherium, Hoplophorus, Eutatus, Neothoracophorus, Plaxhaplous, Holmesina, Propraopus*). There were hippo-sized notoungulates (*Toxodon, Mixtotoxodon, Trigonodops*) and the huge litopterns *Macrauchenia* and *Xenorhinotherium*. These were the last survivors of the two Old Timer groups of mammals (xenarthrans, plus native hoofed mammals) left by the end of the last Ice Age. The third Old Timer group, the giant predatory opossums (sparassodonts), had already vanished, replaced by the dogs, cats, and other invaders.

Of the two great Castaway groups that had originally arrived in the Eocene, there were lots of New World monkeys, including the giant 23-kilogram (50-lb) spider monkey *Protopithecus*, and caviomorph rodents, including the rhino-sized capybara *Neochoerus* (plate 15). Most of the rest of the mammals, however, were invaders from the Legions of the North. These included several types of huge mastodonts (*Cuvieronius, Stegomastodon*), immense short-faced bears (*Arctotherium*) bigger than any bear alive today, diverse horses (*Equus, Hippidion*), and huge llamas (*Hemiauchenia, Palaeolama*), plus other mammals we think of as typical of Latin America today, including numerous tapirs, peccaries, and deer. The predators were also invaders, from a diversity of bears, dogs, foxes, and wolves to saber-toothed cats and weasel and raccoon relatives.

All of this mixed assemblage lived side by side at the end of the last Ice Age, having already survived the shuffling and extinctions when the Legions of the North drove many of the Old Timers extinct. They were successful and diverse and ranged in body size from gigantic sloths and mastodonts to the smallest rodents and bats. Yet, over a few thousand years, nearly all of them vanished. What happened?

The Great Pleistocene Megafaunal Extinction

This pattern of extinction of mostly larger mammals that once lived in South America is mirrored on other continents as well. In North America, a diverse mammal fauna was found in late Ice Age deposits like the La Brea tar pits and many cave deposits in the eastern part of the United States. It ranged from huge mammoths and mastodonts to giant ground sloths, big camels, bison, horses, tapirs, peccaries, deer, and pronghorns. Even the beavers were the size of bears. These herbivores were prey to an impressive spectrum of predators, such as dire wolves, American jaguars, American cheetahs, gigantic short-faced bears, and especially the famous saber-toothed cat *Smilodon*.

About fifteen of these animals vanished from North America between 11,700 and 10,000 years ago, but others died out before or after that time interval.

Australia, too, once had its own Ice Age giants. In addition to its extinct mammals, there were Komodo dragon relatives that reached 7 meters (23 ft) in length and weighed about 2,000 kilograms (4,400 lbs) and huge emulike land birds (dromornithids). Their marsupials were spectacularly large as well (plate 16). There were two-tonne wombat relatives the size of hippopotamuses (diprotodonts). There were gigantic kangaroos twice the size of living hoppers. One of these, the short-faced giant kangaroo *Procoptodon*, was 3 meters (10 ft) tall and weighed about 230 kilograms (500 lbs). There were ground-dwelling koalas and strange clawed marsupials with a tapirlike proboscis (palorchestids). Even stranger looking was the marsupial "lion," *Thylacoleo*. It was the size of a modern leopard, with retractable claws (convergent with the claws that evolved in cats) and even a thumb that could grasp its prey and help the lion climb. However these huge Ice Age marsupials lived, they all vanished during the last part of the last Ice Age. Some appear to have vanished as early as 46,000 years ago, while others persisted until less than 10,000 years ago.

In Eurasia and Africa, there were also extinctions of large mammoths, mastodonts, saber-toothed cats, cave bears, woolly rhinos, "Irish elk," and weird-looking relatives of giraffes, warthogs, and the clawed, horselike creatures known as chalicotheres. But these extinctions were long and drawn out over the entire late Pleistocene, from about 80,000 to about 4,000 years ago, and did not appear to have occurred in a narrow time window like those in the Americas. The number of extinctions was also relatively minor in Africa and Eurasia. In many ways, the megamammals still rule there today. The modern African savanna closely resembles the landscape of the Ice Age megamammals, with elephants, giraffes, rhinoceroses, hippopotami, Cape buffalo, hundreds of antelopes, zebra, and many other large mammals that used to roam much of the world.

Naturally, ever since early naturalists realized in the 1830s and 1840s that there were once mammoths and mastodonts roaming Europe, and lions and hippos in England during the last Ice Age, there has been speculation as to why they vanished. The arguments have been raging for 150 years by this time but have boiled down to just a few reasonable ideas.

Climate Change

Most of the extinctions are concentrated at the end of the last Ice Age (especially between 12,000 and 9,000 years ago), when the earth rapidly warmed out of the wetter, cooler climates of the last glacial episode into the hotter, drier world we have now. Such climate changes mean dramatic changes in rainfall and vegetation, which many herbivores cannot tolerate. In particular, there were some extreme climate swings, such as the Younger Dryas event about 11,700 years ago, when the Ice Age glaciers returned in just a decade after a long warming period, then melted back almost as quickly—a climate shock that seems to explain some of the extinctions. Other scientists have argued that climates went from being more uniform and mild to more extreme and continental, with rapid shifts in temperature typical of the centers of continents far from the moderating effects of the oceans. Critics of the climate hypothesis have argued that there was no similar mass extinction during previous interglacial periods (such as 125,000 years ago), when the climate warmed just as it did 10,000 years ago. But supporters of the climate change scenario have pointed out that the late Pleistocene communities were very different from those at the end of previous glacials, especially with the abundance and extent of certain cold, dry steppe habitats dominated by bison only 12,000 years ago.

The "Overkill" or "Blitzkrieg" Model

Ever since the 1970s, some scientists have argued that humans were the primary agent of mass extinction at the end of the last Ice Age. They point to the first appearance of peoples in North America with sophisticated Clovis-style spear points and arrowheads right about the time that many of the megamammals vanished. We have proof that humans killed mammoths, bison, and horses, but we have no direct evidence of them hunting most other megamammals. In addition, the bison survived the hunters and became the largest species of land mammal left in North America after the others vanished. It appears that many other North American mammals survived for thousands of years after humans first appeared, so if it was a blitzkrieg, it was not a very fast one. Mammoths still survived until 3,700 years ago on polar islands such as Wrangel Island north of the Bering Sea between Alaska and Siberia. Mastodonts survived in North America until about 4,000 years ago. Ground sloths persisted on Caribbean islands until 4,700 years ago. The overkill argument has also been applied to the arrival of Aborigines in Australia, but again it was a complex process, because the megamammals did not die out for thousands of years after people first appeared. Clearly, human hunting is not very important to the animals of Eurasia and Africa, which survived and even evolved for hundreds of thousands of years alongside humans.

Comet Collision

In 2007, a trendy new idea made a splash in all the scientific media: a giant comet allegedly impacted over the Carolina Bays region about 12,900 years ago, which might have caused climate changes that affected North American vegetation and megamammals. However, detailed double-checking and research on the evidence for this impact has pretty well demolished the idea that it ever happened. Even if the evidence for the impact were solid, almost no species vanished at the time of the impact, and it would have had no bearing whatsoever on the mass extinctions on other continents.

The "Keystone" Hypothesis

Some scientists have looked at the megafaunas living in the African savanna today and point out that their diversity is the product of one keystone species. That species is the elephant, which breaks down the trees and prevents the forest from becoming too dense. Elephant damage allows for a much more diverse habitat of trees, brush, scrub, and grasses, which sustains the huge populations of antelopes, zebras, giraffes, and other large megamammals. If something (whether climate or humans) wiped out the mammoths during the last Ice Age, it might have had a cascading effect on the vegetation and wildlife across the continent, especially in North America. This idea is very interesting but seems to be a secondary effect of whatever major cause killed large mammals such as mammoths in the first place.

What about South America's Megamammals?

All this debate brings us back to our starting point: What happened to the huge sloths, glyptodonts, mastodonts, toxodonts, and other megamammals in South America? As in all the other continents, the problem has been debated intensely. However, some unique aspects of the South American story make it different from the rest.

First, improved radiocarbon dating of the fossils show that extinctions in South America were delayed compared to those in North America, occurring as late as 9,000 years ago in the early Holocene, rather than at the end of the last Ice Age, 12,000 to 10,000 years ago, as in North America. This does not support the idea that they died out with the climate changes at the end of the last Ice Age, but it also does not support the human over-kill model. Alberto Cione and Eduardo Tonni of the National University of La Plata in Argentina have proposed the "zigzag" model for South America's extinctions. During most of the last Ice Age, South America's habitats tended to be colder and drier (especially in Argentina, where most of the fossils are found), with rapid zigzags during interglacials to a warmer and wetter climate. This stressed out the mammals adapted to the prevailing cold, dry climate. Each time a zigzag occurred, their populations shrank and became weaker. The last zigzag occurred about 9,000 years ago, and it may have been worse than usual because human hunters slaughtered the already weakened and sparse fauna that had survived previous zigzags.

However, there is another wrinkle: South America has one of the oldest records of humans in the New World. Conventional thinking has long argued that there were no humans in the Americas until people with Clovis spear points crossed the Bering land bridge and swept south about 13,500 years ago. But at a site called Monte Verde in southern Chile, the radiocarbon dates are much older. The oldest level bears charcoal that appears to be 33,000 years old, although this is controversial. Higher levels produce good-quality radiocarbon dates of 14,800 years ago, at least 1,000 to 2,000 years before Clovis people reached the Americas. Most archaeologists believe the Monte Verde people were coastal migrants who traveled from one beach to another in their canoes and did not move far inland with advanced spears and arrows to hunt the megamammals, as did the Clovis people 1,000 years later. However, there are inland sites such as Meadowcroft Rock Shelter in Pennsylvania, which gives radiocarbon dates of 19,000 years ago, and a number of other inland sites in the Americas with pre-Clovis dates as well. The simplistic model of a single big blitzkrieg of human hunters first arriving only 12,000 years ago has clearly become more complicated.

There is another kink as well. The record of fossil bones may not be giving the whole story. In 2009, a group of scientists analyzed samples of soil from permafrost deeply buried in northern Alaska. They found evidence of extinct horse and mammoth DNA in permafrost, which could be radiocarbon dated to be 2,000 years younger than the youngest bones of these animals. Thus, we must be cautious of overgeneralizing and overinterpreting the record of bones, which we know is incomplete. If these data are correct, horses and mammoths survived for thousands of years after human hunters arrived, which does not fit the blitzkrieg or overkill models at all.

People like simple answers, but the truth is often complicated and multifaceted. In particular, Mother Nature is more complex than the simplistic models that so often frame our arguments. In most cases, it is clear that there were effects of climate, weakening and reducing the populations of megamammals as their habitats and diets changed, and possibly human overhunting in some cases. In no case is there an extinction event where only one cause is required.

EPILOGUE
The Sixth Extinction

When Charles Darwin and Alfred Russel Wallace first explored the Amazonian rainforest and roamed the Argentinian pampas, they were amazed at the creatures that no Englishmen had ever seen roaming their own countryside: ferocious jaguars, huge anacondas, prehistoric-looking tapirs and peccaries, pig-sized rodents, giant anteaters and armadillos, unique species of deer and opossums and foxes, and camels without humps, to say nothing of the peculiar sloths and screeching monkeys in the trees. Darwin's fossil finds first proved that these creatures are a pathetic remnant of a landscape that once teemed with huge mastodonts, immense ground sloths, tanklike glyptodonts and pampatheres, horses, saber-toothed cats, short-faced bears, and the bizarre toxodonts and litopterns that confused scientists for decades. South America's native animals are already a shadow of what they were only nine thousand years ago.

The future of South America's wildlife is grim. Paleontologists have been studying the earth's great mass extinctions for close to thirty years now. They point to the "Big Five" mass extinctions that shaped the history of life on this planet, which include the Cretaceous extinctions; the Permian "mother of all mass extinctions," 250 Ma, which wiped out 95 percent of marine life; and the mass extinctions at the end of the Ordovician, Devonian, and Triassic periods. These five extinctions stand out of the background as global events that affected both land life and marine life and wiped out more than 50 percent of species on the planet in a few million years or less.

Biologists and paleontologists are now beginning to talk about a Sixth Extinction, one that is occurring in animals and plants thanks to the explosion of human populations and their effects on the planet. This extinction involves not just the dodo and passenger pigeon, but also the other 875 extinctions that have happened between 1500 and 2009—and those are just extinctions that scientists have documented. This includes 79 species of mammals, 136 species of birds, 22 reptile species, 39 amphibian species, 68 species of fish, 327 species of mollusks, and hundreds of species of plants, among the better-known examples.

Today, humans are wiping out species at a rate never seen in any of the worst extinctions of the geological past. Some scientists estimate that this is occurring at a rate 10,000 times greater than the normal background extinction rate. There are estimates that 140,000 species are being lost each year, counting tiny things like insects that vanish without being documented. Some argue that 50 percent of all species will be gone by the end of the century. Of all the mammal species on earth, 25 percent (1,138 species) are now listed as threatened or endangered. About 13 percent of the birds (1,253 species), 41 percent of amphibians (1,917 species), 29 percent of reptiles (772 species), 23 percent of fishes (2,028 species), 5 percent of mollusks (1,673 species), and more than 8,500 species of flowering plants are on the endangered or threatened list.

Thanks to the incredible rate of slashing and burning in the Amazonian rainforest, one of the richest sources of diversity on the planet, South America is particularly vulnerable to losing the last remnants of its wildlife. The list of endangered mammals in South America is very long and sad, including the Amazonian manatee, the giant armadillo, the giant otter, the maned wolf, several species of primates (bald uakari, golden lion tamarin, mantled howler monkey, and yellow-tailed woolly monkey), and several kinds of wild cats (jaguars, ocelots, margay, and the Andean cat). Hundreds of species of birds are endangered across Latin America, including a wide spectrum of parrots, macaws, toucans, flamingoes, albatrosses, rails, petrels, flycatchers, tanagers, woodpeckers, hummingbirds, doves, pelicans, warblers, owls, finches, mockingbirds, and hawks, not to mention the Galápagos penguin—the northernmost known species of penguin—and the huge harpy eagle, which plucks monkeys and sloths from the tree canopy.

The roster of endangered reptiles is equally depressing, from the crocodiles and caimans of the great Amazon drainage system to the Galápagos tortoise and the wide variety of unique turtles, lizards, and snakes that are found only in the Lost World. Even more threatened are the amphibians, with hundreds of distinct species of frogs vanishing from the rainforest even before scientists have time to describe and document them. A classic case of this was the rare Panamanian golden frog, which was first discovered in 2006 and vanished soon thereafter.

What would Darwin or Wallace think of their beloved South American rainforest without jaguars, ocelots, anteaters, sloths, manatees, monkeys, birds, and so many other creatures? The Lost World has produced some of the biggest and most spectacular creatures the world has ever known, from the biggest amphibians and snakes and crocodiles and tortoises and dinosaurs to giant ground birds and the largest bird that ever flew to the immense ground sloths and glyptodonts. It is tragic to think that, if the present trends continue, the island continent will lose most of its animals. The huge tropical rainforests will be reduced to a barren area of scrub-grasses and sawgrass planted for cattle or biofuels.

The Lost World will be lost forever.

ACKNOWLEDGMENTS

I thank my agent, John F. Thornton, for quickly getting this book to a good publisher, and my editor, Christina Wiginton, and the director of Smithsonian Books, Carolyn Gleason, for their help with this project. Thanks go as well to Matt Litts, marketing director, and Leah Enser, marketing assistant, at Smithsonian Books for their work in the production and promotion of this book. I thank my artists, Nobu Tamura and Mary P. Williams, for the outstanding images that grace many of these pages, and my eldest son, Erik T. Prothero, for his work on some of the figures. I thank my colleagues, especially Mike Woodburne, Ken Campbell, Linda Ivany, Brian Beatty, and Darin Croft, for, among other things, their advice on scientific matters and helping with individual details, their field notes, their images, and their careful review of the manuscript. Many other colleagues, acknowledged in the figure captions, allowed me to use their images.

Finally, I thank my wonderful wife, Teresa LeVelle, for her help and support in this project. I thank my wonderful sons, Erik, Zachary, and Gabriel, for inspiring me to tell this amazing tale of the Lost World.

INDEX

aardvark, 116
Abelisauroids, 18–21, 27, 46
Abelisaurus, 20, 22
Aborigines, 162
Absimo Guy Collet (cave), xiv
Achillesaurus, 27
acid rain, 46, 55
Adams, John, 117
Adinotherium, 104
Aepyornis, 67
aetosaurs, 14
Agate Beach, Oregon, 129
agouti, 130
Agustinia, 22
Airy, George B., 49
Alamosaurus, 45
Alaska, 86, 162
alchemists, 127
Alcidedorbignya, 58
alligators, 66, 68, 86
Allops, 42
Allosaurus, x
alpaca, 105, 141
Alvarez, Luis, 50–52, 57
Alvarez, Walter, 50–52, 56
Alvarezsauridae, 18, 27
Alvarezsaurus, 27
Amahuacatherium, 147
Amargasaurus, 20, 22, 35–37
Amazon Basin, xiv, xvii, 142, 146–48, 152
Amazon giant otter, 141, 166
Amazonian manatee, 166
Amazon rainforest, 134–37, 165, 166
Ameghino, Leontine, 104
Ameghino brothers, 21, 23, 101–04, 140; Carlos, 101–04, 127; Florentino, 101–04, 107, 110, 127, 140; Juan, 102

American Association of Petroleum Geologists, 3–4
American Museum of Natural History, 6, 33–35, 14, 140, 147, 148
American Society of Civil Engineers, 143
ammonites, 7, 47, 53–55
amphibians, xv–xvi, 8–9, 55
Amphicoelias, 39–40
amphisbaenids, 129
Anacleto Formation, 31
anaconda, 74–76, 147, 165
Andagalornis, 60
Andean cat, 166
Andean condor, 70
Andean foothills, 146
Andesaurus, 22, 28
Andes Mountains, 15, 90, 131, 142, 146, 152
Andrews, Roy Chapman, 33
Angel Falls, xiv
ankylosaurs, 45, 46, 109
Anning, Mary, 158
Antarctica, 6, 38, 79, 85–88, 91
Antarctic Peninsula, 53, 83
Antarctodolops, 88
Antarctosaurus, 22, 35, 36, 40
anteaters, 116, 120–21, 141, 151, 165, 167
"antediluvian" world, 158
antelopes, 148, 161, 163
anthracotheres, 144, 145
Apataelurus, 93
Apatosaurus, x, 37, 38, 40–43
Apennine Mountains, 50
apes, 125–26

archaeohyracids, 104
Archaeopteryx, 62–66
archosaurs, 13–16
Arctic Circle, 79, 86
Arctic ice cap, 153
Arctotherium, 160
Argentavis, 69–71
Argentina, 11, 17–21, 57, 58, 97–101, 114, 131, 140, 146, 152, 163–65
Argentinosaurus, 22, 34–43, 45
Argyrosaurus, 35, 40
Arizona, 119
armadillos, 116–21, 141, 160, 165
army ants, 147
Arretotherium, 145–46
Asaro, Frank, 51
Ascension Island, 129
Askin, Rosemary, 87
Asmithwoodwardia, 103
asteroid impact, 12, 46–47
astrapotheres, 108
Astrapotherium, 108
Atlantic Ocean, 2, 5–6, 128–29
Auca Mahuevo, 31–33
Auca Mahuida volcano, 31
Aucasaurus, 34
Australia, 6, 8, 81, 86–87, 91, 152–53
Australian extinctions, 161
Azores, 129

Badlands, 42, 93
Bakker, Bob, 22, 24, 57
bald uakari, 166
Bali, 153
Baluchitherium, 42
bandicoots, 91
Barbouromeryx, 148–49
Barosaurus, 37, 40
Bates, Henry Walter, 135

bats, xv, 82, 144
"Baudo pathway," 151
Bavaria, 62
beardogs, 144
bears, 66
Beatty, Brian Lee, 148
beaver, 131, 160
Bell, Joseph, xii
Bell, Thomas, 139
Bering land bridge, 164
Bering Sea, 162
Big Bang theory, 49
Big Bone Lick, Kentucky, 158
"Big Five" mass extinctions, 165
biogeography, 139–55
birds, 14, 23, 54
The Birds (film), 71
birds of paradise, 152
birth control pill, 49
bison, 160, 162
"blitzkrieg" extinction hypothesis, 164
Bloch, Jonathan, 74–77
"bloody crocs," 14
boa constrictor, 76
Bolivia, x, xiv, 58, 127, 146, 147
Bonaparte, José, 21–25, 35, 36
Bonaparte, Napoleon, 22, 114
bony fish, 8
Borhyaenidae, 142
borhyaenids, 91–93
Borneo, 152–53
Bourque, Jason, 75
Bozeman, Montana, 34
brachiopods, 13, 53
Brachiosaurus, 37, 38, 40
Bradysaurus, 10
Branisa, Leonardo, 127
Branisella, 127
Brazil, xiv, 5–8, 11, 12, 27, 81, 97, 98, 101
British Isles, 154

British Museum, London, 62
brittle stars, 88
brocket deer, 141
Broecker, Wally, 7, 154
Brontops, 42
Brontornis, 60
Brontornithinae, 67
"Brontosaurus," x–xi, 40–43
brontotheres, 42
Brontotherium, 42
Bronze Age shepherds, 159
Bru, Juan Baptista, 114
Bruhathkayosaurus, 39–40
bryozoans, 53
Buckland, William, 158
Buenos Aires, 23, 101–04
Burroughs, Edgar Rice, xiv
bush dog, 141
bushmasters, xv
Button, David, 43

Cadena, Edwin, 77
caenolestids, 86, 90
caimans, 81–82, 147, 166
Camarasaurus, 30, 37, 40
Cambridge University, 95
camels, 105, 144, 150–51, 160, 165
Campbell, Kenneth, Jr., xvii, 69, 127, 147, 149, 151–52
Canada, 23, 46, 86
Cape buffalo, 161
capuchins, 125
capybaras, xv, 130–32, 141, 150–51
carbon dioxide, 13
Carbonemys, 72, 77–78, 80
Carcharodon, 27
carcharodontosaurs, 27–29
Carcharodontosaurus, 27–29
Caribbean Sea, 46, 143, 152, 153, 162
Carloameghinia, 104
Carnegie Quarry, 40–43
Carnotaurus, 17–22, 25, 34, 46, 57
Carolina Bays region, 163
Carolini, Ruben Dario, 28
Carolodarwinia, 103
cassowary, 67
"Castaways," 123–33, 159–60
Catarrhini, 125–26

cats, 66
cave bears, 161
cavies, 130
caviomorph rodents, 123, 130–34, 150, 160
ceboid monkeys, 125
Celebes, 152–53
Central America, 69, 144, 155
Cerrejón, 79–80
Cerrejón Formation, 74
Ceylon, 48
chalicotheres, 161
chalk, 53
Challenger, George Edward, xii–xiii, xvii, 26
Chañares Formation, 13–16
Channel Tunnel, 143
Charactosuchus, 82
cheetahs, American, 160
Chiappe, Luis, 31–32, 34
chickens, 37
Chicxulub, 52
Chile, 133, 146, 164
China, 11, 14, 58, 65
chinchillas, xv, 130
Churchill, Winston, 1
Cione, Alberto, 163
Cladosictis, 91
clams, 152
climate change extinction hypothesis, 161–62
climate classification, 1–2
climbing rats, xv
Clovis-style points, 162, 164
Coates, Anthony, 152–53
coatimundis, 150, 151
cobra, 73
coccolithophorids, 44, 52–53
collarbones, 64
Colombia, 74–81, 146, 152
Coloradisaurus, 22
Colorado, 40, 42
Columbia University, 7, 14, 49, 154
comet impact, 163
comparative anatomy, 111–13
competitive exclusion, 41
competitive superiority, 142
Compsognathus, 64, 65
Conan Doyle, Arthur, viii–xvii, 26
conifers, 37, 43
continental drift, 5–16

convergent evolution, 106–07, 161
Cooper, Merian, xiii
Cope, Edward Drinker, 23, 39–40, 104
corals, 13, 53
coral snakes, xv
Coria, Rodolfo, 28
cornflakes, 49
Corningware, 49
cosmic background radiation, 49
cosmic dust, 50
cougars, 141
coypus, 130
Creation week (biblical), 158
creodonts, 93
crested porcupines, 132
Cretaceous extinctions, 44–59, 165
Crichton, Michael, xiv, 17, 65
crinoids, 13, 53
crocodiles, 8, 14, 21, 37, 66, 77–78, 80–82, 86, 144, 166
Crocodylus, 72, 80
Ctenomys, 130
Cuba, 46
Cuvier, Georges, 101, 111–14, 117, 158
Cuvieronius, 160
"Cuvier's compromise," 158
cycads, 43
Cynognathus, 5, 13

Daily, Bill, 85–88
Darwin, Charles, xi, xvii, 21, 61–64, 95–101, 104, 103, 105, 114–17, 123–25, 130–31, 135, 139–40, 157–59, 165, 167
Darwin, Robert, 95, 159
"Darwin's Bulldog," 64
Deccan lavas, 47–48, 51–59
deer, 141, 148, 160, 165
deinonychosaurs, 27
Deinonychus, 64–65
Deinosuchus, 82
Denisovans, 109
Denmark, 51
Devil (Christian), 113
Devonian extinction, 165
Diadaphorus, 106–07
diatoms, 53
dicynodonts, 11–13
didolodonts, 109

Dimetrodon, 10–11
Dimorphodon, xi
Dingus, Lowell, 31–34
Dinheirosaurus, 23
dinocephalians, 11, 12
Dinodontosaurus, 13
Dinosaur (film), 19
dinosaur eggs, 31–33, 58
Dinosauria, 158
Dinosaur National Monument, 40–43
dinosaurs, 12–16, 44–59
Dinosaur Train (TV show), 19
diplodocines, 38
Diplodocus, 37–40
diprotodonts, 161
dire wolves, 108, 160
Disney Studios, 19
Djadocta Formation, 33
DNA, 108–09
docodonts, 23
dodo, 165
Dodson, Peter, 24
Doedicurus, 118, 160
dogs, 66, 141, 144, 151, 160
D'Orbigny, Alcide, 159
Drake Passage, 87
Dreadnoughtus, 39–40
dromomerycines, 149
dromornithids, 161
"drumstick," 64
dryolestoids, 23, 55
duck-billed dinosaurs, 21, 45, 46, 58, 65, 109
Du Toit, Alexander, 6
dysentery, 137

echidnas, 152
Ecuador, 146
Edaphosaurus, 10–11
edentates, 116
Edops, 9
Edvardocopeia, 103
Egypt, 25, 36, 127
Egyptians, 73
Ekrixinatosaurus, 18, 20
elephants, 41–42, 163
elephant seals, 85
Empire State Building, 143
emus, 67
Endothiodon, 11, 12
England, 154, 161, 165
Eoraptor, 16
Equus, 160
Eremotherium, 159
Eryops, 9
erythrosuchids, 14
"Essay on Man" (Pope), 157–58

Europe, 38
Eutatus, 160
Exposition Universelle (Paris, 1889), 102
extinction, 157–64; fact of, 157–58; rates, 166

Fasolasuchus, 14
Fawcett, Percy, x–xii
fer-de-lance, xv
ferns, 37
fern spores, 54
"filter bridge," 141
finbacks, 10–11
FitzRoy, Robert, 97–98
Flaming Cliffs, 33–34
Fleming, Farley, 87
Florentinoameghinia, 104
Florida, 69, 119, 145, 150–51
floridatragulines, 145
Flower, William, 103
flowering plants, 43
foraminiferans, 44, 53
four-eyed opossum, 89
foxes, 141, 160, 165
Frailey, C. David, 127, 147, 149
French Revolution, 113
frogs, xv–xvi, 166–67
Futalognkosaurus, 35, 37, 40

Gaillard Cut, 144
Galápagos penguin, 166
Galápagos tortoise, 166
Galeamopus, 40
Gallimimus, 27
Garcia, Henry, 74
geckos, 129
Genesis, 61, 157, 159
Geoffroy Saint-Hilaire, Étienne, 114, 125
The Geographical Distribution of Animals (Wallace), 140
Geological Society of America, 51–56
German Naval Observatory, 3
Germany, 1–5
gharials, 80–81
giant armadillo, 166
Giganotosaurus, 28–29
Giraffatitan, 38–43
giraffes, 43, 106, 148, 161, 163
Globidentosuchus, 80
Glossopteris, 5
Glossotherium, 159
Glyptodon, 118

glyptodonts, 116–20, 141, 142, 150–51, 160, 163, 165, 167
Glyptotherium, 119
God's Providence, 157–58
Golden Gate Bridge, 143
golden lion tamarin, 166
Gondwana, xvi, 5–16, 38, 45, 46, 91
gondwanatheres, 23, 55, 88
gorgonopsians, 11
Gracilisuchus, 14
grasses, 37, 43
Great American Biotic Interchange (GABI), 134, 139–55
Great Exhibition of 1851, x
"Great Incognitum," 111
great white shark, 27
Greenland, 1–5, 154
ground sloths, 114–18, 141, 142, 150, 151, 159–60, 162, 165, 167
Gryposuchus, 72, 82
guanaco, 105, 106, 141
Guatemala, 119, 142
Gubbio, Italy, 50–52
Guilielmofloweria, 103
guillotine, 113, 114
guinea pigs, xv, 130
Gulf Coast, 145
Gulf of Mexico, 46, 51
Gulf Stream, 153–54
Guyana, xiv

Haiti, 46
Hamburg, 3
Haplocanthosaurus, 40
Harvard University, 141
Hastings, Alex, 75
Hatcher, John Bell, 103, 140
Hawkins, Waterhouse, x
Hays, James, 7
Head, Jason, 75–76
Heezen, Bruce, 7
hegetotheres, 104–05
Heilmann, Gerhard, 64
Helen (ship), 137–38
Hemiauchenia, 160
Henricosbornia, 103
Henslow, John Stevens, 97–98
Hercules, 73
Herrera, Fabiany, 74
Herrerasaurus, 15–16, 23, 24
Hildebrand, Alan, 52
Himalayas, 49

Hippidion, 160
hippopotamus, 104–05, 110, 158, 161
Hiroshima nuclear bomb, 46
Hitchcock, Alfred, 71
HMS Beagle, 63, 97–100, 117, 123–25, 130–31, 157, 159
hoatzins, 129
Hoffstetter, Robert, 127
Holmes, Arthur, 6
Holmes, Sherlock, ix–xiii
Holmesina, 160
Holocene, 163
Homalodotherium, 104
Homunculus, 127
Hoplophoneus, 93, 118
Hoplophorus, 160
Horner, Jack, 34
horses, 106–10, 142, 151, 157–58, 160, 162, 165
horseshoe crabs, 62
howler monkeys, 124–25
Huanchaca Plateau, x
Huene, Friedrich von, 25
Huincul Formation, 34
human immigration to the New World, 164–65
Huxley, Thomas Henry, 63–65, 103
hyenas, 66, 110, 158
hyraxes, 104

Ibrahim, Nizar, 24–27
Ice Age: Dawn of the Dinosaurs (cartoon), xiv
Ice Age mammals, 157–64
Iceland, 129
Ichigualasto Formation, 13–16
ichthyosaurs, 158
iguanas, xv
Iguanodon, xi
iguanodont, 28, 36
India, 6, 8, 11, 19, 39, 45, 51
Indiana University, 76
Indonesia, 139, 155
Indonesian Archipelago, 152–53
indricotheres, 42
Indricotherium, 42
inkjet printers, 49
inoceramids, 44, 53
"insinuators," 142
interatheres, 104
interglacials, 162
iridium, 12, 50–52
"Irish elk," 161

Irritator, 18, 26–27
"Island Continent," xvii

Jacobs, Louis, 22
jaguars, xv, 141–43, 147, 165–67; American, 160
Japan, 129
Jaramillo, Carlos, 74, 144, 152
Jardin du Roi, 114
Java, 152–53
"Java Man," xii
Jefferson, Thomas, 117
Jobs, Steve, 1
Johnson City College, 127
Jones, Indiana, x, 33
Jordeson (ship), 138
Josephoartigasia, 131
Josepholeidya, 103
Journal of Paleontology, 149
Journey to the Center of the Earth (Verne), xiv
Jura Mountains, 113
Jurassic Park (novel, film), xiv, 17, 27, 65, 108
Jurassic Park II (film), 64
Jurassic Park III (film), 26, 64
Jurassic World (film), 17, 65

Kaatedocus, 40
kangaroo rats, 141
kangaroos, 91, 161
Kannemeyeria, 11
Kelenken, 67–68
"keystone" hypothesis, 163
King Kong (film), xiii
Kirkdale Cave, 158
koalas, 91, 161
Komodo dragons, 161
Köppen, Wladimir, 1–3
KPg boundary, 50–59
Kritosaurus, 23
KT boundary, 50–59

Labrador, 154
La Brea tar pits, 118, 160
La Colonia Formation, 21
Laguna Umayo, 58
La Meseta Formation, 85
Lamont-Doherty Geological Observatory, 7, 49, 50
The Land That Time Forgot (Burroughs), xiv
Langstonia, 82
Laplatasaurus, 45

Lapparentosaurus, 23
La Puente, 74–75
Larsen, Carl Anton, 85
Latin America, 81, 140
laughing gas, 49
Lavocat, Rene, 132
Lavoisier, Antoine, 114
law of correlation of
    parts, 113
leeches, 147
"Legions of the North,"
    141, 151, 159–60
Leidy, Joseph, 104
lemurlike primates, 128
Leontinia, 104
leopard, 161
Lernean Hydra, 73
Lessem, Don, 23, 24
Lestodon, 159
Lewis, Meriwether, and
    Clark, William, 117
Liaoning beds, 65
Ligabueino, 22
Ligabuesaurus, 23
Limaysaurus, 28
Linnean Society, 139
lions, 66
litopterns, 88, 105–09,
    142, 160, 165
lizards, 54
llama, 105, 106, 141–43,
    160
Lombok, 153–53
Lombok Strait, 153
London, 138–39
Lopez de Bertodano
    Formation, 85
Lord of the Rings
    (Tolkien), 120
The Lost World (Conan
    Doyle), viii, ix–xvii, 26
LSD, 49
Luján, Argentina, 101,
    114
Luján Formation, 101
"lumping," 41
Lund, Peter Wilhelm,
    101
lungfish, 8, 21
Luperosuchus, 14
Lydekker, Richard, 103
Lydekker Line, 153
Lyme Regis, 158
Lystrosaurus, 5, 11, 13

Machaeroides, 93
Macrauchenia, 105–09,
    160
Madagascar, 6, 19, 23,
    45, 46
Madrid, 114
magnetic field, 7

magnetic stratigraphy,
    145, 148
magnetrons, 49
Maiasaura, 34
malaria, 137, 139
The Malay Archipelago
    (Wallace), 139
Malaysia, 139
Malone, Edward, xii–xiii
Mamenchisaurus, 37
*Mammalian Fossils in
    the Argentine Republic*
    (F. Ameghino), 102
"mammal-like reptiles,"
    10
mammoths, 41–42, 108,
    158–62
"mammoth steppe," 41
manatees, 167
maned wolf, 141, 166
mantled howler monkey,
    166
mara, 130
Marambio, 85
margay, 166
marine geology, 6–7
marmoset, 125
Marsh, Othniel C.,
    23, 104
marsh deer, 141
marsupial "lion," 161
marsupials, 54, 58, 66, 68,
    83–88, 110, 142, 161
Martill, Dave, 26
Martinez, Riccardo, 16
mastodont, 106–08, 110,
    113, 142, 147–49,
    150–52, 157–58, 160,
    162, 163, 165
Matthew, William Diller,
    140
Matthews, Drummond, 7
McCormick, Robert, 98
Meadowcroft rock
    shelter, 164
Medusa, 11, 73
Megacerops, 42
Megalonyx, 114–18, 159
Megalosaurus, xi
megamammals, 159–64
Megatherium, 114–17,
    159
Menoceras, 145
Menodus, 42
Menops, 42
Mesembriornis, 60
Mesembriornithinae, 67
Mesosaurus, 5, 8
mesotheres, 104
meteor impact, 12
meteorology, 1–5
Mexico, 46, 142, 144

Michel, Helen, 51
microbiotheres, 86, 90
microwave oven, 49
Mid-Atlantic ridge,
    47–48, 128–29
Mihlbachler, Matt, 42
Minoxidil, 49
mioclaenids, 58, 109
Mixtotoxodon, 151, 160
moas, 67
molecular paleontology,
    108
mollusks, 53, 88
Molucca Islands, 139
Mongolia, 14, 19, 27,
    33–34, 46, 58
monito del monte, 86, 90
monkeys, 152
Mononykus, 27
Montana, 79
Monte Hermoso, 130
Montes, Camilo, 152
Monte Verde, 164
Moreno, Francisco, 102
Morocco, 25
Morrison Formation,
    40–43
mosasaurs, 48
mosquitoes, 147
"mother of all mass
    extinctions," 12, 165
Mourasuchus, 72, 81–82
mouse opossum, 89
Mozambique, 11
Mumbai (Bombay), 47
Musée National
    d'Histoire Naturelle,
    114
Museo de la Plata, 102
Museo Municipal
    Carmen Funes, 35
Museo Nacional de
    Ciencias Naturales,
    24, 114
Museum für Naturkunde,
    Berlin, 38, 62
Museum of the Rockies,
    34
muskrat, 131
Mussasaurus, 23
Mylodon, 114–16, 160

naked mole rats, 132
National University of La
    Plata, 163
natural history, 111
Natural History Museum
    of Los Angeles
    County, 127
Neanderthals, 109
Nebraska, 146, 148–49
Neochoerus, 132, 160

Neothoracophorus, 160
Neuquensaurus, 45
New Guinea, 139,
    152–53
New World monkeys, 82,
    125–29, 132, 146, 147,
    165, 167
New York City, 3–4
New Zealand, 67
nightjars, xv
nimravids, 93–94
nitroglycerin, 49
Noah's flood, 61, 157–59
Noasaurus, 22
Nobel, Alfred, 49
Nobel Prize, 50
Nopscaspondylus, 28
North America, 19, 27
North American
    extinctions, 160
North Atlantic, 154
North Dakota, 79
Nothropus, 159
Nothrotherium, 160
notoungulates, 100–09,
    141, 142, 147, 151, 160
nutrias, 130, 131

O'Brien, Willis, xiii
Obruchev, Vladimir, xiv
ocelot, 141, 166, 167
Ocnopus, 159
Oklahoma, 39
Oldfieldthomasia, 103
Old World monkeys,
    125–26
Olshevsky, George, 24
*On the Origin of
    Continents and Oceans*
    (Wegener), 3
*On the Origin of Species
    by Means of Natural
    Selection* (Darwin), 61,
    63, 139, 159
Opdyke, Neil, 7
ophidiophobia, 73
opossums, xv, 83–89,
    110, 165
opportunistic species, 13
Ordovician extinction,
    165
oreodonts, 144
Orinoco River, xiv
ornithomimids, 27
Osborn, Henry Fairfield,
    42, 103–04
ossicones, 43
ostrich, 21, 67
Ostrom, John, 64–65
Othnielmarshia, 103
otters, 141, 142
Ouranosaurus, 36

"overkill" extinction
 hypothesis, 162
Oviraptor, 34
Owen, Richard, 63,
 65, 99–101,103–05,
 116–18, 158
owl monkeys, 125

paca, 130
pacarana, 131
Pacific Ocean, 143, 152,
 153
Pakistan, 51
Palaeolama, 160
palaeomerycids, xvii,
 149–51
Paleopsilopterus, 67
palorchestids, 161
Pampaphoneus, 11–12
pampatheres, 150–51,
 160, 165
Pampatherium, 160
Panama, 69, 139–55
Panama Canal, 143–44,
 149
Panamanian golden frog,
 167
Panama land bridge, 27,
 68, 132–55
Pangea, 5–16, 46, 116
pangolins, 116
Panochthus, 118, 160
pantodont, 58
Paraceratherium, 42
parakeets, xv
Parapanochthus, 160
Paraphysornis, 60
pareiasaurs, 9–12
parrotlets, xv
Pascual, Rosendo, 69, 141
passenger pigeon, 165
Patagonia, 34, 45, 101,
 104, 127
Patagonykus, 27
Patagopteryx, 23
Patterson, Bryan, 141
Paulo Couto, Carlos
 de, 141
peccaries, 141–44,
 148–52, 160, 165
Pedra do Fogo
 Formation, 8
Pelagornis, 70
pelomedusoids, 77–78
Penfield, Glen, 52
penguins, 85–88
penicillin, 49
Pennsylvania, 164
perissodactyls, 109
permafrost DNA, 164
Permian extinction,
 12–13, 165

Permian Period, 5–16
Peru, xvii, 58, 81, 133,
 146
Perupithecus, 128
Perutherium, 58
Peruvian Amazon, 128,
 133
Petrified Forest National
 Park, 9
Phoberomys, 132
phorusrhacids, 60–69, 88,
 141–43, 150–51
Phorusrhacinae, 67
Phorusrhacos, 60
Phugatherium, 132
Piatnitzkysaurus, 22
pigs, 141
Piper Cub airplane, 70
piranhas, 147
Pithecanthropus, xii
Pitman, Walter, 7
pit vipers, xv
placentals, 54
Planet of the Reptiles, 80
plankton, 52–53, 152
Plateosaurus, 37
plate tectonics, 128–29
Platyrrhini, 125–29
Plaxhoplous, 160
plesiosaurs, 21, 48, 158
Pliometanastes, 150
Plutonia, xiv
pocket gophers, 141
Polly, David, 76
polydolopids, 88
Pope, Alexander, 157–58
porcupine, 130–32, 141,
 151
Port Julian, 105
Portugal, 23
potassium-argon dating,
 145
Pratt, John Henry, 49
prehensile tail, 125
The Princess Bride (film),
 131
Princeton University,
 140–41
Prionosuchus, 8
Proborhyaena, 92
*Proceedings of the National
 Academy of Sciences*, 102
Procoptodon, 161
pronghorns, 148, 160
Propachyrukhos, 105
Propraopus, 160
prosauropods, 37
proteins, 109
Proteopithecus, 127
protoceratids, 144, 145
Protoceratops, 34
protomammals, 5–16

Protopithecus, 160
Provelosaurus, 9
Provence, France, 33
Psilopterinae, 67
Psilopterus, 60
pterodactyls, 62, 65
Pterodactylus, xi
Pterodaustro, 23
pterosaurs, 63, 70
pudu, 141
Puertasaurus, 45
Punta Alta, 98–99, 130
Punta Peligro, 58
Purussaurus, 72, 81–82
pyrotheres, 107–08
Pyrotherium, 107
python, 76

Quartermain, Allan, x
Queztalcoatlus, 70

rabbits, 104–05, 110, 141
raccoons, 150, 160
radiocarbon dates, 164,
 163
radiolarians, 53
rafting on vegetation, 129
rauisuchids, 14
rayon, 49
Rayososaurus, 23
Raytheon, 49
Reig, Osvaldo, 15
Reign of Terror, 113,
 114
reptiles, 9–16, 54–55,
 72–82
retractable claws, 161
rhea, 67
rhinoceroses, 42–43, 105,
 106, 108–10, 144, 145,
 152, 158
Rhynchippus, 104
rhynchosaurs, 14
Ricardolydekkeria, 103
Ricardowenia, 103
Riggs, Elmer, 43
Rio de Janeiro, 124
Rio do Rasto
 Formation, 9
Riojasaurus, 23
Rio Negro, xiv, 136–37
rodents, xv, 82, 104–05,
 129–33, 147, 152
"rodents of unusual size,"
 131
Romer, Alfred, 25
Romer-Simpson Medal,
 25
Romero-Pittman, Lidia,
 147
Roosevelt, Theodore, 147
Rosario, Argentina, 23

Roxton, Lord John, xiii
rudistids, 44, 53
Russia, 14
Rutherford, William, xii
Ryan, Bill, 7

saber-toothed cats, 108,
 119, 141, 160, 161, 165
saber-toothed mammals,
 92–94, 110
safety glass, 49
saki, 125
salamander, xv
Salgado, Leonardo, 28
Salla beds, 127
Saltasaurus, 21, 23, 45
Salvador, Bahia, Brazil,
 123
San Juan Basin, 45
Santa Cruz beds, 127
Santana Formation, 27
Santa Rosa fauna, 133,
 147
Sarcosuchus, 82
sauropods, 30–43, 45–46,
 65
Sauroposeidon, 39
Saurosuchus, 14
Scelidodon, 160
Scelidotherium, 114, 116,
 160
Schaff, Chuck, 22
science journalism, 55
Scotchgard, 49
Scotland, 154
Scott, William Berryman,
 103, 104, 140
sea anemones, 13
sea cows, 145
sea level, 47–48
sea scorpions, 7
sea stars, 88
sea turtles, 48
sea urchins, 53
secretary birds, 67
Sedgwick, Adam, 97
seed fern, 5
serendipity, 48–49
Sereno, Paul, 14–16,
 24, 25
seriema, 60, 67
Seymour Island, 53–54,
 83–90
sharks, 8, 54
short-faced bears, 160,
 165
shrew opossums, 86, 90
shrews, 141
shrimp, 62
Siberia, 109, 162
Siberian volcanoes, 12–13
"side-necked" turtles, 78

sigmodontine rodents, 150
silicoflagellates, 53
Silly Putty, 49
Simpson, George Gaylord, 6, 25, 41, 103, 104, 133, 140–41, 146–47
Singapore, 139
"Sixth Extinction," 165–66
skinks, 129
skunks, 141
sloths, 116–21, 163, 167
Smart Car, 160
Smilodon, 160
Smith, William, 61
Smithsonian Institution, 74
Smithsonian Tropical Research Institute, 144
Smith Woodward, A., 103
snails, 152
snakes, xv, 21, 54, 66, 68, 73–77, 147
sociology of science, 55
Solnhofen limestone, 62, 64
South Africa, 6–7, 8, 11, 12
South Carolina, 119, 151
South Dakota, 42, 146
sparassodonts, 91–93, 142, 160
spectacled bear, 141
Spencer, Percy, 49
spider monkeys, 125, 160
spiders, 147
Spielberg, Steven, 17
Spinosaurus, 17, 25–29, 36
spiny rats, 130
"splitting," 41
squirrel monkeys, 125
Sri Lanka, 48
Stallard, Robert, 152–53
Stegomastodon, 160
Stegosaurus, x–xi
Stirtonia, 82
Strand Magazine, ix–xi
Stupendemys, 72, 78–80, 82
Summerlee, Professor, xii–xiii
Sunda Shelf, 152–53
Superglue, 49
super-greenhouse climate, 13
Supersaurus, 40
Surameryx, 148–49, 152

Suuwassea, 40
Swedish Antarctic Expedition, 85
swifts, xv
Sykes, Lynn, 7
synapsids, 9

Tanzania, 11
tapirs, xv, 106–09, 141–43, 148–52, 160, 165
Taylor, Louis, 22
tectonics, 152
Teflon, 49
tegu lizards, xv
Telicomys, 132
temnospondyls, 9, 15
tepuis, xiv–xvi
Ternate, 139
Tertiary, 50
Texas, 46, 69, 119, 145, 150, 151
Tharp, Marie, 7
thecodonts, 64
theoretical equilibrium dynamics, 143
therizinosaurs, 27
Thermodynamics of the Atmosphere (Wegener), 2
theropods, 17–29
Thinobadistes, 150
Thoatherium, 106–07
Thomas, Oldfield, 103
Thomas Farm fauna, 145
Thomashuxleya, 103, 104
"The Three Princes of Serendip" (story), 48
Thylacoleo, 161
Thylacosmilus, 92–94
tinamous, xv
Titanis, 68–69, 150
Titanoboa, 72–79, 80
titanosaurs, 30, 38, 45, 57
Titanotherium, 42
Tiupampa fauna, 58, 90
TNT, 49
Tolkien, J. R. R., 120
Tonni, Eduardo, 69, 163
Torres, Manuel, 114
tortoises, 129
Toxodon, 99–101, 104, 109, 160
toxodonts, 104–05, 163, 165
tree kangaroos, 152
tree sloths, 165
T. rex and the Crater of Doom (Alvarez), 56

Trialestes, 14, 23
Triassic, 9–16
Triassic extinction, 165
Triceratops, x, xi, 34, 45
Trigodon, 104
Trigonias Quarry, 42
Trigonodops, 160
trilobites, 13
Troodon, 34
Tschopp, Emanuel, 40–43
tsunami, 51, 129
tuco tuco, 130
Tunisia, 25
turtles, 21, 54, 77–78
tyrannosaurs, 27, 65
Tyrannosaurus, xi, 17–20, 25–29, 45, 46

uakaris, 125
University of California, Berkeley, 50
University of Chicago, 14
University of Edinburgh, xii, 95
University of Florida Museum of Natural History, 74–77, 144
University of Graz, 3
University of Hamburg, 3
University of Marburg, 1
University of Michigan, 76
University of Toronto, 75
University of Tucuman, 24
Unquillosaurus, 18, 27, 46
Uranus, 49
Uruguay, 68, 99
Urumaco, 80, 81
Utah, 40

vacant ecological niches, 142
Valley of the Moon, Argentina, 24
Vancouver, 56
Velociraptor, 27, 28, 46, 64–65
Velocisaurus, 22
Venezuela, xiv, 80, 146
Verne, Jules, xiv
Viagra, 49
vicuña, 105, 141
Vine, Fred, 7
volcanic ash dates, 148
voles, 141
Volkheimeria, 23
Volkswagen Beetle, 118

Von Humboldt, Alexander, 135, 140, 145
Voyage of the Beagle (Darwin), 114–17, 130–31

Wallace, Alfred Russel, 134–55, 165, 167
Wallace Line, 152–53
warthogs, 161
weasels, xv, 141, 151, 160
Webb, S. David, 141
Weddell seals, 85
Wedgwood, Josiah, 98
Wegener, Alfred, 1–7
Western Interior Seaway, 48
West Virginia, 117
whales, 145
White Cliffs of Dover, 50
Whittaker, George, 147
Wilberforce, Archbishop Samuel, 63
Wing, Scott, 74
Winge, Herluf, 101
wolves, 110, 160, 161
wombats, 91
Wood, Albert E., 132
Woodburne, Michael, 85–88, 151
woolly monkeys, 125
woolly rhinoceroses, 161
World War I, 3, 39
World War II, 6, 49
Wormtongue, Grima 120
Wrangel Island, 162
Wyoming, 40, 79

xenarthrans, 111–21, 159–60
Xenorhinotherium, 160

Yale University, 64
yapok, 90
yellow fever, 137
yellow-tailed woolly monkey, 166
Younger Dryas event, 162
Yucatán, 46–47, 52, 142

Zambia, 11
zebra, 161, 163
"zigzag" model, 163–64
Zimbabwe, 11
Zinsmeister, William, 53–54, 86–88
Zoological Museum, Copenhagen, 101